*THE STATIONERS' COMPANY
AND THE BOOK TRADE
1550–1990*

PUBLISHING PATHWAYS

Previous Titles in the Series

Edited by Robin Myers & Michael Harris

Development of the English Book Trade 1700-1899. OPP, 1981

Sale and Distribution of Books from 1700. OPP, 1982

Author-Publisher Relations in the Eighteenth and Nineteenth Centuries. OPP, 1983

Maps and Prints: Aspects of the English Booktrade. OPP, 1984

Economics of the British Booktrade 1605-1939. Chadwyck-Healey, 1985

Bibliophily. Chadwyck-Healey, 1986

Aspects of Printing from 1600. OPP, 1987

Pioneers in Bibliography. St Paul's Bibliographies, 1988

Fakes and Frauds. Varieties of deception in print and manuscript. St Paul's Bibliographies, 1989

Spreading the Word. The distribution networks of print 1550-1850. St Paul's Bibliographies, 1990

Property of a Gentleman. The formation, organisation and dispersal of the private library 1620-1920. St Paul's Bibliographies, 1991

Censorship and the Control of Print in England and France 1600-1910. St Paul's Bibliographies, 1992

Serials and their Readers 1620-1914. St Paul's Bibliographies, 1993

A Millennium of the Book: Production, Design & Illustration in Manuscript and Print (900-1900). St Paul's Bibliographies, 1994

A Genius for Letters: Booksellers and Bookselling from the 16th to the 20th Century. St Paul's Bibliographies, 1995

Antiquaries, Book Collectors and the Circles of Learning. St Paul's Bibliographies, 1996

THE STATIONERS' COMPANY AND THE BOOK TRADE 1550–1990

Edited by
Robin Myers and Michael Harris

ST PAUL'S BIBLIOGRAPHIES
WINCHESTER

OAK KNOLL PRESS
NEW CASTLE, DELAWARE

© 1997 The Contributors

First published 1997 by
St Paul's Bibliographies
West End House
1 Step Terrace
Winchester
Hampshire SO22 5BW

Published in North and South America
and the Philippines by
Oak Knoll Press
414 Delaware Street
New Castle
DE 19720

ISBN 1-873040-33-4 (UK)
ISBN 1-884718-45-0 (USA)

Library of Congress Cataloging-in-Publication Data

The Stationers' Company and the book trade, 1550–1990 / edited by
   Robin Myers and Michael Harris.
      p.   cm.
   Includes bibliographical references and index.
   ISBN 1-884718-45-0 (hc)
   1. Stationers' Company (London, England)--History--16th century--Congresses. 2. Stationers' Company (London, England)--History--17th century--Congresses. 3. Stationers' Company (London, England)--History--18th century--Congresses. 4. Book industries and trade--England--London--History--16th century--Congresses. 5. Book industries and trade--England--London--History--17th century--Congresses. 6. Book industries and trade--England--London--History--18th century--Congresses. I. Myers, Robin. II. Harris, Michael.
Z329.S79S74 1997
070.5'0941--dc21   97-40367
                                                                     CIP

Typeset in Garamond by Ella Whitehead, Munslow, Shropshire
Cover designed by Eric Dent
Printed in England by St Edmundsbury Press, Bury St Edmunds

Contents

List of Contributors vi

Introduction vii

List of those attending the Conference xi

Ann Saunders	*The Stationers' Hall* 1	
Peter Blayney	*William Cecil and the Stationers* 11	
D. F. McKenzie	*Stationers' Company Liber A: An Apologia* 35	
Jean Tsushima	*Members of the Stationers' Company who served in the Artillery Company before the Civil War: Ralphe Mabbe and his network* 65	
Ian Gadd	*The Mechanicks of Difference; a study in Stationers' Company Discourse in the Seventeenth Century* 93	
Robin Myers	*George Hawkins (1705-1780): Bookseller and Treasurer of the English Stock of the Stationers' Company* 113	
Warren McDougall	*Smugglers, Reprinters and Hot Pursuers: The Irish–Scottish Book Trade and Copyright Prosecution in the Late Eighteenth Century* 151	
Philip Henry Jones	*Wales and the Stationers' Company* 185	

Index 203

Contributors

PETER W. M. BLAYNEY is Distinguished Resident Fellow at the Folger Shakespeare Library, Washington DC, and is working on a history of the Stationers' Company, 1501-1616. He has gained an international reputation for his work on the London book trade in the sixteenth century.

IAN GADD is at Pembroke College, University of Oxford, working on the Stationers' Company between 1557 and 1660. He has studied at the University of Edinburgh and the University of Pennsylvania.

PHILIP HENRY JONES lectures at the College of Librarianship, Wales. He has been widely recognized for his work on Welsh printing and is currently co-editing *A Nation and its Books*, the forthcoming history of the book in Wales.

DON MCKENZIE has recently retired as Professor of Bibliography and Textual Criticism in the University of Oxford. His three volumes, recording some 17,000 Stationers' Company apprentices enrolled between 1605 and 1800, have become an indispensable aid to research. His work in bibliography has transformed the field and he is currently editing a key text in the Company archive, Liber A.

ROBIN MYERS is currently President of the Bibliographical Society (London). She has been Hon. Archivist of the Stationers' Company since 1978, is a liveryman of the Company and author of the standard account of the archive.

WARREN MCDOUGALL is an Honorary Fellow of the Faculty of Arts, University of Edinburgh. He is editing the eighteenth-century volume of the projected *History of the Book in Scotland*.

ANN SAUNDERS is Hon. Editor of the London Topographical Society and President of a number of organizations concerned with the history of London. She has written and edited a variety of highly acclaimed works on the subject.

JEAN TSUSHIMA is Archivist Emeritus of the Honorable Artillery Company. She is currently working on a history of the HAC and a biographical dictionary of its members from 1537 to 1914. She is an authority on, and collector of, early military manuals, many of which were printed by members of the Stationers' Company.

Introduction

THE STATIONERS' COMPANY, like the organizations centred on other crafts and commercial activities in London, attempted over centuries to protect its status and privacy by excluding scholars and researchers from its records. However, as individuals were given access from the eighteenth century it became increasingly difficult to hold the line. Now, with the entire archive available through microfilm publication to all scholars with an interest in the English book trade, it seemed time to focus on the Stationers' Company in our series of volumes on book-trade history. It also seemed appropriate that the papers should be presented at a Conference in the magnificent setting of Stationers' Hall itself, where the force of association more than offset the problem of acoustics.

The Company has, from its foundation in the mid-sixteenth century, provided a powerful focus for the conduct of the trade in print. While never a leading City Company in terms of precedence, standing only 47th in priority, the interest of its members in the materials which formed the primary medium of public communication gave it a special importance within the public sphere. Booksellers, stationers, printers, binders and other producers and dealers in print coalesced within the Company which was, from the first, more closely aligned with the interest of the state than most others.

This political relationship is examined by Peter Blayney. In his ground-breaking study of William Cecil, he traces the sometimes subterranean links between the minister and the trade both before and after the granting of the Royal Charter in 1557. Through a close examination of Cecil's activities as Licenser, Principal Secretary and aristocratic landowner, he is able to identify an interest in the control of printed materials which has not appeared in previous studies.

In trade terms, the Company was from the first engaged with issues of control. By overseeing apprenticeship, limiting the number of master printers, restricting the production and sale of the printed materials registered in its Entry Books, the Company was as closely concerned with its members' commercial interests as with those of the state. The character and effectiveness of the Company's interventions in the interlocking areas of politics and commerce has become the subject of some debate.

On one hand, scholars have emphasized the limitations of the power exercised by the Company over the production and publication of print. This was the position taken by Sheila Lambert in her paper in a previous volume in the series, *Censorship and the control of print* (1991). On the other, scholars have seen the actions of the Company as pervasive and influential. This is the line taken by Jean Tsushima in this volume. Through a close study of a specific sector of the membership in the mid-seventeenth century, those who were also members of the Honourable Artillery Company, she suggests the way in which the Stationers' Company played an active part in relation to publishing. In particular, she focuses on Ralph Mabbe, indicating how the Company was closely linked to political and religious networks during the Tudor and Stuart periods.

The key to unlocking the role of the Stationers' Company lies mainly in the records which are held at the Hall and which have recently been described and classified by Robin Myers (*The Stationers' Company Archive, 1554-1984* (1990)). Within this wealth of material, one of the most important and enigmatic items is the manuscript volume known as Liber A. This is the last of the Company's early records to remain unpublished and it presents particular difficulties to the editor. This task has been undertaken by the most notable exponent of seventeenth-century bibliography, Don McKenzie. In his contribution to this volume he assesses some of the difficulties and opportunities that are involved in editing the material and he demonstrates, in a particularly effective way, how valuable detailed work on the Company records can be in illuminating its cultural status.

If the printed product gave the Company its special character, its members have consistently claimed a distinctive position within the general structure of the City Companies. This difference, real or imagined, is the subject of Ian Gadd's analysis. Through a close reading of texts, including petitions from the Company and printed works on trade practice, he teases out the elements of what he calls 'the mechanicks of difference'.

His chronological focus on the Company in the late seventeenth century overlaps with Ann Saunders's account of the Hall itself. She provides a view of the origins of the Company's interest in property adjacent to St Paul's Cathedral, whose use and form was established in relation to the aristocratic London households of the middle ages. However, the rebuilding of the Hall after the Great Fire of London (1666) provides the main thrust of her investigation. By a close reading of the

Company records, she traces each stage of the rebuilding and the emergence of the fully operational livery hall by 1700.

Robin Myers investigates the life and work of one of the Company's important but largely unknown officials during the eighteenth century, George Hawkins. A bookseller working his way up through the London trade, Hawkins became Treasurer of the English Stock, the main source of the Company's wealth over a long period. Using a wide range of materials extending from newspaper advertisements to some of the minor manuscripts held in the archive at the Hall, she follows his career from its Fleet-Street origins into the potentially calmer waters of Company service.

The Stationers' Company was fundamentally metropolitan in interest and character. Even so, in line with the general trade in print, its influence extended much further afield. Two of the contributions to this volume follow the lines of interaction between the London Company and its activities within the trade, into other parts of the British Isles. Philip Jones explores the links between the Welsh and London book trades from the sixteenth to the nineteenth centuries. He suggests how entry in the Company registers was used over a long period to protect Welsh materials as well as providing a clear indication of how Welsh printers engaged with the London trade. Through a number of case histories, he indicates how a period of apprenticeship and training could be followed by a return to Wales but also how individuals could achieve considerable success through a career based in London.

This suggests a type of integration; the Company establishing a framework within which individuals from any part of the country could be accommodated. Warren McDougall, on the other hand, in a study of the eighteenth-century Scottish trade, reveals a relationship characterized by conflict and opposition. Through a variety of customs records and evidence gleaned from strings of prosecutions in the Scottish courts, he uncovers a network of booksellers engaged in the attempt to break free of London regulation whilst developing a clandestine trade with Ireland.

The history of the Stationers' Company in the nineteenth and twentieth centuries has not, in general, been the subject of much analysis or research. The conference offered the opportunity to signal a change in the approach to this period, ratified partly by an upswing in academic interest, but in particular by the announcement of a multi-author history to be edited by Robin Myers. This will consist of essays examining the history of the Company from 1800 to 1990 and several of the contributors spoke on the structure and content of this work (Robin Myers, Michael Harris, Ann Saunders, Richard Bowden).

Once again, we are extremely grateful to the British Academy for providing a grant in support of the conference.

Michael Harris and Robin Myers
London, May 1997

List of those attending the Conference

Jean Archibald
Librarian, Edinburgh University Library

Bernadette Archer
Librarian, National Art Library, Victoria & Albert Museum

Dr Marie Axton
English Faculty, Unversity of Cambridge

Iain Bain
Liveryman, Stationers' Company

Dr Maureen Bell
Lecturer, School of English, Birmingham University

Charles Benson
The Library, Trinity College, Dublin

Mark Bland
Post-doctoral researcher on the early book trade

Richard Bowden
Archivist, contributor to History of the Stationers' Company *(1800-1990)*

Alan Cameron

Andrew Cook
Archivist, India Office Library and Records

Karen Cook
Curator, British Library Map Library

Robert Cross
Publisher, St Paul's Bibliographies

Mary Jane Edwards
Professor of English, Carleton University, Ottawa

Christine Ferdinand
Librarian, Magdalen College, Oxford

Antonia Forster
Professor of English, University of Akron

Janet Ing Freeman
Bibliographer

Roy Fullick
Master, Stationers' Company

Gay Fullick

Anna Greening
Archivist, Fawcett Library

David J.Hall
Liveryman, Stationers' Company; Deputy Librarian, Cambridge University Library

Judy Edwards
Headmistress

Bob Hasenfrutz
Lecturer, Department of English, University of Connecticut

Captain Peter Hames
Retired clerk, Stationers' Company

Donna B. Hamilton
University of Maryland at
College Park

John Hewish
Retired librarian

Paul Hopkins
Spencer archivist, Northampton-
shire Record Office

A. W. Huish
MA student, Royal Holloway
College, London

Lynn Hulse
Research fellow, librarian
archivist, Clare Hall, Cambridge

Arnold Hunt
PhD student, Trinity College,
Cambridge

David Hunter
Music librarian

David Lewis Jones
Liveryman, Stationers'
Company, Librarian, House of
Lords

Colin Lee
Book collector

Geoff Kemp
Graduate student, King's College,
Cambridge

Elisabeth Leedham-Green
Cambridge University Archives

Christina Mackwell
Lambeth Palace Library

George Mandl
Past Master, Stationers' Company

Giles Mandelbrote
Curator, The British Library

Arthur Marks
Art historian, University of
North Carolina

Judith Marks
Bookbinding historian

Miriam Miller

Martin Moonie
D.Phil student, Somerville
College, Oxford

Gaye Morgan
Librarian, Early Printed Book
Project, Oxford University

Charles Parry
National Library of Wales

Margaret Payne
Librarian, Kent

Esther Potter
Bookbinding historian

James Raven
Mansfield College, Oxford

Peter Rippon
Past Master, Stationers' Company

C. T. Rivington
Past Master, Stationers' Company

Ian Robinson
PhD student, School of English,
Birmingham University

J. R. Russell
Treasurer, Stationers' Company

Eva Sessions
The Ebor Press, York

William Sessions
Liveryman, Stationers'
Company, The Ebor Press, York

Terence Shapland
Liveryman, Stationers' Company, publishers' print production

Marion Sherwood

Alison Shell
Research fellow, University College, London

Julianne Simpson
Librarian, Early Printed Book Project, University of Oxford

Dr Marja Smolenaars
Sir Thomas Brown Institute, Leiden

David Stoker
University of Wales, Aberystwyth

Mr S. Takenouchi

Ruby Reid Thompson
Archivist, Clare Hall, Cambridge

Kuzuo Tsushima
Retired UN official

Ann Veerhoff
Sir Thomas Brown Institute, Leiden

Peter Waanders
MA student, history of the book, Centre for English Studies, London University

Veronica Watts
Bookseller

Anne Watts

John Walwyn-Jones
Bookseller, Questor Rare Books

Eva Weininger
Collector, courtesy literature

Nigel Wheale
Anglia Polytechnic University, Cambridge

Ian Willison
Senior Research Fellow, Centre for English Studies, University of London

Laurence Worms
Bookseller, Ash Rare Books

Peter Wright
Retired lecturer in librarianship

Fig.1. Stationers' Hall, from a drawing by Howard Penton.

The Stationers' Hall

Ann Saunders

FEW OF THOSE passing up and down Ludgate Hill are aware of the presence of the historic building that lies behind the tawdry shops and anonymous offices lining the way to St Paul's Cathedral. Turning north along Warwick Lane and glancing casually to the west, all the passer-by is likely to notice is a concrete superstructure and a sloping space for parked cars. Only the unusually perceptive will observe that on the far side of the car park is a substantial stone-clad edifice, the Stationers' Hall. Those who venture towards it will see other, rather grand buildings to their right, and will notice that an alleyway leads under another building and gives access to an attractive little garden, across which a path with steps at irregular intervals marks the way to the working entrance of the Hall.

This substantial plot, nearly three-quarters of an acre in area, was acquired by the Stationers' Company on 26 March 1611 from the Earl of Abergavenny and his two sons for £3,500.[1] The buildings on it were destroyed on 4 September 1666, the most apocalyptic day of the Great Fire, along with St Paul's Cathedral and all the other precious buildings around the precinct. Over the next decade, the Stationers rebuilt their premises – the Hall, offices and warehouses – and have since then remained faithful to the site.

Before considering the post-Fire rebuilding, it might be as well to think about what the Stationers wanted from their Hall, what it was that they acquired in purchasing Abergavenny House, and how and why it suited their particular needs.

First, they wanted somewhere in which to meet as a Company and where they could transact Company business. This meant that they needed a large Assembly Hall, of sufficient size to accommodate the whole Livery – and their wives (who were specifically mentioned at the time of purchase) – and that they also needed smaller rooms for court meetings and in which the Master, Wardens and Clerk might confer in privacy.

Secondly, they wanted storage space, storage for books, bound and unbound. Paper is bulky to store; it weighs heavy and is easily damaged by damp. Luxury binding materials such as vellum are of serious interest to rats and mice.[2] Volume of publication had increased steadily, relentlessly, since Caxton's beginnings in the 1470s; precious stock needed careful shelter; solid buildings were required.

Thirdly, the Stationers looked to provide themselves with a comfortable income from the property. A handsome hall could be let out, at a price, to the other hall-less companies for their assemblies; it could be used for ward motes, weddings and wakes, even for church services. And the houses around the perimeter could be rented, which would provide an income and, every twenty years or so, a substantial sum of money in the payment of a fine on renewal of the lease. Through their records, it becomes clear that the Stationers collectively had a very sharp eye to the main chance.

So – on what did they lay out their £3,500? It was not their first Hall; that had been acquired about 1554 within the Precinct of St Paul's Cathedral. It consisted of what had once been Peter College, a residence for chantry priests. They later rented additional premises in Milk Street. The first Hall was conveniently located across the road from the mansion which they acquired in 1611 and where the members of the Stationers' Company still meet. It seems that, in acquiring Abergavenny House, they made a shrewd and long-lasting bargain. What exactly was it that they bought?

Abergavenny (or Bergavenny) House was one of the many 'inns' in London belonging to the higher clergy or nobility. These premises were the largest private structures in the capital and were fitted out with the proper comforts. Their use was geared to the individual responsibilities of the men and women who filled the major offices of state and who might be called on to play a part in the council, attend to general duties at court or respond to the commands of any member of the royal family. Perhaps above all, the inns provided repositories for the accumulation and dispersal of commodities required both to satisfy the owners' need for personal display and to support the organization of large-scale households and far-flung estates. London was well established by the later middle ages as an international *entrepôt* for luxury imports and specialist crafts. To the inns came a steady flow of silks, velvets and cloths of gold; they were conveniently near to the merchants such as the mercers and goldsmiths whose services underpinned the social rituals of the nobility. The inn increasingly became associated with the forms of manners and military training which themselves denoted high status.[3]

The complexity of this sort of social and economic activity was modified in the owner's absence. However, at these times a London inn could fulfil a second range of functions which required the engagement of a permanent staff. This centred on maintaining contacts with, and providing support for, the dispersed elements of an individual estate whose components were scattered across the country. Aymer de Valence, Earl of Pembroke and proprietor of what was to become known as Abergavenny House, owned property in 631 different places. In such cases the London inn became the accounting office for the estate as a whole. Staff would collect and store goods arriving inwards from distant properties, retaining them for local use or selling them on and remitting the money to the owner. These overlapping functions of display and administration were reflected in the lay-out of the inns, making them peculiarly suitable for use by such organizations as the Stationers' Company. The Great Hall, substantial storage space, security (usually an outer wall and gatehouse), stabling and a network of rooms compactly organized on a site of about three-quarters of an acre in the centre of London provided the accommodation that they needed. Finally, the town house itself might produce an income. Parts of it could be let out – and this is exactly what the Stationers were going to do with their property.

Among the owners of Abergavenny House in its heyday was Marie de St Pol, the daughter of Count Guy St Pol and Marie of Brittany, and a very remarkable person. Born about 1304, she was married in July 1321, aged 17, to Aymer de Valence, Earl of Pembroke, and cousin to Edward I. Marlowe gives him a trenchant minor role in *Edward II*. He was then in his 50s and recently widowed. It was a brief marriage. On 23 June 1324, Aymer, in France on a diplomatic mission, dropped dead, probably of an apoplectic stroke, and Marie was left one of the richest widows in England or in France. She buried her husband in a superb tomb on the left-hand side the Sanctuary in Westminster Abbey, resisted all attempts to provide her with a second spouse, and lived on in single blessedness for another 53 years, dying at last in March 1377. She was buried not beside her husband in the Abbey, but at Denny, a religious house she had founded near Waterbeach in Cambridgeshire, and her great wealth went into establishing Pembroke College, in Cambridge.

Throughout her long life, when she came to London, she used Pembroke Inn and I cannot think that the accommodation there would have been anything other than well-built and well-maintained. It stood in a particularly desirable position, near to St Paul's Cathedral and towards the summit of the fashionable western hill – the eastern, Leadenhall slope did not become a sought-after position till the middle of the next, the fifteenth, century when the great merchant princes from Sir John Crosby to Sir Thomas Gresham began to build their mansions there. Most conveniently, the City wall provided protection on the western boundary, and St Martin's Church and the shops up what we know as Ludgate Hill did the same to the south. The Inn buildings themselves formed the northern boundary, backing on to the Earl of Warwick's Inn lying towards Smithfield, so the Countess only needed a wall and gatehouse to the east, facing on to Ave Maria Lane; a bar across the entrance still controls access to car-parking space. There must have been a Great Hall and, with so much property from her husband, scattered as it was over eleven English counties (Berkshire, Buckinghamshire, Essex, Hertfordshire, Kent, Norfolk, Northumberland, Nottinghamshire, Suffolk, Yorkshire and Wiltshire) as well as in Wales and Ireland, a substantial amount of storage space might well have been essential.

When the Countess died in 1377, her will was proved in the City's Court of Hustings,[4] as well as in the Church Courts, presumably because of her London property. She ordered specifically that her executors might remain in Pembroke Inn for up to two years to settle all the legal matters in connection with the will, and that it should afterwards be sold; it passed to the Neville family, the Earls of Abergavenny who were related to her husband's family. But times changed and by the early seventeenth century such a large and cumbersome London property was beginning to be an unnecessary and unwelcome expense. I believe, though I cannot be absolutely certain, that we may have a glimpse of it in its final aristocratic days on Wyngaerde's Panorama of London of c.1544, the south end of the Hall showing up square just behind St Martin's Church. In March 1611 the Abergavennies sold out to the Stationers.

They may have been renting the buildings even before they bought them, for the Court Minutes contain an entry for 4 November 1606 saying that the Company Clerk may use the room on the south side of the yard next to the great warehouse for his own purposes. Four days later the old Hall in St Paul's Precinct was leased out to Edward Kynaston, vintner, for 21 years at £40 per annum, which implies that the Company had somewhere else to meet.[5] The sale was finalized in March 1611 and was entered on the City Corporation Hustings roll; the money for the purchase was provided by the partners in the English stock. By May, repairs and alterations to the house were under way; the entries in the minutes are tantalizingly, frustratingly brief, so we do not know what they were actually doing. This is a problem that besets all our investigations into the history of the Hall itself. The Stationers were simply too busy to record the minutiae of running their property. What mattered were the books, the English Stock, their main source of income. We must piece together our history of the Hall from the briefest of entries, the mere snippets that got noted down almost in passing. The most frequent relevant entries are those to the appointment of fresh feoffees or trustees for the Hall, for the partners in the English Stock continued to own it, and to charge the Company rent for it, down to 1773.

Over the next 55 years, the passing references tell us that Ralph Wedgwood was permitted to rent the kitchen, buttery and a room adjoining for his own and his wife's lifetime for 5s a year, to be paid half-yearly,[6] that Mr Hobson might make a water course through the courtyard, provided he dismantled it when requested,[7] and that a new portal was to be made out of the Council Chamber 'with all convenient speed'. In March 1632, the old house was giving trouble and Mr Williams the bricklayer was instructed 'to take down the chimney in the Council Chamber on the west side of that room with the staircase' and the kitchen chimney.[8] The work was going to cost £90 and Mr Williams was urged to 'doo the same substantially'. In spite of all this, in October 1654

the Hall being very muche out of repaire, the Renter Warden was desired to appoint some other convenient house for the Dinner to be made on the next Lord Maior's Day.[9]

So much repair was needed that in the following year Foxe's *Book of Martyrs* had to be sold off to pay for the work; but little seems to have been done, so that in 1664 there was no fit place for the annual reading of the Ordnances. All in all, it may have been something of a relief when the old buildings were swept away with the rest of London in the Great Fire of 2-5 September 1666.

The subsequent relevant entries in the Court Book D are intriguing. There was no meeting until almost a fortnight after the fire had been more or less brought under control. Then the Clerk, the Wardens and three other members gathered to discuss the case of Richard Lambert who owed £40 for printing unauthorized almanacs in York;[10] the Hall was not mentioned. The first full Court was on 2 October when it was

Ordered that the Wardens provide labourers for the digging up and searching the ruins and rubbish of Stationers' Hall. And that the same bee watched day and night, at the doing thereof.[11]

Later Court meetings took place in St Bartholomew's Hospital, one of the few buildings that remained intact around the perimeter of the stricken City. On 21 December, the Court ordered that all ground owned should be cleared and measured; Widow Ward, who had occupied the Darke House beside Billingsgate, had already been permitted to build a shed among the ruins so that she could continue in business, whatever that was. But they were far more concerned about Company and apprenticeship matters and, above all, about stock.

Others were concentrating on the restoration of London, with the King himself as the prime mover. Commissioners were appointed for the rebuilding, Sir Roger Pratt, Hugh May and Christopher Wren for the Crown; Peter Mills, Edward Jarman and Robert Hooke for the City. Every man was ordered to clear his own site and then to apply to the City for a surveyor to inspect and confirm his boundaries and old foundations, if any survived. The task was immense, 13,200 houses had vanished, besides 87 churches, 44 Company Halls and most public buildings; the work was carried out by Peter Mills, Robert Hooke and John Oliver. On 2 April 1667 the Master and Wardens were summoned to the Guildhall to hear His Majesty's pleasure concerning the rebuilding,[12] and a Mr Robert Wapshott, a bricklayer, was approached to construct a new, possibly temporary, 'tenement in the garden'. Presumably something was built for on 3 March 1669[13] Warden Hunt was instructed that he

doe forthwith provide and pay for such hangings, tables, stooles and other furniture as may be fitt to furnish the Roome in the new Built Warehouse in Stationers Hall garden now intended for the use of the Company untill the Hall be rebuilt.

That summer, on 9 July 1669, it was

Ordered that the foundation for the Building of the Hall to be Surveyed and Mr Milles to be imployed therein.[14]

And accordingly, on 13 August, Mr Mills came. The entry in his *Survey of Building Sites* runs:

Five foundacions set out the day abovesaid scituate in Avemaria Lane belonging to the said Company containing upon the front North and South 96 foot from the middle of each party wall and in depth East and West 40 foot.[15]

A rough sketch plan stored in Box G may be related to the post-Fire rebuilding.[16]

Clearly, the old foundations of the medieval Inn were re-used and it is probable that the present Stationers' Hall stands on the site of what had once been the Countess of Pembroke's Great Hall. At the beginning, the work went on fast and on 3 December 1669 it was agreed that leave be

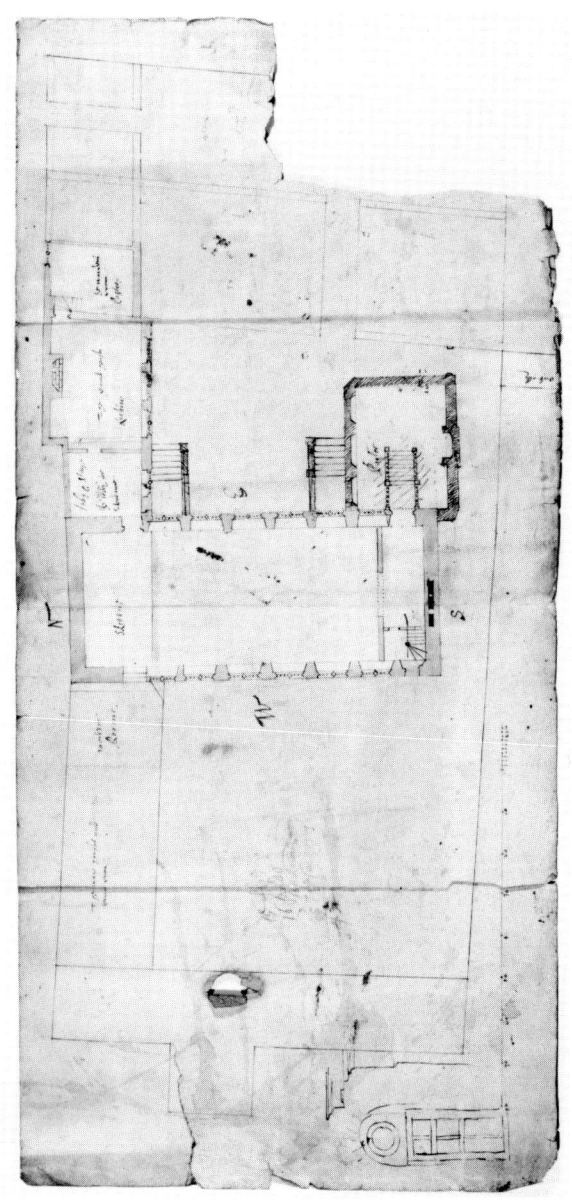

Fig.2. Post-Fire plan of Stationers' Hall and adjacent buildings. *Miscellaneous Records, Series I G21 i.*

given to the Aldermen of the Ward of Farringdon Within, to keep their Ward Moote in the Hall of this Company.[17] But by the next year, activity had died away, even though it was resolved to give Mr Mills £5 'as a gratuity for what he hath done for this Company'.[18]

There was then a two-year breathing space when very little seems to have happened, but on 5 August 1672 the Court reproached themselves that, though the foundations were laid, the Hall had not risen above a single storey. It was ordered that all debts should be called in, to pay for the construction, and work began in earnest so that on 24 October 1673, the Court Book entry runs:

> Ordered Mr Warden White to take care to provide Baize and other necessaries convenient to hang round the Hall on this Lord Mayors day onely. For the better ordering of the Company it is likewise ordered that every man wth his wife take place in the Hall according to theire seniority and as they shall be called by the Beadle.[19]

It would appear that they were expecting a large gathering and possibly a high level of confusion on this special and triumphant occasion.

The bills were settled – £905 to Robert Wapshott for brickwork, drains, slating and plastering, £732 for the carpentry work to Henry Foord, and £33 to Mr Pollard the painter. As far as I am aware, none of these men worked on any of the Wren churches and it is not possible to add any colourful personal details to the bare accounts. The Stationers had a snug, tight brick building for their Company and warehousing needs.

In the following year they decided to add a touch of grandeur to the surroundings. An entry for 6 November 1674 runs:

> It was this day ordered that Mr Colledge shall have the wainscoting of the Hall belonging to this Company. And that he shall enter into Articles with this Company to do it with well seasoned & well marked wainscot according to the Modell by him given, he the said Colledge being to have for doing the same three hundred pounds, out of which there is to remain in the Companies hands one hundred pounds for one whole yeare after the worke is done it being to remaine as cautionary money.[20]

Wren's epitaph – *Si Monumentum requiris, Circumspice* – can be applied to the Hall, standing as a monument to the craftsman Stephen Colledge. Seven years after it was completed to the Company's satisfaction, Colledge was on trial for his life, accused of writing and publishing a treasonous song, *The Ra-ree Show*, criticizing the King during the Succession Crisis which was gripping the nation. He was tried close by at the Old Bailey where the jury found no case, so the prisoner was removed to Oxford and there a packed jury found him guilty and he was promptly hanged.

There was plenty of demand for such a splendid Hall, and in September 1676, the Court fixed the charges and the officers' remuneration for its letting:[21]

To the Poor	1.	0.	0.
To the Clerk		10.	0.
To the Beadle		5.	0.
To Briggs the Porter		2.	6.
To Judith Gally for cleaning the Hall		2.	6.

For six months from March till Michaelmas 1678, the congregation of St Martin's was allowed free use of the Hall for divine service, presumably while work on the Church was completed. The arrangement may have ended in friction for the Order of 9 September 1678 which ended the neighbourly arrangement also required the Wardens

to send to the workmen to know by what Authority they make this Companies Gardens a lay stall.[22]

In conclusion, it may be useful to take a look at the Hall as it was before the Company employed Robert Mylne to face it in Portland Stone at the end of the eighteenth century. In 1674 the Company employed William Leybourne, an eminent surveyor, to make a book of plans of all the Company's property and, though it gives us less information than we would wish about the Hall, it reveals the adjacent, lettable buildings. The Hall itself shows up clearly on the Ward map which illustrates John Strype's edition of Stow's *Survey of London* published in 1720; it is a trim, substantial building, a proper headquarters for a senior City Livery Company.

References

All references are to documents in the Stationers' Archives, unless otherwise stated.
1. Court Book, C, f.27a.
2. When cleaning up Lambeth Palace Library after the bombing of the last war, it was noticeable that the mice had gone for the vellum bindings every time.
3. See particularly an article by Caroline Barron in *The London Journal* for 1995 where she discusses the aristocratic London house in the middle ages; the list of references is invaluable.
4. Sharpe, Reginald B. ed., *Calendar of Wills proved and enrolled in the Court of Hustings AD 1259-1688*, 1890, Part II, pp.194-6.
5. Court Book C, f.11a.

6. Court Book C, f.67b.
7. Court Book C, f.71b.
8. Court Book C, f.123a.
9. Court Book C, f.294a.
10. Court Book D, f.123b.
11. Court Book D, f.124a.
12. Court Book D, f.130a.
13. Court Book D, f.152a.
14. Court Book D, f.160b.
15. Corporation of London Record Office, *Survey of Building Sites* by Peter Mills, vol.2, f.52b.
16. Series I Box G, item 21 i.
17. Court Book D, f.165a.
18. Court Book D, f.169b.
19. Court Book D, f.222a.
20. Court Book D, f.240b.
21. Court Book D, f.267b.
22. Court Book D, f.326b.

William Cecil and the Stationers

PETER BLAYNEY

ON 13 AUGUST 1549 the Privy Council made two decisions connected with the book trade. The first was very specific: Oliver Dawbeney, citizen and tallowchandler of London, and John Mardeley, yeoman, were bound in the sum of forty pounds to guarantee that neither Mardeley nor anyone acting for him would

> at any tyme hereafter publishe or set foorth in writing or print, or cause to be published or set foorth in writing or print, any boke, ballet or other woork then siche as he or they shalbe licensed to sett foorth by my Lord Protectour and the rest of the Kinges Majestes Counsaile, the same woorke or woorkes to be first subscribed with the hand of William Cicill, esquier.[1]

Dawbeney seems to have left no other visible mark on history, but John Mardeley is known as the author of three pamphlets published in 1548-49.[2] The Lord Protector, as yet unaware that he would soon be ousted from that office, was Edward Seymour, Duke of Somerset, and William Cecil esquire was his personal secretary.

The basic rules governing the licensing of books had been laid down in 1538 by Henry VIII. At that date Henry's main concern had been with imported books, so he had elected himself sole licenser for importation. The responsibility for approving books for publication in England he had given to 'some of his grace's Privy Council, or other such as his highness shall appoint'.[3] So whether or not they had actually licensed anything else since the beginning of the young Edward's reign, the councillors were hardly breaking new ground in appointing themselves to license any future book by Mardeley. And it was well within the Lord Protector's authority to require the validating signature of his private secretary, Cecil.

The Privy Council's concern for the public welfare did, however, extend beyond merely protecting readers from unfiltered doses of John Mardeley, and later in the same meeting a more comprehensive order was issued:

that from hensforth no prenter sholde prente or putt to vente any Englisshe booke butt suche as sholde first be examined by Mr. Secretary Peter, Mr. Secretary Smith, and Mr. Cicill, or the one of them, and allowed by the same.[4]

Unlike Cecil, his fellow licensers were Secretaries with a capital S: the councillors Sir William Petre and Sir Thomas Smith were the two Principal Secretaries to the King.

After quoting the text of that second Council order, Petre's biographer commented that

Here, in company, are three of the Fathers of the Civil Service, all bibliophiles. Their task, however, was no literary one, but the suppression of seditious books and pamphlets. Within two months the trio was broken up and Petre was the sole censor for the rest of the reign.[5]

But while it is true that the trio was soon broken up, Petre was certainly not the sole licenser for the rest of the reign.

When the Duke of Somerset was arrested on 10 October, Smith and Cecil were among those also detained, and three days later Smith was removed from the Privy Council. None of the prisoners, however, remained in custody more than a few months. Cecil was in the first group to be released, on 25 January 1550,[6] and may have resumed his licensing duties immediately; if not, he may have done so when Somerset was reinstated to the Council in April. If the Council order is interpreted strictly, then Petre would have been the only person entitled to license books until Cecil rejoined him; if it was meant to apply to any and all Principal Secretaries, then Nicholas Wotton would have shared the job with Petre for nearly a year. In either event, Cecil would certainly have resumed that responsibility no later than 5 September 1550, when he became a Privy Councillor and replaced Wotton as secretary. Licensing books was not quite among the most important functions of a secretary of state, so given Petre's years of seniority it seems reasonable to guess that the newly appointed Cecil did most of whatever licensing was needed during the few months that the order remained in force. But on 28 April 1551 a new requirement superseded it:

that from henceforth no printer or other person do print nor sell within this realm . . . any matter in the English tongue . . . , unless the same be first allowed by his majesty or his Privy Council in writing signed with his majesty's most gracious hand or the hands of six of his said Privy Council.[7]

As councillors, both Cecil and Petre could still play a part in licensing books for publication, but the responsibility was no longer theirs alone.

Cecil's relatively brief career as licenser for the press came to an abrupt end with the accession of Mary Tudor. Sir William Petre was reappointed by Mary as both councillor and secretary, but Cecil was not. By all accounts he enjoyed Mary's good opinion,[8] and he apparently took part in at least two diplomatic missions abroad. He served the county of Lincolnshire in various capacities, and was a member of Mary's fourth Parliament. But although his abilities were widely recognized, and some predicted that he might succeed Petre as secretary, he never held any office of state under Mary.[9] When Elizabeth acceded in November 1558 she reappointed Cecil to the Council and made him sole secretary, but the comparatively minor function of licensing was probably not among his duties. Mary, who of all the Tudors probably had most to fear from the press, had taken the right to license books out of the hands of the Council, and had reserved it to herself alone. And when Elizabeth issued her *Injunctions* of 1559, she gave that power to the ecclesiastical rather than the secular authorities – principally to the Bishop of London and Archbishop of Canterbury.[10]

All told, then, Cecil was a designated licenser for at most about seventeen months, although as a Privy Councillor he was qualified to participate in the process for two additional years. If, therefore, his relations with the book trade had been confined to his licensing activities, this paper would now be over.[11] But during his two terms as Principal Secretary, Cecil had other duties that sometimes brought him into contact with Stationers, and it is those connections that I plan to explore here. As background, though, I need first to sketch a brief history of privileges.

The first known royal privileges to be issued for books by an English monarch were granted by Henry VIII to Richard Pynson in late 1518. Each was for a topical Latin oration: one by Cuthbert Tunstall, prebendary of York; the other by Richard Pace, Dean of St Paul's.[12] Each gave Pynson two years' protection from competition, and each is known only from a summary of its terms printed in the book itself. Neither was granted by a process that left any trace in the more accessible parts of the extant public records.

During the next three decades Henry issued numerous other book-related privileges and grants. Some, like those of 1518, protected specific texts for a specified number of years. Others apparently covered more than one text: sometimes a small number of specified titles; sometimes the works of a particular author; occasionally even a whole class of books, as in 1543 when Grafton and Whitchurch were given a privilege for all liturgical books of Sarum use.[13] By the 1530s Henry had apparently also begun to grant broader privileges to individual publishers, giving protection for a specified term to any and all books published at the costs of the privileged person. By 1538, indeed, so many books of all kinds were claiming to have been printed *cum privilegio regali* that Henry found it necessary to order that all such claims should thereafter be qualified by *ad imprimendum solum*.[14] In other words, the privilege was for printing only, and did not necessarily imply royal approval of the book's contents.

Like the first two grants of 1518, however, many of Henry's privileges are known only from texts or summaries printed in the books themselves – while virtually all the others are known only by deduction from the use of *cum privilegio* in imprints or colophons. Not even the printed claim that a privilege was granted by letters patent guarantees that it will be found on the Patent Rolls or among the Privy Seal warrants.[15] Even the office of King's Printer, which Henry may have granted to Richard Faques and certainly bestowed successively on Richard Pynson and Thomas Berthelet, was apparently not granted under the Great Seal. The surviving patent of 1530 that is usually described as appointing Berthelet King's Printer in fact does nothing of the kind: in granting him an annuity of four pounds it describes him as already holding that office.[16]

By contrast, however, most of the book privileges known to have been granted by Henry's successors were granted by letters patent under the Great Seal, and were duly registered on the Patent Rolls. The procedure by which such a patent finally acquired the Great Seal was laid down by a statute of 1536.[17] After the monarch had approved and signed a draft of the intended grant it was given to one of the Principal Secretaries, who kept it as evidence that it had in fact been signed. First, though, he had it copied by one of the four Clerks of the Signet, and sent the copy under the Signet as a warrant to the Keeper of the Privy Seal. Retaining that bill as evidence for the Signet, one of the clerks at the Privy Seal Office copied it out again and had the copy sealed. That writ of Privy Seal was sent to the Chancery as the final warrant for the Great Seal itself. Retaining the writ as evidence, one of the six Clerks wrote out the actual patent, to which the Great Seal was then affixed in the appropriate fashion. Finally the writ was copied again, this time on to the Patent Roll as a register copy for the archives.

That, at least, is how the procedure is usually described in its simplest form,[18] omitting the various registers, docquets, and indexes that were also generated. But what is less often considered is what had to happen *before* the royal signature set the bureaucratic machinery in motion. If, for example, John Bodley wanted a patent for the Geneva Bible, he had to do rather more than simply write out a request, hand it to Elizabeth in person, and watch her read and sign it. The Elizabethan Patent Rolls record an annual average of more than a thousand grants. To that total must be added the contents of the Close Rolls, the Pardon Rolls, and the Confirmation Rolls; the leases and grants issued directly under the Privy Seal, or under other seals such as that of the Duchy of Lancaster – to say nothing of the unknown number of requests for the royal signature that were considered but rejected. We can hardly imagine that each bill was usually handed to the sovereign by its applicant, or that the sovereign usually read each one through and considered its individual merits. That was what secretaries were for.

A bill submitted for the sign manual had first to be approved by a secretary of state,[19] who had to ensure that it was a legal and appropriate request, that it was drawn up in correct legal form, and that it was accompanied by a summarizing docquet that the monarch might actually read. I do not know how much discretion each secretary was given to turn away obviously unsuitable requests on his own authority, or how often each monarch either added or withheld a signature against a secretary's advice. But advising was part of the job, and it can hardly be doubted that a Principal Secretary could exercise considerable influence over the number and nature of the patents issued during his term of office.

The book-related patents granted in the first half of the reign of Edward VI were similar in nature to many of those granted by his father. In April 1547, three months after the accession, Richard Grafton and Reyner Wolfe were respectively appointed King's Printer and King's Typographer for Latin, Greek, and Hebrew, in each case for life. At the same time Grafton and Edward Whitchurch were given a seven-year privilege for all authorized service books – this being the Protestant replacement for the grant of Sarum liturgies they had obtained from Henry four years earlier. A few months later Walter Lynne received a seven-year patent for a specific anti-Catholic book and for 'all other maner of bokes consonant to godlines' to be produced at his own charges, and about a year later John Oswen was licensed to produce service books for seven years for use in Wales and the marches – with the usual addition of any other books to be initiated by him. And in July 1550 Stephen Mierdman was given a five-year privilege for any books to be produced at his own expense, but with no particular work specified.[20] At about the same time Nicholas Udall *nearly* received a seven-year grant that would have included 'the Bible in English as well in the large volume for the use of churches as in any other convenient volume'. Since various versions of the Bible were already in progress, that might well have caused some major conflicts of interest – but it would appear that the Udall patent was intercepted at the last minute, probably at the request of an interested party with a powerful friend. A writ of Privy Seal exists, but it lacks any indication that it was sealed and delivered; the grant was copied on to the Patent Roll, but with neither a date of delivery nor any note of the warrant under which it was issued.[21]

William Cecil became a Principal Secretary to Edward VI in September 1550, and during his term of office five book-related patents were issued. The first two, however, were grants directly sponsored by the King and Privy Council, and are unlikely to have been influenced at all by the identity of the secretaries. The first was an eight-year privilege to Richard Jugge for a royally authorized revision of Tyndale's New Testament. The first edition in quarto appeared about a year and a half later, when the Council fixed the price at 22 pence.[22] The second patent was more of a ban than a grant. Cosmo, Duke of Florence, had hired Laurence Torrentinus to print *The Digests and Pandects of the Civil Law* from what was believed to be Justinian's original manuscript, and had asked King Edward to forbid all printers in England, of whatever nationality, to print any version of that work for seven years without Torrentinus's permission.[23] Given the overall character of English printing during the 1550s, the precaution was probably unnecessary. Almost two years passed before the next Edwardian book privilege was issued – and then, in less than six weeks, three were granted in quick succession. Those three patents would help to shape the future of the Stationers' Company – and Cecil was personally involved in at least two of them.

The founding of the English Stock in 1603 was one of the most significant events in the Company's history after the charter, and the principal assets of the Stock were the rights derived from four patents. Three of those were surrendered by their then owners in 1603, and were combined in a single new grant to the Company itself in October. Those were the patent for almanacks and prognostications originally granted to Richard Watkins and James Roberts, the patent for primers, psalters, and books of private prayer originally granted to William Seres, and the varied collection of rights accumulated during the long and acquisitive career of John Day. And while the founder members of the English Stock were still trying to organize themselves, in 1605 Thomas Wight suddenly agreed to sell them the remaining 24 years of the patent for books of common law, originally granted to Richard Tottell.

Every one of those ancestral patents was first granted while Cecil was secretary. The almanack patent was one of the last three book privileges issued while he was sole secretary to Elizabeth. The last three issued during his first secretariat, only months before Edward died in July 1553, were as follows: primers to William Seres on 6 March; Ponet's catechism and the ABC with the Brief Catechism to John Day on 25 March, and books of common law to Richard Tottell on 12 April.[24]

I have found no evidence of any special relationship between Cecil and either of the almanack patentees. In the case of lawbooks, although those who held the patent in the 1590s were evidently under Cecil's protection, the evidence regarding Richard Tottell himself is mixed. With the special exception of Reyner Wolfe (who remained Typographer for Latin, Greek, and Hebrew under both Mary and Elizabeth), Tottell was the only book patentee whose privilege was renewed by Mary Tudor. Since both the original and the renewed patent were signed while Sir William Petre was one of the two secretaries, Tottell may have been Petre's *protégé* rather than Cecil's. It is certainly true that when Tottell later tried to obtain two different grants, his petitions were either submitted directly to Cecil or referred to him by a later secretary for advice – but it is also true that both were rejected. The undated bills survive among the Cecil papers, one requesting a seven-year privilege for all books or tables of cosmography and the other a 31-year monopoly for making paper in England. But whatever he thought of the merits of those two requests, Cecil was nevertheless the secretary through whom Tottell's lawbook patent was renewed for life in the first book privilege granted by Elizabeth.[25]

In 1571 Cecil was elevated to the peerage as Baron Burghley, and in 1572 he was appointed Lord Treasurer. Nearly six years later, the reversion of the lawbook patent was granted to one of the Clerks of the Signet, Nicasius Yetsweirt, for 30 years after Tottell's death.[26] The Principal Secretary at the time was Sir Francis Walsingham – but since Yetsweirt had held his clerkship under Elizabeth, Mary, Edward VI, *and* Henry VIII, he had known and worked for a dozen secretaries, and he enjoyed Elizabeth's personal favour. It may also be worth noting that as Clerk of the Signet he had probably written out the Signet Bill for at least one of Tottell's grants with his own hand, so he would have known exactly what he was requesting.

While Cecil was secretary, Yetsweirt was granted an office in Somerset and several pieces of real estate[27] – but no matter how deserving he may have been, I do not believe that Cecil would have recommended the lawbook reversion for signature. All but three of the book privileges issued during his terms of office were granted to active members of the book trade. Two of the exceptions were grants of dictionaries to their compilers; the other was a seven-year patent for the Geneva Bible to John Bodley, who had apparently been one of the principal financial contributors to the venture.[28] Seven years, however, was enough. When Bodley later requested that his patent be renewed for twelve more years, Cecil sought the opinions of the Bishop of London and Archbishop of Canterbury – but although both of them approved, the request was nevertheless denied.[29] During Cecil's secretariat, no book privilege was ever granted to anyone unconnected with either the particular book or the book trade in general. That, unfortunately, could not be said of his successors.

I have been unable to discover precisely when in 1593 Nicasius Yetsweirt died, but it was probably before 8 July. On that date the Privy Council wrote to the Stationers' Company to warn them that although Tottell was now lately deceased, 'the benefitt of the saide graunt is to come to Charles Yetsuerte, sonne of the saide Nicasius'. Having been informed that 'certene persons are in hande with the printinge of the Rastall and Poulton's abridgement of the statutes', the Council ordered the Master and Wardens to 'comaunde and inhibit the saide persons . . . that they forbeare to proceede any further'.[30]

There were two problems with that order. First, while the Rastell and Pulton abridgements had first been printed at Tottell's expense,[31] and were consequently covered by the terms of his patent, the right to print books of statutes belonged to the office of Queen's Printer. In 1577 the Company had ruled that during Tottell's lifetime the abridgements should be shared equally between the rival patentees, but that the imprints should identify only the Queen's Printer.[32] The 'certene persons' who had already started printing Rastell's abridgement in 1593 were the deputies of Queen's Printer Christopher Barker, exercising what they believed was now their right. The other problem was that whoever had told the Company and the Council in July that Tottell was lately deceased had been exaggerating: he did not die until 1 September.[33]

When the lawbook patent was finally granted to Charles Yetsweirt in March 1594, it included a quite extraordinary passage in which Elizabeth claimed to remember having *meant* to include the two abridgements in the reversion of 1577:

the sole and onlie imprinting of which two Abridgmentes . . . was by vs (as we of o^r certen knowledge do remember) ment and entended of o^r especiall grace, and fauo^r, to haue ben graunted to the aforesaid Nicasius and his Assignes by o^r said *lettres* patentes to him made, but by reason of some defect or ambiguitie of wordes in the aforesaid *lettres* patentes . . . it is affirmed by divers, and so geven out, that the same did not passe by o^r said *lettres* patentes.[34]

In Charles's new patent those two books were therefore expressly named and included.

Yetsweirt immediately set up a press and began to print, and among the books he produced during his first working year was an edition of Rastell's abridgement that appeared early in 1595. Meanwhile, however, the deputies of Christopher Barker were finishing the edition that the Privy Council had tried to stop.[35] Yetsweirt therefore began to enlist the support of some powerful allies.

By late March the question of the lawbook patent had already been referred to Sir John Puckering, Lord Keeper of the Great Seal, and on the 27th the Earl of Essex wrote to him in support of Yetsweirt. Less than a month later, however, Yetsweirt died, and the matter passed into the evidently capable hands of his widow Jane. Five days later, Jane Yetsweirt sought the aid of Cecil's son, Sir Robert, reminding him of favours he had formerly done for Charles and explicitly assuming that he already knew the essential details of the case. Within the next few days she wrote on her own behalf to Puckering, who soon received another letter from Essex to confirm that he supported Jane no less than Charles. She also wrote to Cecil himself, again invoking past assistance to the Yetsweirt family and assuming some degree of familiarity with the proceedings.[36] Cecil's favours to Nicasius had in fact been mentioned by Charles Yetsweirt as long ago as 1569, when he wrote to ask if he could become one of Cecil's servants.[37] Even if that request is not interpreted quite literally, Charles and Jane Yetsweirt can certainly be numbered among Cecil's *protégés*.

By 1595 the Yetsweirts seem also to have acquired some claim to the attention of the Earl of Essex, and perhaps of Puckering as well. It is therefore worth pointing out that the contest over the abridged statutes was not the only feature of the new patent that would have upset the Stationers. The celebrated clause in the 1557 charter that restricted printing to members of the Company included the proviso that the Crown could always grant exceptions by letters patent. But nothing could compel the Stationers to *like* such exceptions, and they would have been far from happy when Yetsweirt set up a new printing house. There is reason to suppose that the printer who actually managed the business for the Yetsweirts was the man who would eventually acquire the patent for himself: the Draper, Thomas Wight. And even though Wight himself was in good standing with the Stationers, the case of Simon Stafford would soon illustrate just how little the Company liked the idea of Drapers setting up as printers.[38] Worse still, the patent did not even restrict Yetsweirt to lawbooks alone, but included the usual clause about other books produced at his own cost.

The new printing house did indeed print books of other kinds – no fewer than six before the end of 1594, though none thereafter. One was *Of the Interchangeable Course, or Variety of Things in the Whole World* (STC 15488), translated from French by Robert Ashley and dedicated to Sir John Puckering. Another was a work in Spanish with a fictitious imprint (STC 19624.5), intended to be sold surreptitiously in Europe. It was written by the exiled former secretary to Philip II, Antonio Perez – who was now in the service of (and who dedicated the book to) the Earl of Essex.[39] A third was the anonymous *Arraignment of the Whole Society of Jesuits in France* (STC 779–9.5), which has no dedication but could have been sponsored by almost anyone. The remaining three were all versions of a single book: two editions in English and one in French of *A True Report of Sundry Horrible Conspiracies of Late Time Detected, to Have (by Barbarous Murders) Taken Away the Life of the Queen's Most Excellent Majesty* (STC 7603–3.5, 7580). The author was William Cecil, Lord Burghley.

But while Cecil certainly took a personal interest in the fortunes of the Yetsweirts, as I mentioned earlier I know of no special relationship between him and the first lawbook patentee, Richard Tottell. The case of John Day, however, is rather different. In September 1552 the Duke of Northumberland wrote to Cecil about John Ponet's newly-written catechism:

I haue thought good to requier yo^u to be a meane for the kinges ma^{tes} lycens for the printinge of the same, And that this poore man, who hathe byn allwaies A furderer of godlie thinges, may by his highnes gracius goodnes be auctorised for the onlie printinge of the same for A certein space soche as shalbe thought mete by his ma^{tie}, wherin the poore man shal haue caus to pray for his highnes.[40]

Poverty is of course relative, and John Day seems to have had something of a knack for persuading the powerful that he was more unfortunate than he seemed to others.

Cecil was evidently successful as 'a meane for the kinges ma^{tes} lycens', because when the patent was finally delivered six months later, it included not only Ponet's catechism (which had meanwhile been officially authorized by Edward for use in schools), but also the ABC with the Brief Catechism extracted from the Book of Common Prayer, plus any and all future works by either Ponet or Thomas Becon to be compiled or produced at Day's charges.[41] In the case of the two catechisms this patent overrode that of the King's Printer, to whom all authorized service books in English otherwise belonged. And whether by intent or by another 'defect or ambiguitye of wordes', the patent neglected to mention any 'certein space soche as shalbe thought mete', and could therefore be argued to be for life.

In view of Day's undisguised Protestant sympathies, it is hardly surprising that he was granted no privileges by Mary Tudor. Lacking an expiration date, his first patent can be presumed to have revived automatically on Elizabeth's succession. A year later he obtained a second grant – this time an explicitly lifelong patent for William Cuningham's *Cosmographical Glass* coupled with a seven-year privilege for any other books to be produced at Day's charges. The second part of that patent had been expired for a full six months before Day secured his next grant, but the new terms were even more comprehensive. Only two books were specified by title – 'the psames of David in englyshe mitre with notes [*and*] the A.B.C. with the lytle catachysme' – but the privilege included not only all books to be published at Day's expense during the next ten years, but also all books so produced in the past.[42]

That was the last Day patent to be issued during Cecil's term as secretary, but far from the last time Day came to his attention. In 1568 John Foxe wrote to request, in the interests of speeding the revised *Acts and Monuments* through the press, that Day be allowed to employ more than the permitted maximum of four alien workmen.[43] Cecil's response is not on record. In 1572 Matthew Parker wrote a letter that has often been quoted, complaining that the City authorities were preventing Day from setting up a shop in St Paul's Churchyard. He has turned to Cecil, he explains, 'for that yo" of the Councell haue written to me, & other of the [*High*] Commission, to helpe Daie' – but unfortunately the circumstances are unknown. In this case Cecil probably did exert a little influence, because the Privy Council subsequently wrote to the Mayor and Aldermen on Day's behalf – but the City nonetheless prevailed, and the shop was never built.[44] Day remained, however, a topic that Archbishop Parker assumed would interest Cecil, and in 1573 he wrote another often-quoted letter to report that a workman named Asplyn had attempted to murder Day and his wife.[45]

Given the broad terms of Day's 1567 privilege it is unclear why he felt he needed a separate grant in 1574 for two catechisms and all subsequent works by Alexander Nowell, Dean of St Paul's.[46] When the 1567 patent finally expired he obtained one last privilege: a lifetime grant in survivorship to him and his son Richard for *The Psalms in English Metre, The ABC and Little Catechism,* Nowell's catechisms and other works – and, inevitably, for

all suche bookes whatsoeu[r] as the saide Iohn and Richard or either of them hathe imprynted or shall imprynte beinge compiled or translated and set oute by any lerned man at the procurement costes and charges of the said Iohn Daye & Richard or either of them.[47]

Cecil, of course, was no longer secretary when those last two privileges were granted, and we have the word of Christopher Barker that the second of them was procured by the Earl of Leicester,[48] son of the duke who had urged Cecil to secure the first Day patent 25 years earlier. But while Cecil was not Day's only influential supporter, he was certainly instrumental in helping to create the collection of rights that would eventually pass from Richard Day to the English Stock.

The first of the four major English Stock patents to be granted, albeit the last to be discussed, was the one with which Cecil was most closely connected – the patent for 'all man[r] of bookes of private prayers called . . . prymers' granted to William Seres for six years in March 1553.[49] This being the reign of Edward VI, the contents of those primers were extracted from the Book of Common Prayer, and included the ABC, the Brief Catechism, and a selection of psalms. The accession of Mary therefore left Seres with a privilege for books that were soon to be banned, and presumably also a large stock of increasingly unsaleable primers – and by the end of October the Catholic equivalent of his patent had been granted to John Wayland.[50] Seres is known to have been imprisoned during Mary's reign, and it is a reasonable guess that he had failed to concede defeat with sufficient grace or alacrity. But a few months after Elizabeth came to the throne he received a new and expanded lifetime privilege for 'aswell all maner of bookes of private prayers vsually . . . called . . . primers and also psalters . . . in Latine or englishe'.[51]

Before I continue with the story of the Seres patent it will be useful to consider the question of conflicts of interest, because there was always a tendency for the larger book privileges to overlap. I have already noted the controversy over the Rastell and Pulton abridgements, to which both the Royal Printer and the law patentee could lay claim. When the ABC and the Brief Catechism were printed as parts of the Book of Common Prayer they belonged to the Royal Printer, when included in a primer they belonged to Seres, and when printed alone they belonged to John Day. When included in an English Bible, the Book of Psalms belonged to the patentee for that particular translation, but psalms included in the

Book of Common Prayer belonged to the Royal Printer. Separate psalters in prose, and any psalms included in a primer, belonged to Seres, but metrical translations of them belonged to John Day. The patents granted during Cecil's secretariat did, therefore, sometimes lead to disputes – but they were usually easy to settle, and the parties usually honoured the settlements.

The conflicts that caused the Stationers so many problems in the 1570s and '80s were of two different kinds. During the sixteenth century the Company had devised its own system and rules for conferring and protecting publication rights. The problems of the mid-1570s were caused mainly by the grant of royal privileges for texts already owned under Company rules by someone else. No such patent was issued while Cecil was secretary. The piracy problems of the early 1580s, on the other hand, were largely catalysed by the grant of major book privileges to people outside the book trade. And as I have already noted, apart from the compilers of two dictionaries and a financial backer of the Geneva Bible (each of whom received only a short-term privilege for a single text), during Cecil's secretariat no book patents were granted to outsiders.

Near the beginning of this paper I noted that when Sir Thomas Smith's brief term as secretary was terminated in 1549 by the fall of Somerset, he was also removed from the Privy Council. After more than twenty years out of office he was finally restored to the Council in 1571 – and to celebrate that promotion, the Mayor and Alderman promptly made him free of London by redemption. A year later, when Cecil was appointed Lord Treasurer, Smith became sole secretary in his place. And for the book trade, the consequences were little short of catastrophic.

The first book privilege ushered through the system by Smith was granted to Thomas Marshe in September 1572, and caused two kinds of trouble. It gave Marshe a twelve-year privilege for two Latin schoolbooks, for two stated reasons: first, because Marshe had 'procured more pro-porcyonable and apte le*tt*res [*i.e., type*] then heretofore hath byn occupied' in England; and second, because the official restrictions on importation had hindered the use of those texts in schools.[52] Neither claim was accurate – and the second was blatantly dishonest, because most of the texts had been printed in England comparatively recently, and already belonged to others.[53] No minutes of the Court of Assistants survive from before 1576, so the precise dimensions of the upheaval cannot be known – but some of the consequent arbitrations were still being invoked several years later.[54] It can be said with some confidence that Cecil would probably not have recommended such a grant. In 1569 Archbishop Parker had approvingly passed on a request from Henry Bynneman for 'a privilege for Prynting two or 3 vsual bokes for Grammarians, as *Therence*, *Virgile*, or Tullys Office etc.',[55] but Cecil had wisely ignored it. Virgil was not included in the Marshe privilege, but both Terence and Cicero were.

The other problem was that in addition to giving Marshe the exclusive right to print those books or cause them to be printed, the patent also gave him the sole right to 'sett [*them*] forth to sale', and ordered that nobody else should import or sell other editions. That brought the patent into direct conflict with the jealously-guarded privileges of the City itself, and on 27 January 1573 the following entry was written in the Repertory:

It is informed this courte by Thom[a]s norton gent that Thomas Marshe, Stacion[r] hauth obteyned *lettres* patentes for sale of bookes against the lib[r]ties of this Citie & that there is good hoppe to haue the same *lettres* patentes repealed And for that end the wardens of Stacion[r]s were willed to exhibite there bill into there [*sic*, for *the*] Chauncery and a bill was drawen to haue bene exhibited accordinglie by lycence of this courte Since w[ch] tyme the wardens haue surceased there attempted suyte. Therefore it is ordered that S[r] Alexander Avenon & S[r] Rowland Hayward shall call the wardens of the Stacion[r]s before them to knowe why the said suyte is not proceded & that m[r] Norton be there also to charge the said Stacion[r]s w[th] there necgligence.[56]

Two years later the City was still trying to persuade the Company (which had meanwhile arbitrated its internal disputes, and was presumably content to let sleeping dogs lie) to explain why nothing had yet been done.[57]

In April 1573 two book privileges were issued, one of them an uncomplicated eight-year grant to Lodowick Lloyd for his translation of Plutarch. The other gave Thomas Vautrollier two Latin books for ten years.[58] Some stationers may have resented the fact that Vautrollier, who was only a brother of the Company and not a freeman,[59] thereby gained the unchallengeable right to run a printing house. But he had already printed a handful of books since 1570 without having his press seized, so the Company appears to have had no serious objection to his setting up as a master printer – and since neither of the books had been printed before, the privilege may not have raised many hackles. A year later, however, the emboldened Vautrollier obtained a second patent – this time for several Latin books including a version of the Bible, another version of the New Testament, and all the works of both Ovid and Cicero.[60] This grant, too, included books that were already owned by others – and to add insult to injury, allowed Vautrollier to hire as many as six alien workmen to help him print them.

Midway between the two Vautrollier grants, a patent was issued that would become one of the most frequently infringed of all book privileges during the unruly 1580s. Reyner Wolfe had finally died, leaving vacant the lucrative office of Queen's Typographer for Latin, Greek, and Hebrew, which included the rights to Lily's Grammar. And on 15 December 1573 that office was granted for life to a non-Stationer, Francis Flower. A year later another patent was granted outside the Company when Thomas Tallis and William Byrd received a 21-year privilege for books of music and printed music paper.[61] A year later still, somebody attempted to obtain what would have been the most inappropriate patent yet. The applicant may well have been John Wolfe, then still a freeman of the Fishmongers, and who (according to Christopher Barker) once 'sued for a priuiledge wch was thought vnreasonable by some serving her Maiestie'. The sheer effrontery of the petition is certainly reminiscent of Wolfe, because the patent being sought was for 'all balades Damaske paper and bookes in prose or meetre from the quantitie of one sheete of paper to xxiiij^{tie}'. To be fair to Sir Thomas Smith, there is no direct evidence that he would have recommended that bill for signature. But the Stationers evidently thought him capable of doing so, else they would hardly have thought it necessary to send a petition to Lord Treasurer Cecil.[62]

A comparison between the book privileges issued respectively by Cecil and Smith, therefore, appears to support my suggestion that a Principal Secretary could exercise considerable influence over the kinds of patent granted during his tenure. Viewed from the book trade, and by contrast with Cecil's, Smith's secretariat was a disaster whose consequences were felt for years, or even decades. That is ironic – because when Smith had been made free of London in 1571, the company he had chosen to join was the Stationers.[63]

To return to William Seres: less than a year before Cecil was succeeded as secretary by Smith, he procured an enlarged grant to Seres and his son William in survivorship. This included

all manner of booke and bookes of priuate prayers primers psalters and psalmes bothe in greate volumes and small in Englishe or latine . . . As allso all and every other booke and bookes wch the said willm Seres the elder and willm Seres the younger or either of them haue or hath imprintid or at anie time hereafter shall imprinte wch haue ben or shall be sett forthe by anie learned man of this o^{r} Realm . . . , whether the same or any of them shall be in Englishe or Laten.[64]

Cecil's personal role in this grant is doubly attested. When William Seres junior petitioned him in 1582 for assistance against the piracies of John Wolfe and others, he began by reminding Cecil that my late father by the good meanes & favour of your honor obteyned of our late sovereigne lord kyng Edward the sixte a certen priviledge . . . W^{ch} priviledge was taken from him in quene Maryes time & synce that by the further helpe & goodnes of your honor was eftsoones graunted to hym & to me.[65]

And when Christopher Barker wrote a commentary on the privileges for Cecil in the same year, he described the Seres patent as having been

procured by yor hono^r to that vertuous honest man yor Lordships late seru^{a}nt William Seres the elder, and his sonne.[66]

Twenty years after it was granted, the validity of the 1571 patent was questioned on the grounds that no record could be found in Chancery of the surrender of the previous grant (of 1559). A new patent was therefore sought to resolve the ambiguity, and the draft submitted to Solicitor-General Egerton has survived. It bears Cecil's autograph endorsement: 'forasmuch as some question is made touchynge ye form^r Grant, I pray you to cause a new book to be made W Burghlye'.[67] In this context, 'book' is the contemporary technical term for any draft, bill, or warrant preceding the final letters patent.

When Barker referred to Seres as 'yor Lordships late seru^{a}nt' he was not just using an empty formula – because Seres was, quite literally, Cecil's servant. His origins are unknown, but since he was listed as a 'Stranger' in the lay subsidies of 1564 and 1577 he was presumably alien-born,[68] and his known connection with Arnold Birckman in the 1550s may perhaps suggest what first brought him to England. He was made free of London by redemption as a Stationer on 18 September 1548 – and since he was already a trusted servant by November, he may perhaps have owed his redemption to the growing influence of the 28-year-old William Cecil.

Among the Lansdowne Manuscripts is a memorandum book kept by Cecil in 1552–7 in which Seres's name occurs frequently. On one page he appears in a list of servants and 'reteynors'; on another he is found in a list that apparently records the provision of new blue livery coats. He is often found collecting rent from various tenants, especially one Andrew Skarre, and making payments on Cecil's behalf to a variety of people including (on more than one occasion) the treasurer of 'ye aduentur of Russia'. Seres also made many purchases for the household, including food, wine, apparel, bows for the armoury, a variety of miscellaneous household goods, and quantities of blue cloth for liveries.[69] Additional evidence, as if it were needed, is found among the Cecil Papers at Hatfield House, including two miscellaneous bills submitted by Seres for payment in which he calls Cecil 'my maister', and two accounts in Cecil's hand in which his own obligations for the quarter are balanced against Seres's debts.[70] Books feature in all four documents, and there is also a separate bill for books purchased throughout 1554 and 1555, endorsed in Cecil's hand as 'Seress and birkmans bills for bookes'.[71]

When Northumberland began scheming in 1553 to put his daughter-in-law on the throne, Cecil realized that he might need to flee London at short notice, and made plans accordingly. Twenty years later his former clerk, Roger Alford, wrote him an account of what he remembered of those days. The preparations, he recalled, included conveying all Cecil's papers, plate, and money 'to one Nelsons howse in London and Seres howse yor servante'.[72] Evidently, then, Seres was an unusually trusted retainer. He was also, of course, a bookseller, a publisher, and (for at least a few years) a printer, and as his career flourished his services to Cecil presumably became less frequent. One can hardly deduce very much from the scarcity of evidence outside the Lansdowne memorandum book – but the only services for which I have found evidence after the 1550s are the collection of some rents in February 1564 and the delivery of a letter in 1577.[73] The *earliest* known transaction between Seres and Cecil, however, (which happens also to be the first recorded association between Cecil and Sir William Petre), has proved to be fairly well documented, and is worth examining in some detail.

In February 1548 Cecil was commissioned, with his Lincolnshire neighbour Lawrence Eresby, to enquire into the former chantries in that county.[74] All chantry properties had been seized by the Crown the year before,[75] and what Cecil and Eresby had to do was to have those in Lincolnshire surveyed and valued for the Court of Augmentations. Soon afterwards they decided to purchase a particularly tempting chantry property in London for themselves. Most of the chantries were considerably smaller and more affordable than the monasteries seized by Henry VIII, and the Court of Augmentations preferred to sell them in batches rather than singly. Cecil and Eresby therefore joined forces with ten other applicants. They included one of the commissioners for London chantry properties (Hugh Losse), a colleague of Cecil's father's from the King's Wardrobe (Robert Robotham), Secretary Sir William Petre, Petre's steward John Keyme, and Keyme's brother Richard. A comparable syndicate of insiders today would delight an investigative journalist – but for its time the transaction was unexceptional.[76]

The fourteen properties sought by the group were duly granted to the nominal applicants, John and Richard Keyme, on 24 November for apayment of £1,154 15s. Next day each of the other members of the

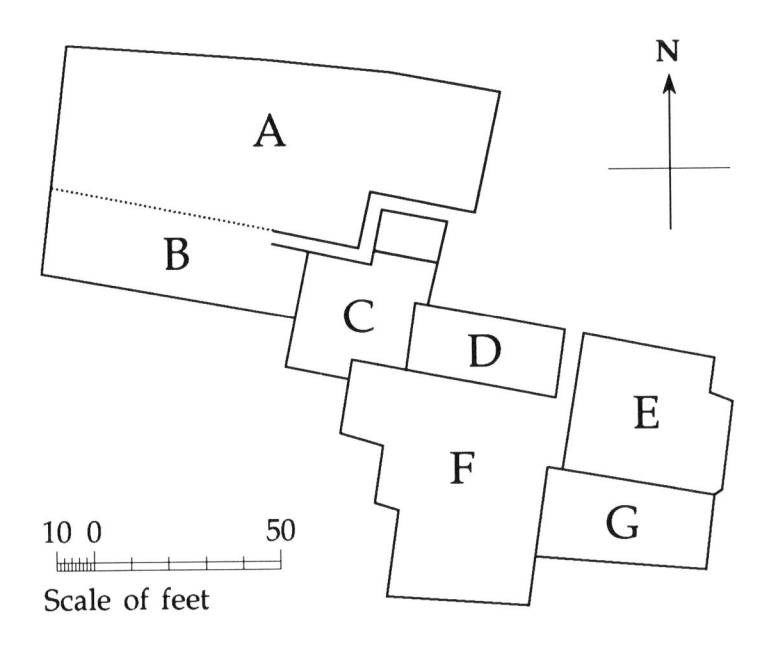

Fig. 1. Chantry property purchased in 1548 by Cecil and Eresby.

syndicate purchased his own designated real estate from the Keymes. The conveyance to Cecil and Eresby does not specify the price, but their property had accounted for £72 10s. of the total. In order for the transaction to be legally completed someone had to take possession, and neither Cecil nor Eresby was available to do so in person. The conveyance therefore records that possession was taken by two designated proxies or 'attornati'. They were Cecil's clerk Roger Alford and William Seres.[77]

By the following March, Seres had apparently established himself in one of the buildings on the property, probably that marked C in Figure 1. In the lay subsidy for 1549 he is listed as a resident in the parish,[78] and a year later Cecil formally granted him a lease as of Lady Day 1549. The deed included a covenant that Seres was not to alienate or sell any part of the lease to his wife or children, but that he could purchase the fee simple for eighty pounds at any time during the next ten years.[79] Part of the western section of the property (A, and perhaps part of B) was sold in May 1551 to William Sparke, merchant taylor, and John Battene, and less than a year later Eresby conveyed his share of what remained to Cecil, leaving him sole owner.[80] Another building (probably G) was sold to one John Killigrew at about this time,[81] while B, D, and E were leased to various tenants. Parcel F was sold in the autumn of 1554 to a committee of trustees acting on behalf of one of the unincorporated City companies.

In 1556 Cecil granted a second lease to Seres, for 25 years from December 1555, and including all the remaining Cecil parcels except the one already leased to him.

which leace is made onely vppon trust to ye sayd w^m seress y^t therby he maye seme to haue an int^{r}est th^{r}in and so to gath^r my rents ye bett^r as appereth by an obligation of his.[82]

The tenants from whom Seres was to gather those rents included a merchant taylor named John Pount,[83] who had been renting building D since June 1555 and who eventually purchased it in 1559, and probably a skinner named Adam Bland who purchased building E in March 1557.

Such, then, was the relationship between Cecil and William Seres – and it remains only to explain whereabouts in London this piece of real estate lay. The property in question originally comprised the buildings and grounds of Peter College, and was bounded by the Deanery, Creede Lane, Ludgate Street, and St Paul's Churchyard, as shown in Figure 2. The company to whose trustees Cecil sold parcel F – which the company could not own as a corporation until a charter *made* it a corporation – was the Company of Stationers, and what Cecil sold them was the site of their first Hall.

I shall try to resist the temptation to conclude this paper with an exaggeration. Among the vast surviving quantities of Cecil papers, documents mentioning books or stationers are comparatively rare. It would therefore be foolish to suggest that Cecil ever spent much of his time championing the interests of – or even thinking about – the book

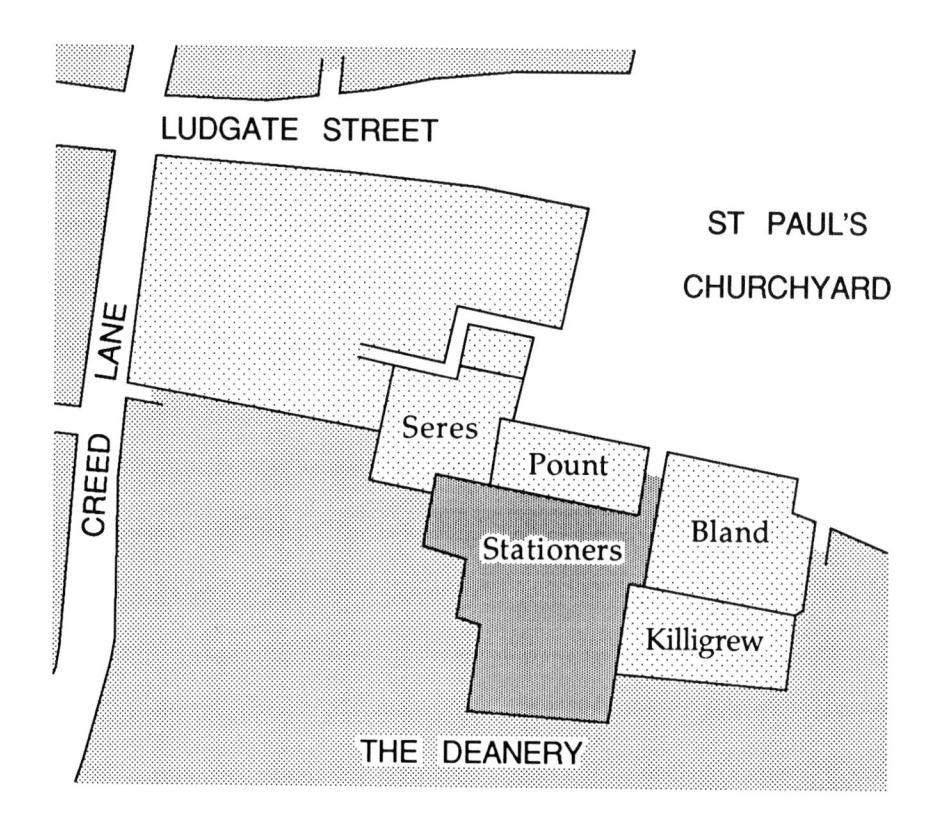

Fig.2. The property in context, *c.*1560.

trade. But when one holds the kind of power that Cecil wielded so skilfully and for so long, even an occasional thought and a little effort can have far-reaching consequences. I do not believe it is exaggerating to claim that William Cecil, as licenser, Principal Secretary, and landowner, influenced the history of the book trade in general – and of the Stationers' Company in particular – more than has hitherto been appreciated.

References

1. *Acts of the Privy Council*, pp.312–13.
2. The title of STC 17317 includes the date 1548; STC 17318 and 17319 are undated.
3. *Tudor Royal Proclamations*, ed. Paul L. Hughes and James F. Larkin (1964–9), no.186 (esp. pp.271–2).
4. *Acts of the Privy Council*, II, p.313.
5. F. G. Emmison, *Tudor Secretary* (1961), p.75.
6. *Acts of the Privy Council*, II, pp.343–4, 372.
7. *Tudor Royal Proclamations*, no.371.
8. According to David Loades, when Cecil joined Mary at Ipswich on 25 July he 'was committed to prison' (*Mary Tudor: A Life* [1989], p.185). I have found no evidence to support that claim, and much to contradict it. The account of Robert Wingfield (*Camden Miscellany* 28 [1984], p.270) is corroborated by that of Cecil's clerk Roger Alford, who adds that Cecil was among the first to kiss Mary's hand at Ingatestone on the 31st (Strype, *Annals of the Reformation* [1824], IV, p.489). He was also free to attend the funeral of Edward VI on 8 August (PRO, SP 11/1, no.6).
9. Conyers Read, *Mr. Secretary Cecil and Queen Elizabeth* (1955), pp.103–13.
10. *Tudor Royal Proclamations*, nos. 390, 460 (esp. pp.128–9).
11. Cecil did, in fact, authorize three more books for publication in 1588–91 while he was Lord Treasurer: see Arber, II, pp.502, 532, 599.
12. STC 24320 (see Elizabeth Armstrong, *Before Copyright* [1990], pp.10–11) and 19081a.
13. *Letters and Papers*, XVIII, i, 100, no.31.
14. *Tudor Royal Proclamations*, no.186 (esp. p.272); Arthur W. Reed, 'The regulation of the book trade before the proclamation of 1538', *Transactions of the Bibliographical Society* 15 (1917–19), 157–84, pp.178–82.
15. STC 15988, for example (*A Goodly Prymer in Englyshe*, printed in 1535 by John Byddell for William Marshall), claims on T4^v to be protected 'by [Henry's] letters patentes', but no trace of such a grant has been found among the public records.
16. *Letters and Papers*, IV, iii, 6248 (22). The patent was delivered on 22 February, not the 2nd as misprinted by Greg (*Transactions of the Bibliographical Society* 8 (1904–06), p.187) and repeated by Colin Clair (*Gutenberg-Jahrbuch* 1966, p.179) and the revised *STC* (vol.3, p.97).
17. 27 Hen. VIII, c. 11 (An Act Concerning Clerks of the Signet and Privy Seal).
18. For example, by W. P. W. Phillimore, *An Index to Bills of Privy Signet, Commonly Called Signet Bills, 1584–1596 and 1603 to 1624* (1890), p.v; Sir H. C. Maxwell-Lyte, *Historical Notes on the Use of the Great Seal of England* (1926), pp.90–7; Graham Pollard, 'The Company of Stationers before 1557', *The Library*, 4th ser., 18 (1937–8), 1–38, pp.32–3.
19. Maxwell-Lyte, *Historical Notes*, pp.94, 97.
20. *Calendar of the Patent Rolls, Edward VI* (1924–6), I, pp.100, 187, 61, 269; III, p.314.
21. *Ibid.*, III, p.315; Public Record Office, C 82/921; C 66/830, m. 40.
22. *Ibid.*, III, p.227; *Acts of the Privy Council*, IV, p.73. There is a reference to this order in one of Cecil's notebooks: PRO, SP 10/14, no.53, fol.1^v.
23. *CPR, Edward VI*, IV, pp.106–7.
24. *CPR, Elizabeth* (1939–86), V, no.1952; *CPR, Edward VI*, V, pp.50–1, 43, 47.
25. BL, MS Lansdowne 105/33; PRO, SP 12/184, no.69; *CPR, Elizabeth*, I, pp.62–3.
26. *CPR, Elizabeth*, VII, no.3674.

27. *Ibid.*, II, p.26; III, nos.1159, 1219, 1798; IV, no.397; V, no.1320.
28. *Ibid.*, V, no.2682; II, pp.518, 218.
29. BL, MS Lansdowne 8/62 (Arber, II, p.64).
30. *Acts of the Privy Council*, XXIV, pp.369-70.
31. STC 9306 (1557) and 9526.7 (1577).
32. BL, MS Lansdowne 48/82, fol.190^r (Arber, I, p.115).
33. Henry R. Plomer, *Abstracts from the Wills of English Printers and Stationers* (1903), p.34.
34. PRO, C 82/1565; C 66/1415, m. 7.
35. STC 9319 (Deputies of Barker, '1594'), 9320 (Yetsweirt, '1595').
36. Susan M. Allen, 'Jane Yetsweirt (1541–?) claiming her place', *Printing History* 9 (1987), 5-12, pp.7-9, citing (and unreliably transcribing) BL, MS Harley 6997, nos.2 (fol.3^r: Essex to Puckering, 27 March 1595), 9 (fol.16^r: Essex to Puckering, 7 May), 10 (fol.18^r: JY to Cecil, 7 May), and 11 (fol.20^r: JY to Puckering, n.d.); Hatfield House, Cecil Papers 32/5 (JY to Sir Robert Cecil, 29 April). Jane wrote again to Sir Robert on 24 August 1596 (Cecil Papers 44/8) concerning some 'billes signed by her Maiestie in ye monethes of Mr Yetsweirt, my late husbandes waytinge', but it is unclear whether those bills had anything to do with the lawbook patent.
37. PRO, SP 12/49, no.52 (fol.103^r): 'Quapropter si visum fuerit Honori tuo me in seruorum tuorum numerum recipere'.
38. Gerald D. Johnson, 'The Stationers versus the Drapers: control of the press in the late sixteenth century', *The Library*, 6th ser., 10 (1988), 1-17, pp.10-14.
39. Denis B. Woodfield, *Surreptitious Printing in England, 1550-1640* (1973), pp.36-7, 107-9 (in which the printer is wrongly identified as Richard Field).
40. PRO, SP 10/15, no.3 (fol.5^r). In the revised *Calendar of State Papers, Domestic Series, 1547-1553* (1992), C. S. Knighton wrongly identifies the 'poore man' as Reyner Wolfe (p.257, n.). As King's Typographer for Latin, Greek, and Hebrew, Wolfe already had the right to print the Latin version.
41. Three additional points are worthy of note. First, according to Strype (*Ecclesiastical Memorials* [1822], II, ii, p.251), the March patent was preceded in September 1552 by a licence for Ponet's catechism alone, both in Latin and English. I have been unable to verify this, but since Cecil apparently had to adjudicate conflicting claims by Day and Reyner Wolfe to the Latin version in early October (Hatfield House, Cecil Papers 151/46) I see no reason to doubt it. Second, although Day interpreted the patent as allowing him to print 'aswel this Catechisme . . . as also an A.B.C. with the Brife Cathechisme' (STC 4812, sig.A4^v), and apparently printed the two as separate books, both the warrant and the Patent Roll copy clearly specify 'a Cathechisme . . . *having thereunto annexed* an A.B.C. with the brief Cathechisme' (PRO, C 82/962/23 [my italics]; C 66/938, m. 7). Third, a 'typical' Day patent combines the grant of a particular work with a general licence for subsequent Day publications by the same author (Ponet in 1553, Cuningham in 1559, Nowell in 1574). It may therefore be legitimate to infer that the Brief Catechism (in 1549 and/or as revised in 1552) was the work of Thomas Becon.
42. *CPR, Elizabeth*, I, p.4; IV, no.675; quotation from PRO, C 82/1176/9.
43. BL, MS Lansdowne 10/211.
44. BL, MS Lansdowne 15/50 (Arber, I, p. 454); *Acts of the Privy Council*, VIII, p.89. C. L. Oastler mistakenly identified the shop in question with William Jones's existing shop at the other end of the churchyard, which Day eventually leased in 1576 (*John Day, the*

Elizabethan Printer [1975], pp.31-2). See my 'John Day and the bookshop that never was', in *Material London, ca. 1600*, ed. Lena Cowen Orlin (forthcoming).
45. BL, MS Lansdowne 17/56 (Arber, I, p.466).
46. *CPR, Elizabeth*, VI, no.1181.
47. *Ibid.*, VII, no.1537; quotation from PRO, C 82/1318.
48. BL, MS Lansdowne 48/82, fol.190^v (Arber, I, p.116).
49. *CPR, Edward VI*, V, pp.50-1; quoted from PRO, C 82/962/31. Although William's surname is now usually mispronounced *sears* it was certainly disyllabic, and was probably pronounced *series* or *cerise* rather than *serries*. Given the customary pronunciation of names such as Pepys, Sandys, and Wemyss, the occasional *Serys* or *Serrys* spelling carries little evidential weight – but the fact that Cecil always wrote *Seress* is more significant. The sporadic appearance elsewhere of the spelling *Ceres* probably indicates the same pronunciation as the harvest goddess – as suggested also by the extraordinary *Searese* in the lay subsidy of 1577 (PRO, E 179/145/252).
50. *CPR, Philip and Mary* (1937-9), I, p.277.
51. *CPR, Elizabeth*, I, pp.54-5; quotation from PRO, C 82/1066.
52. *Ibid.*, V, no.2445; quotation from PRO, C 66/1082, m. 18.
53. To be precise: six of them are known to have been printed since 1570 (STC 700, 4770.4, 4845.5, 5295, 19139, 22981) and two others at least once since 1567 (STC 171.5, 25878.5). Given the low rate of survival of schoolbooks it is extremely likely that comparable editions of the other two have been lost.
54. W. W. Greg and E. Boswell, *Records of the Court of the Stationers' Company, 1576-1602, from Register B* (1930), pp.9, 11. See also Arber, I, pp.272, 359, 418.
55. Bodleian Library, MS Ballard 62, p.35. I am grateful to Mark Bland for drawing my attention to this letter, and to Ian Gadd for transcribing part of it for me.
56. Corporation of London Records Office, Rep. 17, fol.435^{r-v}.
57. CLRO, Rep. 18, fols.350^r, 368^v (Arber, II, p.747).
58. *CPR, Elizabeth*, VI, nos.401, 398.
59. Arber, I, p.279.
60. *CPR, Elizabeth*, VI, no.1445 (Arber, II, pp.746-7).
61. *Ibid.*, VI, nos.1556, 2898.
62. BL, MS Lansdowne 48/82, fol.193^r (Arber, I, p.144); 48/76, fol.176^r (Arber, I. p.468).
63. CLRO, Rep. 17, 143^r; Arber I, p.447.
64. PRO, C 82/1234 (*CPR, Elizabeth*, V, no.2126).
65. BL, MS Lansdowne 48/80, fol.184^r (Arber, II, p.771).
66. BL, MS Lansdowne 48/82, fol.191^r (Arber, I, p.116).
67. J. Payne Collier, *The Egerton Papers* (1840), pp.138-43, esp. p.139.
68. PRO, E 179/145/219 and 252 (Castle Baynard ward, parish of St Gregory).
69. BL, MS Lansdowne 118, fols.27^r, 36^v, 43^{v}-4^r, 45^{r-v}, 54^v, 57^r, 60^{v}-2^v, 64^r, 65^v, 67^v, 71^r, 73^{r-v}, 75^{v}-8^r, 79^{r-v}.
70. Hatfield House, Cecil Papers, Bills 1, nos.1, 130 (Cecil's accounts); 2, 67 (Seres's bills). Seres is also mentioned in nos.18 and 69.
71. Hatfield House, Cecil Papers 143/91.
72. BL, MS Cotton Titus B. ii, fol.376^r (Strype, *Annals of the Reformation* [1824], IV, pp.487-8).
73. PRO, SP 12/33, no.13 (fol.40^r); SP 12/112, no.45 (fol.171^r).
74. *CPR, Edward VI*, II, p.136.
75. 1 Edw. VI, c. 14 (The Act for Chantries Collegiate, 1547).

76. It should not be imagined that commissioners such as Cecil, Eresby, and Losse joined such syndicates in order to conceal their identities: each of them openly applied for similar grants in later years (*CPR, Edward VI*, II, pp.354–62; IV, pp.457–9). The remaining syndics were John Swift and Arthur and Ralph Bedfield, gentlemen, Stephen Coke, haberdasher, and Nicholas Howard, butcher.
77. PRO, C 54/462, m. 46.
78. PRO, E 179/145/174 (Castle Baynard ward, parish of St Gregory, 'Will'm Sheres'). He is mistakenly listed as if a citizen rather than a stranger.
79. BL, MS Lansdowne 118, fol.21^v.
80. Unless otherwise specified, information about the property in the 1550s comes from one of four sources: an eighteenth-century abstract of title for parts of A-- among the deeds belonging to the Friends' Provident Life Office (Box 73, file 18); the conveyance of an as-yet-undetermined part of B–C in 1585 from John and Mary Seres to James and Sara Farrington (CLRO, Husting Roll 267/40); the conveyance of parcel E in 1591 from Adam and Joan Bland to William Bland (Husting Roll 271/44); and the conveyance of parcel D in 1612 from Henry Pount to William Childe (PRO, C 54/2141, no. 4). I am extremely grateful to the Friends' Provident Life Office for allowing me to examine and to cite the deeds in their possession, and to Mr R. W. V. Holland for his generous assistance in the search.
81. BL, MS Lansdowne 118, fol.10^r.
82. *Ibid.*, fol.21^v.
83. *Ibid.*, fol.21^r.

Stationers' Company Liber A:
An Apologia

D. F. MCKENZIE

ANYONE WHO HAS DONE graduate work at Cambridge will know that the most productive place in the University Library is, or at least was, its Tea Room. Oxford, to the eternal regret of all who have made the translation, has nothing comparable. Still, measured by the time it takes me in the Bodleian Library to negotiate the southern staircase to or from Duke Humfry, it has perhaps some claim to rival the UL's Tea Room as the locus of quite a few scholarly transactions. Certainly it was while I was descending that staircase in Graham Pollard's company twenty years ago that he casually said it did not look as if he would get round after all to editing Liber A for the Bibliographical Society, as he had hoped to do, and asked if I would take it over. The loss to scholarship in his surrender has to be weighed against the many other things he did do in his later years, and one can see the wisdom of his decision, if not of his choice. Indeed this paper might well have been called 'On *Not* Editing Liber A'. Edward Arber was not allowed to, Graham Pollard didn't, and I am sorry to report that, as yet, I haven't.

We must all regret that Pollard really did not in the end have time to bring his incomparable knowledge of the Company to bear on the one major set of documents which, apart from the later court books, is still largely unpublished. Everything he wrote had an authority which compelled assent, and he had no equal in seeing the trade steadily and seeing it whole. It was that strength which he brought in his early thirties, indeed *the* early thirties, to his research on the Stationers' Company.

In the introduction to her book on the Company's archives Robin Myers reminds us that Pollard first went to Stationers' Hall with John Johnson in 1933 when searching for book trade documents for Johnson's 'a modest chrestomathy of the principal documents' for the history of the book trade down to 1830.[1] Esther Potter's excellent account of that venture and of Graham Pollard's part in it absolves me from commenting further, except to say that the plan to edit Liber A had its place in his own understanding of the fundamental importance of such evidence for any proper history of the book trade, and it helps also to define the difference between his interest in such materials and the essentially literary concerns of most of his predecessors.[2] For them and for the Company itself the entrances of copies were understandably of the greatest significance in documenting many of the finest works of Elizabethan and Jacobean literature. It may well be the case that there are still fewer professional historians, political or economic, interested in the history of the Company than there are those whose training has been literary.

That bias has a long history and is partly the reason that Liber A is still unedited. Since Robin Myers has given us an admirable account of Stationers' Company bibliographers from Joseph Ames to Edward Arber, I need not recall very much of it except to remind you, first, how selective the early editors were in their common concern to establish (as she says) 'the Shakespeare canon and chronology, or unearthing titles of old popular literature for antiquarian researches'; and, second, how protective the Company was of its records of domestic management such as Liber A.[3] These clearly had no literary interest.

The Company's defensiveness, perhaps even hostility, is implied in the comment by Joseph Ames as early as the 1740s, when he said he wished he might 'get some of the same favour at Doctors' Commons and Stationers' Hall &c.' as he had had elsewhere in London.[4] As Robin Myers notes, 'Ames never came to Stationers' Hall, never saw the Entry Book of Copies and collected all his material elsewhere.'[5] By contrast with the Company's slow recognition of its role in scholarship is the far-sighted proposal by the antiquary William Oldys ('that admirable man', as Arber calls him), almost certainly again in the 1740s and before the founding of the British Museum. Reporting on the library resources in London, he included Stationers' Hall and made a plea not only for easier access to the records there but for an actual library at the Hall.

> It were to be wished, [he wrote,] the Stationers' Company would erect a library to their Hall, it being commodiously enough situated for resort from all parts; and so many of them having got estates by the learned, it would demonstrate some gratitude to the sciences, and repay their expenses sufficiently in honour and reputation. And this might be easily effected, if every one at first would give one book of a sort; and that of all pamphlets published weekly, six of a sort might be contributed here, to be sold or exchanged for bound or other books, reserving one of the pamphlets of a sort for the library.[6]

It is in effect a proposal for a public library, created at the very source of supply, and although he does not single out the Stationers' own archives as a unique resource, Oldys's general purpose was certainly to have the Company recognize its responsibilities to scholarship and build up a collection in which the trade and its products (from the most enduring to the most ephemeral: he goes on to cite George Thomason's precedent) could be fruitfully studied.

Some 30 years after Joseph Ames was rebuffed, George Steevens did make an entry at Stationers' Hall – in more ways than one, if we can trust his starred initials and date ('G*S 1774') against a Shakespeare item in Liber B. Certainly by the time his second revision of Johnson's Shakespeare appeared in 1778, Steevens had not only been furnished with, as he put it, '*the* three volumes of the records of the Stationers' Company', but was supplied 'with the accommodation which rendered the perusal of them convenient to me'.[7]

I must skip over the succession of other scholars who used the records, except quickly to say that Malone too wished to see 'all three volumes', and that George Chalmers was given 'liberty to inspect at the Hall the Books of Entries for the years 1576 to 1599', as was Alexander Chalmers a year or two later.[8] While this selective access to the registers of copies (Liber C taking them up to 1620), and the publication of extracts from them, certainly brought the Company's records into the main line of Shakespearian scholarship, it contributed only incidentally to the history of the trade. Even those like John Nichols and Charles Rivington, who were themselves engaged in it and who, as members of the Company, were genuinely interested in its history, were far too protective of their mystery and of the Company's good name to open up these other books. It is true that on 4 July 1780, John Noorthouck, a liveryman of the Company, had been voted £80 for indexing the court books and Liber A, but that was for domestic purposes only.[9] Had William Herbert lived longer, he might well have been one who, being interested in the history of printing and the revision of Ames, would have moved beyond literary to more broadly historical interests in his use of the records.[10] Most, however, came to consult the *entry* books, indeed 'the three books', namely Register A, Liber B, and Liber C.

In 1842, after the Livery Companies had been required in the 1830s and early 1840s to give an account of themselves and justify their continuing existence, George Woodfall proposed that a committee examine the records of the Company with a view to publishing 'such particulars of its Literary and other History as may be likely to prove interesting to the Reading Public and which may be found not injurious to the interests, or derogatory to the dignity of the Company'. They said they needed 'a

Gentleman for Editor on whose experience, ability, integrity and honour the Court may place the most implicit reliance.'[11] They chose their own Clerk, Charles Rivington, but he made no progress with it. Robin Myers pertinently cites the cautionary comment of Rivington himself about a Company history: 'It would need much discrimination and judgement . . . with reference to the interests of the Corporation and English Stock[,] in printing what when once given to the public cannot be recalled; and that if undertaken by a stranger . . . would require strict superintendence on the part of the Court'.[12] It is a tortuous sentence: one in which perhaps his anxiety has proved deeply prejudicial to his rhetoric.

The next move towards editing the archives came from F. J. Furnivall. Understandably, given his interest as an editor for the Early English Text Society, he thought an edition of the Company's documents of vital importance to his own larger project. The *Athenaeum* of 14 May 1870 notes, however, the still limited scope of the records he might be permitted to edit:

The authorities of the Stationers' Company have given Mr. Furnivall leave to copy and print the whole of the entries relating to Licences and Fines for printing books, that are contained in the first volume of their Registers. It is hoped that one of the officers of the Company will, some day, compile a history of it, before as well as after it was chartered, in 1556 [sic], with extracts from the many curious and valuable old documents that the Company possesses.[13]

In fact Furnivall's work for the EETS forced him to surrender the task of editing the Company's records (and finding subscriptions for their publication) to Edward Arber, who took it in hand on 8 October 1873. The first volume was published on 1 January 1875, the second on 1 October the same year; volume 3 was published on 1 July 1876 and volume 4 on 1 May 1877. In volume 2 Arber noted: 'The *Transcript* is the labour of mere vacant moments; and is realized concurrently with the discharge of onerous and responsible duties in a busy official life: working early and late that it may be accomplished.'[14] In volume 4, he thanks Furnivall and hopes that he 'may rejoice to see the accomplishment of that which he himself attempted'.[15] Given Arber's industry, I hardly know whether we should all lower our heads in honour or hang them in shame.

I should like to stress two related points about Arber. First, his recognition that, as he put it, 'THE time has now come when the English Printer and the English Publisher must take their due places in the national estimation.'[16] He would have been an honourable successor to both Ames and Herbert as an historian of the trade in all its dimensions, and perhaps our first genuine historian of the book. But my second point is that he must have felt deeply frustrated in his hopes of the larger history he knew to be needed. Tactful though he was in noting the limitations placed upon him, there is no disguising his disappointment in the following comments:

> It is to be quite understood that in the preparation of this *Transcript* we are not permitted to see any other Register or Book whatever belonging to the Company besides those we reprint herein . . .
> The last section of the Decrees and Ordinances is . . . not allowed to be reprinted in this *Transcript*.
> [With the exception of four extracts supplied by C. R. Rivington,] *permission has not been granted by the present Court of the Company to reprint this section of this Register, occupying from folio 427 to folio 486.*[17]

Noting that Register C is mostly a record of entries and reveals little about the domestic organization of the Company, he is reduced to citing a few titbits from John Nichols's *Literary Anecdotes*.[18]

Greg described Liber A as 'a rather mysterious folio'.[19] Certainly it was one which, in this whole history, led a highly secret and fugitive existence. Though denied permission even to see it or to transcribe any of the records of the Court, Arber was allowed to reprint, in volume 5, C. R. Rivington's anodyne paper on the history of the Company which, as Blagden tactfully puts it, 'draws on this material and which underlines – in various ways – the mistake of denying it to Arber.'[20]

If my remarks so far seem to be a way of delaying a direct discussion of the actual editing of Liber A, let me test your patience even further by turning now to the early history of the Company. Given the presence of so many here more expert than I am on the 1550s and 1560s, I do so hesitantly, and yet I think it essential if we are to see where Liber A fits into the pattern of record keeping and to assess the extent to which its function might be seen as fulfilling an already established role in the Company's corporate life in the City.

As we all know, on 4 May 1557 the Stationers became a royally incorporated fellowship (the Charter of incorporation is so dated). This was a consummation for which it had been wishing, devoutly or not, since at least 1542, when it was discussed at a session of the Convocation of Canterbury. Four years later, on 8 July 1546, a proclamation provided that every book should bear the author's and the printer's name, and exact date of printing, and that the printer should present a copy to the mayor of his town, before he began general distribution.[21] On 3 June 1557, the Stationers were formally recognized as a Company of the City of London by the enrolment of their Charter among the City Records, and on 6 September the Company was granted its arms. Two years later, on 10 November 1559, the new Queen confirmed the Company's Charter. Her 'Injunctions' of the same year name the Stationers and set up a system of ecclesiastical licensing.

They were created a Livery Company by the Lord Mayor on 1 February 1560, and there is a statement which suggests that this action was merely giving formal recognition to the way in which the Company already functioned: it was said on 30 June the same year that the Livery had been 'New begonne and Revyued againe'. Another suggestion of continuity may be found in Anthony Clerke's payment, on 16 May 1561, of 16 years' quarterage, a span which, as Arber remarked, puts the Brotherhood back to at least 1545.[22] When, on 28 September 1561, the Company was granted place and precedence in all processions etc. after the Poulterers, that too merely confirmed an existing order: in November 1531 the Brotherhood appears to have had a Livery and attended the Mayor's feast at Guildhall in 27th place, after the Poulterers. In 1562 the Company's ordinances 'being somewhat defective' were confirmed 'wth some alteracions and addicions'. The wording itself implies a much older set of ordinances, ones first formulated perhaps in 1403; and if the inference is sound (since it must be drawn from the much later text of 1678), they provided that the Wardens should be elected according to 'ancient usage'. On 9 October 1526, two Stationers' Wardens had been named as then taking office.

Some of the most persuasive evidence deployed by Graham Pollard in his account of the Stationers' earlier years was analogous material drawn from the records of other Companies. His account of the procedures followed in the lead-up to incorporation, for example, significantly qualified the older view, indeed one put by Greg himself, that there was a special understanding between the Stationers and the Crown – a view even that the Crown, in the interests of securing a more efficient control over blasphemous and seditious publications, was an equal partner in the move.

Greg's claim is well known: 'The Charter of the Stationers' Company, granted in 1557, is now commonly regarded as in the main a master-stroke of Elizabethan politics.'[23] Pollard makes it clear how unusual this would have been ('it was the first and last City Company to be thus favoured'), that the Charter was wholly the Company's initiative for the better control of its own organization, and that it passed through the conventional stages of petitioning the Crown for such incorporation. Not only does he see the master-stroke theory as improbable when set against the background of the evolution of London Companies, but he makes two more serious objections: it would have required a degree of mutual understanding between the executive and the leading Stationers; and the Charter would need to be interpreted as the *ipsissima verba* of the Crown. In fact, on this last point, earlier proclamations in Mary's reign are far from complimentary, nor are Elizabeth's Injunctions of 1559. In a sentence which I greatly enjoy, since it sums up my own view of much current writing about censorship in the 17th century, Pollard wrote: 'the development of the book-trade, like the development of motor-cars, may be more completely understood by studying the mechanism of the engine rather than that of the brake.'[24]

Now, while it is clear from the fascinating detail in Peter Blayney's account of William Cecil and the Stationers that a major revisionist history of this period is pending, I was also taken with his concession that for all his help to individual Stationers, and his crucial role in the granting of privileges, there is little evidence that even Cecil was in any sense a driving force in establishing a corporate identity for the Company, and it is simply inconceivable that Mary had the political acumen implied by Greg.

While incorporation doubtless had the *effect* of being to the mutual benefit of both political and commercial interests, within the continuum of the Stationers' history as a craft guild, dating perhaps from as early as 1403, the act of incorporation in 1557 remains, in my view (following Pollard), a quite natural stage in its evolution. It was Pollard's recognition that the procedures for approval of the ordinances of 1562 were like those for any other Company, and that, with only minor changes, they had also been those of the formerly unincorporated Company, that led him to remark: 'It was at this point that I began to suspect that I was making an unnecessary fetish of the date 1557.'[25]

Since Peter Blayney by contrast tells me that the act of incorporation was in his view an absolutely crucial event in the Company's history, I should like to suggest that, if we focus not on the Charter but on the ordinances, then such a conflict of views is more apparent than real. As Pollard makes clear, though the incorporation was of fundamental importance from a legal point of view, to the Stationers themselves it was a means to securing the *power to act* in control of their trade through their ordinances. The power they sought can be seen in 'The artycles contayned in a boke for the stacioners drawen out in forme of lawe by Master Rychard ffaulsete' some time before November 1559.[26] Besides the powers we might expect (the limitation of printing and bookselling to members of the Company, allowance of printing by the Stationers themselves, power of arrest, etc.), it includes a clause: 'The stationers to make orders for pryntinge and bokesellinge and them to change as occasyon shall serue'. In fact, they cannot have got their way, and Elizabeth's Injunctions of 1559 laid down a different form of control. In 1561 there are entries of payments to Norton 'for his counsell in Drawynge our ordenaunces', and 'for confyrmynge of our ordenaunces'.[27] In the next year's accounts, Edward Cater was paid for 'velome to wryte the *Constitutions* in'; red ink was bought, and a further payment made 'for the wrytinge in the ordenaunces into the boke fayre Wreten'.[28] These constitutions are not in Liber A and have in fact disappeared. Their powers, however, were extended in certain ways by ordinances decreed in 1566, but the Stationers' concern to extend their freedom to act legally under their ordinances, surfaces again in 1584 when, in the period leading up to the Star Chamber decree of 1586, they resolve to 'make an experymente by course of lawe or otherwise of the force and validytie' of their confirmed ordinances.[29] Although a decision of the Court, this resolution is not in Register B but is recorded only in Liber A. When in 1641 and 1643 the Company addressed Parliament in the hopes of resecuring its control of the trade following the abolition in June 1641 of the Court of High Commission, its strength was seen to lie in its ordinances under the Charter.

At least in one sense the Company had literally turned over a new leaf when it received its Charter: it made several new books for its records. As we have noted, when Edward Cater copied out the ordinances of 1562 in the Company's records, he did so in red ink in a vellum book specially made 'to wryte the *Constitutions* in'. This was evidently the Red Book to which there is another allusion in the Wardens' accounts for 1591-2: '*Item* paid to the Clerke for wrytinge the Decrees of ye starre chamber into the red booke'.[30] It appears again in Register B on 19 January 1598: 'Also yt is ordered that these ordon*n*ances against excessiue pryces of book*es* and against printinge for forens to this Company shalbe wrytten in the Redd booke and publiquely Redd to this company wi[th] thother ordon*n*aunces on the vsuall quarter Dayes'.[31] Clearly it was this, not Liber A, which, in Greg's words, was 'the formal repository of the ordinances of the Company as enacted by its governing body'.[32]

There is also a single entry relating to a White Book. This was one of the items in the inventory of property handed over to the incoming Wardens in 1559-60: 'The nombre of all suche Copyes as was lefte in the Cubberde in our Counsell chambre at the Compte . . . as apereth in the whyte boke for that yere *anno* 1560 xliiij'.[33] Such a custom of listing copies received by the Company of books printed by its members each year is further implied by an entry for 1575 when there were 'Deliuered into the hall certen copies which haue ben printed this yere. As by a particuler booke thereof made appearithe'.[34] Instead of keeping all such books and forming a library of them, as was later recommended by William Oldys, they were probably sold from time to time. Greg cites the accounts for 1561-62: '*Item* for bookes, balledes and other papers brought in as copyes accordynge to our ordenaunces xx^s'.[35] Pollard cites from W. D. Macrae's *Annals of the Bodleian Library* a decree of the Court of Assistants of 28 January 1612, whereby every printer was to deliver to the Under Warden a copy of every new book, or old book with new additions, printed for himself or for others, 'within ten daies next after the finishinge of the first ympression thereof and the putting of the same to sale'.[36]

Records of the Company's varied business were doubtless kept in far more books than are so alluded to, and certainly in many more than now survive. One which is still extant, however, was (by inference) Register A, the Wardens' accounts book. This includes a summary of receipts for 1554-57, and then details of income and expenditure (for example entrance of copies, bindings of apprentices, freedoms, fines for offences, contributions to dinners, quarterages and rents, payments out for repairs, and for food and equipment for musters). As from 22 July 1571, however, this Register contains only the summary accounts of the Wardens' receipts and payments and none of the other information. It was closed when full on 2 August 1596 and is reprinted in its entirety by Arber.

Another, which has not survived, must have been used from July 1557 to note decisions of the Court, and then from July 1571 it may also have been used for the detailed entries of copies, bindings, freedoms, fines, and livery. The only clue we have to its contents, however, is an entry in the Wardens' accounts for 1571-72 for money 'Received for Lycenced Coppies as doth appeare by the Register in the Clarkes booke'.[37] Greg suggests that this volume, which he described as 'essentially a minute book' and in effect Court Book A, was full by July 1576.[38] As it was later lost, it is impossible to be quite sure how comprehensive its entries were. In any event we now have hardly any records of the Court's deliberations before July 1576, and for the five years from July 1571 to July 1576 we also lack information about copies entered, men bound or made free, or fines levied, etc.

The first reference to Register B appears in the Wardens' accounts for 1576-77: a payment of 6s for 'a booke of entrances for the clarke'.[39] At some point it was labelled 'Lib. B'. It was divided into sections, allowing 17 folios for occasional notes at the beginning; then 117 folios for apprentices; 185 folios (the major part) for the entry of copies; 85 for freedoms; 11 for fines; 12 for admissions to the livery; and a final section of 61 folios which, although headed 'Decrees and Ordinances', contains records of decisions of the Court from July 1576 until the end of 1602. It was this last part which Arber was not allowed to reprint, but which Greg and Boswell edited and published in 1930 as Register B.

As the several sections filled up at different dates, a new series of volumes, each devoted to a particular class of record, was begun in 1595. The first, a new book bought that year and described in the Wardens' accounts as specifically 'for the entrance of Copies', was indeed so labelled: 'Entry booke of Copies – Liber C' and it records such entries from 1695 to 1620.[40] A separate Court Book was begun in 1602 and somewhat confusingly was also described as 'Liber C'. It is a fair copy of the orders of the Court from the end of 1602 until March 1655. The entries to the end of 1640 were edited by W. A. Jackson.[41] In 1605 new volumes were started for apprentices, for freemen, and for the recording of fines; and in 1606 a separate volume was used for calls on the livery. The new book of fines, the entries in which run from mid-1605 until mid-1640, was also reproduced by Jackson.

Finally, there was Liber A. Peter Blayney has done a calculation of the paper bought and used for the Wardens' Book (Register A) and for Liber A and suggests that they were made at the same time. Clearly Liber A was seen from the beginning as having a function in some ways parallel to that of the Wardens' Book and the Clerk's Book in the day-to-day running of the Company, but different from that of the Red Book of constitutions.

Despite its later title, 'ORDERS OF | PARLIAMT. & LD. MAYOR | LIBER | A', its initial function was almost certainly that of a book of precepts as communicated to the Company in letters from the Town Clerk on the order of the Lord Mayor, conveying decisions or instructions from the Court of Common Council. It is therefore in the most literal sense a Company book in acknowledging that the Stationers, as a Livery Company of the City of London, had to administer other ordinances besides their own. As Pollard said, 'Before 1557 their whole authority was derived from the City of London; and even after that date they continued to be part of the City administration.'[42]

Liber A is clear proof of Pollard's argument that the Stationers were a Company like any other and of the relevance of, for example, Ian

Gadd's research into the further implications of the Company's broader relationships and responsibilities. The present title of Liber A, at least in referring to orders of the Mayor, is in that sense justified. The word 'Parliament' is more problematic. Greg has suggested that it might refer to any assembly, in particular here to the Court of Common Council, but the volume was rebound and probably given its present title at the end of the seventeenth century when such a general sense seems less likely.[43]

Although the earliest entry is a copy of an order of Common Council dated 16 May 1522 stating that strangers are not to keep shops in the city, this was probably copied into Liber A in 1558 or 1559 when the volume was newly begun. The first of the main series of entries, which are pretty much in date order, is one for 27 July 1559.

The volume as a whole contains roughly 350 distinct items. About 130 of them fall in the period 1559 to 1601; another 150 in the years 1604 to 1640 (these are the ones which were printed by Jackson together with his edition of Court Book C); there are some 64 between 1641 and 1700; and then about half a dozen for the years 1744 to 1777.

If we look first at the content of the earlier unpublished material, that up to 1602, we see at once the great frequency of orders from the Mayor as communicated in letters from the City Clerk. For example, some 90 of the entries up to 1601 have solely to do with the civic responsibilities of the Company and much of this material can doubtless be found replicated in the records of the other Companies. It includes the raising of loans for the purchase of corn, for the provision, equipping, and training of soldiers; the exacting of subsidies demanded of the City by the Crown and solicited in turn by the City from its various Companies; assessments for the supply of weapons, horses, and ships, for the purchase and safe keeping of gunpowder, the relief of Nantwich, the repair of Yarmouth, and so on.

There are also such letters which refer more directly to Company matters and conditions of trade: reports of freemen living beyond the city limits and not therefore paying their lot and skot, establishing the precedency of the Company in civic processions (next after the Poulterers), matters affecting the livery (on 1 February 1560 the Stationers were allowed livery and hoods and ordered to have them made quickly so that they might wait upon the Lord Mayor), returns of the value of lands and plate, the use of offensive language, the standard of materials and workmanship. And of course apprenticeship itself, with its implicit promise of freedom of the City and the liberty then to practise any trade within it, was very much a civic affair.

I doubt if there has yet been any investigation of the implications of many of those matters: for example, the economics of assessments and taxes as these might bear on the income levels and financial obligations of members of the Company; nor have those named in the assessment lists in Liber A in the sixteenth century been methodically checked against other details of their careers and dates (between 1569 and 1598 there are some 21 such lists, all dated, averaging 55 names each – one has 125). Jean Tsushima's paper about Stationers' Company printers in the Artillery Company before the Civil War has its partial parallels in the sixteenth century. How many altogether of those earlier men interrupted their work to be made into soldiers we cannot exactly say, but their masters had to sustain the loss of their labour at various times, and the men themselves, as members of a citizens' army, had to develop skills remote from printing and bookselling.[44]

In November 1580 the Company was informed that in the past year a force of 800 Londoners, including 9 Stationers, had been equipped and sent for service into Ireland. Their 9 coats, paid for from the Chamber of London, cost 8s each, 'whereof hir m*aie*stie hath allowed iiijs. for eu*ery* Cote'. The Company of course, answering to the contrary at its peril, had to fund the difference of 36s, which meant yet another charge on its members to an end which had more to do with the keeping of books than the making of them.[45]

For all that, Liber A has some 40 entries before 1602 which do relate directly to the trade, among them several which bear on some of the points being made by Peter Blayney in discussing patents and the origin, in them, of the English Stock. Here, as Blagden has shown in his brilliant article demonstrating that the constitution of the English Stock in 1603 merely formalized a commercial activity which had been developing within the Company for about twenty years, the crucial evidence is to be found mainly in Liber A.[46]

In January 1578, for example, the Court, in answer to petitions of the poor men, said it would give favourable consideration to any of the poor brethren of the Company who asked to be allowed to print an unclaimed copy. On 29 October 1578 a conflict of interest between William Seres and Henry Denham and John and Richard Day, father and son, about an overlap in their patents for printing the psalms in metre with notes, was resolved, and on 18 January 1580 ratified by the Court. But only in Liber A is it recorded. Other conflicts also marked the early 1580s. On 7 February 1582 John Day began his action in Star Chamber against Roger Ward and William Holmes for printing the *ABC with the Little*

Catechism.[47] On 15 May 1582 Christopher Barker had met John Wolf, who was leading the opposition to the patentees.[48] Shortly after, the Queen appointed a Commission to look into these differences, and the Court of Aldermen ordered four of their number to report on the printers' complaints of poor wages and shortage of work.[49]

In October 1582 John Wolfe with 18 others appealed to Lord Burghley against the unfair behaviour of Thomas Norton who, as counsel to the Company and City Remembrancer, was open to the charge of giving advice prejudiced in favour of the patentees. The endorsement on their paper made the terms of the case fairly clear: 'The Stacioners of London against ye priviledged persons'.[50] In December 1582 Barker reported to Burghley.[51]

After October 1582, however, there is evidence of the dispersal of work: Henry Denham took seven young men to join with him, and John Day spread his work among seven or eight householders of the Company.[52] On 26 March 1583 the Court made it a condition that in return for entering to Henry Bynneman Aristotle's works and Homer in Greek and Latin, and a Greek New Testament, he should from time to time take any five of the Company to be partners in printing them.[53] On 18 July 1583 the Commission made its report: 'Those that haue presses and complaine against the patenties are not aboue iiij / Wolf hath acknowleged his error and is releved with worke'.[54] Then early in 1584 the patentees, on a hint from the Commissioners and on the lead given by the Court in January 1578, made a gift of copies for the use of the poor.[55]

An order of the Lord Mayor for resolving the differences between the complainants on the one part and the patentees on the other provided that any books not printed by the patentees be brought into the Hall, that they be free to sell them, but that the remaining books of the patentees be not printed by those with no rights to them, the master and wardens to give work at reasonable wages to those printers lacking it, that all suits be stayed meantime, and that the number of apprentices bound be limited. When John Day died on 23 July 1584, his son Richard nominated five assigns, including Wolfe, all of them men who had begun by opposing his father. On 18 January 1585 the Court allowed Thomas Purfoote the printing of the first leaf of *The Little Catechism*.[56]

On 29 October 1584 the Court had approved expenditure by the Wardens to promote an Act of Parliament for the confirmation of the Charter 'or any other good aucthorytie on matters tendinge to ye commodyty of the house'. This Company initiative led in 1586 to the 'The newe Decrees of the Starre Chamber for orders in printinge', just as in 1643 a petition from the Company to Parliament would resecure its powers. There followed other results: the payment of 6*d* in the pound to the poor – a practice so well established by 1603 that the English Stock then paid £100 to the poor each year; and the printing of copies to the use of the Company, that is with various members investing a part of the paper stock needed for an edition and taking their return pro rata. Then certain other entries of copies were conditional upon the printing being done by nominated printers: Robert Robinson and Valentyne Simmes, for example, were thus given the right to print certain copies. Even as early as 9 June 1575 a plan had been devised for the printing of Bibles and New Testaments by ten members of the Company.[57] Decisions relating to the Statutes at Large and the homilies on 15 June 1587 and to the Psalms in metre on 29 October 1588 suggest other attempts by the Company to spread work by printing 'in common' certain books controlled by royal letters patent.[58] Another effect was to ensure that anyone benefiting from such work was a member of the Company.

More significantly for the future English Stock, when the various partners in the Day/Seres privilege met on 12 October 1591 they already had a treasurer (Mr Watkins), and a common stock. On 18 March 1594, after a meeting of the Court, the Master, Wardens, four Assistants, and ten members of the Company, met as 'many of the partners' in the Day/Sere privileges, and elected a Treasurer (Watkins), and four Stock-keepers. It was in effect the English Stock in all but name.[59] Latin and Irish Stocks had still to come, as had almanacs, but primers and psalters were put out as before under the general direction of the Court, and stocks were warehoused by the Company.

There is in Liber A but not in other extant Company records an item of 25 May 1560 relating to the infringement of William Seres's privilege to print primers and psalters in English and Latin, and Richard Jugge and John Cawood are to discover who is pirating them. In an entry of 25 June 1573 noted by *STC*, John Hart is given an extended privilege to print his *Methode or Comfortable Beginning for All Unlearned to Read English*. This of course was in phonetic spelling. It was 'Graunted by consent of the whole Table the daie and yere above videlicit the xxv° Iunij 1573.[60] This last decision was clearly one made by the Court but like the others noted here, falls within the period for which records of the Court are otherwise lacking. There is also a list of eleven members of the Company living outside London in 1571, and in 1574 of 26 free denizens. And it is also in this period for which the Court Book is missing that we find detailed entries about Jugge's right to print Bibles and testaments and his release of some of these, in certain formats, to others in the Company. There is another the same year – 1575 – on Christopher Barker's Bible privileges, and then much later, in April 1578, an agreement between Seres and Barker. On 20 October 1578 there is an entry of the resolution of a contention between William Seres the elder and William Seres the younger on the one hand and John and Richard Day on the other. Several entries record decisions made 'at a court holden this day' which have no counterpart in Greg's edition of the Court orders for 1576 to 1602. Another matter not recorded in Register B at the time is an entry of 1585 which, given the imminence of the Star Chamber Decree in 1586, is highly significant. It reveals the Master and Wardens seeking greater freedom of search and seizure and suggesting they test the limits of the existing ordinances in the hope of extending them. There is a reference of 1584 to the seizure of Robert Waldegrave's equipment which is not in the Court Book; another document of 31 July 1584, headed 'Complainants v. Patentees' and peculiar to Liber A, is crucial to Blagden's argument about the evolution of the English Stock.[61]

When in 1954 Greg wrote to Graham Pollard to seek some information he needed in preparing his Lyell Lectures, he said he had found the two articles in *The Library* for 1937 invaluable.[62] In reply, Pollard thanked him for mentioning 'those old articles of mine on the Stationers' Company' and added: 'They need some revision, particularly on the Company regulations about stitching books because I had missed an illuminating document from Liber A which was printed by Miss Prideaux at the end of her book on the history of bookbinding.'[63] The original entry of 25 March 1586 is most informative, but how Miss Prideaux gained access to Liber A in 1893 I have no idea. In his essay on the records of the Company, C. R. Rivington cites various extracts from Liber A denied to Arber. These include a return of presses for July 1586 and a letter of 30 August 1591 from Whiftgift to the Company about Thomas Orwin.[64] Greg's note in his *Companion to Arber* comments: 'Very inaccurately printed [he really meant 'transcribed']: 'remitte' should be 'comytte' and 'favou^r' should be 'tuicôn'.'[65]

Although they have been published by Jackson, I must briefly mention the entries in Liber A which fall in the period 1604-40. Most of them are letters from the Mayor but there are several which relate to the trade. In 1611 Nathanael Butter, who 'most vniustly, vndutifully, and deceiptfully and deliberatly, wittingly, and willingly, offended' by printing primers abroad, is obliged to forfeit his yeomanry share in the English Stock.[66] In 1615 an interesting letter from the Archbishop of Canterbury asks the Lord Mayor of London, to whom complaint had been made by two men whose books had been seized, 'whether it appertayneth vnto yo^u to iudge of matters concerning bookes' since these fall within the jurisdiction of the Commission for Causes Ecclesiastical.[67] This year too the excessive number of foreigners and strangers is cause for concern.[68] A little later, in 1618, Francis Bacon gets involved in supporting the complaints of poor members of the Company deprived of opportunities for work when foreigners are employed in their place.[69] There are several copyright cases, including one relating to the printing of primers and psalters to which Christopher Barker had the rights.[70] There is a petition of 1621 from Bonham Norton against Cantrell Legge's action in printing grammars in Cambridge.[71] In 1622 several entries are devoted to George Wood's infringement in printing almanacs and primers on an unlicensed press.[72] There are entries relating to negotiations with Cambridge in 1623 and 1629, and to the 1637 agreement with Oxford.[73] But the Star Chamber Decree of 1637 is not even mentioned, and there are only two or three references to significant books, although Raleigh's *History of the World* is one of them and Foxe's 'Booke of Martyrs' another.[74] Finally, there is one document, 'The Case betwixt the Printers of London and the Printers of Cambridge', specifically Thomas and John Buck, which is not printed by Jackson but perhaps should have been noted. It relates to negotiations between the Company and the University of Cambridge in the late 1620s and in its original form would have been prepared just after 10 February 1628. It appears out of order in a much later hand at the end of Liber A as one of a series of documents relating to discussions between the Company and the University of Oxford in the 1690s.[75]

In the 1640s, where we move again into the unpublished parts of the volume, there are numerous letters from the Mayor, but these cease in 1650 and reappear only some 35 years later when questions arise about the livery. Given the upheavals in the trade following the abolition of the Court of High Commission in 1641, it is surprising perhaps to find so few entries relating directly to the general state of the Company at the time. In 1643, however, there are two documents which are important in complementing others for that highly significant year. One records a decision of 19 July to seize Thomas Harper's presses, just a few weeks after the infamous decree of 14 June 1643 which re-established licencing and to which we owe Milton's *Areopagitica*. Another of 20 June names the licensers appointed by the Commons under that order.[76] A copy of the Company's petition of 19 August 1644, appending 254 names, about Bible printing is to be found here in Liber A, as is a copy of a further petition to the Mayor, dated 14 June 1645, appending 226 names, which summarizes the Company's history and incidentally notes that its ordinances were approved 'about five years after' the Charter was granted, a clue which led Pollard to confirm 1562 as their date. C. R. Rivington supplied Arber with the text of this latter petition but without all the names.[77]

There was in fact, as Ian Gadd reminds me, an even earlier ordinance, of 12 March 1641, not in Liber A but recorded in the Lords Journals, which also confirms that date, and adds that, by those ordinances, 'no Man shall print any Book unless the Copy be first assigned by the Master and Wardens of the Company of Stationers'.[78] As Ian Gadd has suggested to me, the word 'assigned', as distinct from merely 'entered', may carry interesting implications of the Court's active participation in the printing and publishing processes, perhaps even in the form already noted in the allocation of certain copies to specific printers in the gradual evolution of the practices embodied in 1603 in the English Stock. In both the ordinance of 1641 and the petition of 1645 we also find a claim that the Company itself had been in continuous existence for 240 years, confirming other evidence of its effective creation in, what must in fact have been, 1403.

One would have thought that following the Restoration, and given the activities of Roger L'Estrange as Surveyor of the Press and the successive renewals of the Printing Acts, there would have been a good deal for the Clerk to enter in Liber A. Surprisingly it is quite innocent of any entry at all from 1650 until 1685 when, under James II, the Livery was in a constant state of flux. Since it was ordered that the names of those rejected and those admitted should be recorded, there is a rash of entries in 1685, and again from September 1687 until June 1690. These orders are mostly in the name of the Mayor but derive really from the King and have little to do with the Company's corporate commitments. The year 1685 also sees a substantial part of Liber A being taken up with a record of various letters between the Company and the Bishop of Oxford, and in March 1689 with a copy of the articles of agreement between the University and Parker and Guy for Bible printing. In the light of recent attempts by the International Association of Scholarly Publishers to protect the copyright of critical editions by having them recognised as creative works, it is interesting to note that a very similar point had been raised in September 1685 in the negotiations between the Company and the University of Oxford: namely whether, in classical authors, 'the property be really altered by Annotations, and the Letter and forme of printing'.[79]

Three other documents in this later section of Liber A are worth brief mention. One is alluded to in Arber by C. R. Rivington who noted the committal, in 1692, of the Master and Wardens (Edward Brewster, John Simms, and William Phillips) to Newgate where they lay sticking to their principles for nearly two months. They had refused to elect Giles Sussex to the livery, although he was a member of the Company, because he was a packer by trade.[80] In 1744 there is an extensive *resumé* and analysis of the 1710 copyright act, and in 1771-77 a further clutch of documents relating to the Company's real estate and, in response to the publication in 1771 of annual memorandum or pocket books, to the infringement of the Company's rights in almanacs.

As Greg wrote, 'The book is obviously of great importance for the history and constitution of the Company, and would need to be carefully studied before any final opinion on these subjects could be formed.'[81] And again: 'The volume has not been reprinted, nor, so far as I know, has it ever been properly studied, but it is clearly important and a closer acquaintance with its contents might appreciably extend and possibly modify our understanding of the history and working of the Company. It will, however, need careful editing, for it is a very disorderly collection of miscellaneous records covering two centuries and a half . . .'[82]

I should be surprised if, even in the mid-1930s and perhaps as part of his thinking about the chrestomathy of documents relating to the book trade, Graham Pollard had not already some thought of turning his attention to Liber A. But it is not until we find him much later, on the Council of the Bibliographical Society, that I am aware of his making any direct reference to its editing.

On 7 June 1956 he drew up a list in his own hand of books the Bibliographical Society might or might not publish. In it is Liber A of the Stationers' Company, followed by the note: 'Only considered likely to be a slim volume. To be considered when Court Book C has been published.'[83] At a further meeting of 21 January 1957, the item comes up again: 'Liber A of Stationers Company. No editor yet in sight. To be reconsidered when Court Book C is published.'[84] Then in a later memorandum on the publications policy of the Bibliographical Society, dated 8 August 1958, he includes Liber A under his first section of 'Projects which we have some continuous moral obligation to undertake'. His description of it is incorporated as a possible longer term project in the Report on Publications Policy of 4 December 1958, signed by F. C. F[rancis]. It is there described as follows:

Liber A. This was really the precedent book of the company and contained documents to which particular importance was attached at the time. It starts before Greg and Boswell, *Records of the Court of the Stationers' Company 1576-1602*, and includes some interesting XVIIIth century matter. The proceedings of the Court recorded in this book between 1603 [sic] and 1640 have been printed by Jackson, but none of the rest of it. It would make, perhaps with the addition of some cognate documents, a large quarto volume rather thinner than Greg and Boswell.[85]

And then, in the Minutes of the Publications Committee of the Bibliographical Society for 1 October 1959, we find the following entry: 'An offer from Mr Graham Pollard to edit Liber A of the Records of the Stationers' Company was gratefully accepted.'[86]

A transcription was made by Walter Mitchell in 1966, and this was in turn indexed in great detail by Michael Pearson in 1979-80.[87] The transcription and the index have both now been keyed and copies can be supplied to any *bona fide* researchers. There is a printed index to Liber A which was published in 1902.[88] By Robin Myers's calculation it has 88 subject headings and indexes only 14 personal names: Pearson by contrast has 2,150 subject headings and indexes all names. And then for the period which overlaps with Jackson, Pearson's index is much more detailed (and accurate).

W. A. Jackson, as we know, edited the entries from Liber A for the years 1604 to 1640 and included these along with his edition of the entries in Court Book C up to the end of 1640, together with the Book of Fines. His proposal to edit Court Book C is referred to in correspondence between R. B. McKerrow and Graham Pollard in 1937. (I am not at all clear who put him on to it, but photostats of the whole of C had been supplied to the Society by 1930 and in 1932 Greg noted that some of them were then 'in the hands of a transcriber', as if an edition was already being planned at that stage.[89]) A couple of months after Pollard had given his second paper on the early constitution of the Company (he had delivered it on 18 October 1937), McKerrow wrote to him mentioning Jackson's plan to edit Court Book C, but saying Council would much prefer Pollard to do it.[90] Pollard in reply noted that he would prefer collaboration and said that there were other decrees and ordinances not in Court Book C which should be included. He was also insistent that it be the full text, not extracts, and that it be published by the Society.[91]

What Pollard had in mind were the relevant entries from Liber A. I am not wholly sure about the wisdom of that decision. The inclusion of the Liber A material may be thought to imply its status as essentially part of the business of the Court, which with a few exceptions in an earlier period it is not. Its omission from any future edition of Liber A would also inevitably misrepresent that volume as a whole in its function as a book of precedents and diminish now the cumulative force of the materials relating to City affairs.[92] Those problems are in a minor way compounded by the title *Letter Book* which Jackson gives to this section drawn from Liber A, although the orders from the Mayor were in a sense letters. Still, there can be no question that it was a great service to supply all the Liber A entries for 1604 to 1640 along with the transcript of Court Book C for the same period – indeed I am sure that it was done on Pollard's insistence.[93]

In 1931 Pollard had written to Greg to seek permission to quote part of his introduction to the edition of Court Book B. He received in reply the following curt card: 'Dear Sir, As far as I am concerned you can quote what you please. For permission from the Stationers' Company, you had better apply to the Clerk, Stationers' Hall, EC4. Yours faithfully WW Greg'.[94] When in 1954 Greg was preparing his Lyell Lectures, the boot was on the other foot. In his letter to Pollard of 11 March, as noted earlier, Greg complimented him on his two articles in *The Library* for 1937, which he said he had found invaluable, and ended by writing:

I hope you will forgive me if I am making excessive calls upon your courtesy, but I shall be exceedingly grateful for any assistance you can give me. Yours sincerely, WW Greg[95]

Indeed, some promise of the riches of which we have been deprived can be seen in those two essays in *The Library* on the early history of the Company, 'The Company of Stationers before 1557', published in June 1937, and 'The Early Constitution of the Stationers' Company', which appeared the following December. To keep some association between Liber A and Pollard's own hopes of editing it, it would not be inappropriate to reprint the essays as an introduction, with such additions or qualifications as later scholarship demands.

The work of the quartet of scholars whose work I have most mentioned – Arber, Greg, Pollard, Blagden – like anything we ourselves may leave behind, will need revision. But in saying that, I am reminded of what Goethe said of Euripides: When we criticise such men, let us do it on our knees. My abiding sense as I look back at their contributions is of immense gratitude for what they have given us and some regret that Liber A, although much more accessible now as a typescript, on disk, and through Michael Pearson's excellent index, has not yet quite reached the stage that Pollard in particular had hoped for it.

References

It is a pleasure to record my gratitude to Peter Blayney, Christine Ferdinand, Ian Gadd, Robin Myers, and Esther Potter for their several kindnesses and valuable advice during the preparation of this paper.

1. Robin Myers, *The Stationers' Company Archive: An Account of the Records 1554-1984* (Winchester: St Paul's Bibliographies, 1990), xxvii-xxviii.
2. Esther Potter, 'Oxford Books on Bibliography', in Robin Myers and Michael Harris (eds), *Pioneers in Bibliography* (Winchester: St Paul's Bibliographies, 1988), 101-17; for Pollard's participation in the plan for a chrestomathy, see p.106.
3. Robin Myers, 'Stationers' Company Bibliographers: The First Hundred Years: Ames to Arber', in Myers and Harris, *Pioneers in Bibliography*, 40-57.
4. Joseph Ames, *Typographical Antiquities*, rev. William Herbert. 4 vols (London, 1810); at i. 36 in the copy annotated by Thomas Frognal Dibdin, cited in Myers, 'Stationers' Company Bibliographers', 40.
5. Myers, 'Stationers' Company Bibliographers', 40.
6. [J. Yeowell], *A Literary Antiquary: A Memoir of William Oldys* (London: Privately Printed, 1862), 84-5.
7. George Steevens, *Prolegomena to the Dramatick Writings of Will. Shakespeare* (London, 1788), 295; cited in Myers, 'Stationers' Company Bibliographers', 47. My italics.
8. Myers, 'Stationers' Company Bibliographers', 47-8.
9. Myers, *The Stationers' Company Archive*, pp. 52-3, 77.
10. Myers, 'Stationers' Company Bibliographers', 48-50; see also Robin Myers, 'William Herbert: his library and his friends', in Robin Myers and Michael Harris (eds), *Property of a Gentleman. The formation, organisation and dispersal of the private library 1620-1920* (Winchester: St Paul's Bibliographies, 1991), 133-58.
11. Cyprian Blagden, *The Stationers' Company: A History, 1403-1959* (London: George Allen & Unwin Ltd, 1960), 260-1.
12. Myers, 'Stationers' Company Bibliographers', 49.
13. *Athenaeum* (14 May 1870).
14. Edward Arber (ed), *A Transcript of the Registers of the Company of Stationers of London, 1554-1640 A.D.* 5 vols (London and Birmingham: Privately Printed, 1875-94), ii. 30. Hereafter Arber.
15. Arber, iv. 28.
16. Arber, i. xiii.
17. Arber, i. xxii, ii. 26, 879.
18. Arber, iii. 20 (Arber's notes are from Nichols, *Literary Anecdotes of the Eighteenth Century*. 9 vols (London, 1812-16), iii. 573-4).
19. W. W. Greg, *Some Aspects and Problems of London Publishing between 1550 and 1650* (The Lyell Lectures 1955; Oxford: Clarendon Press, 1956), 26.
20. *The Stationers' Company*, 261.
21. STC 7809. Paul L. Hughes and James F. Larken (eds), *Tudor Royal Proclamations*. Volume 1. The Early Tudors (New Haven and London: Yale University Press, 1964), No.272 (i. 373-6). Blagden, *Stationers' Company*, thought the proclamation drafted within a day or two of the meeting of Convocation, citing *Letters and Papers of Henry VIII*, vol.17, no.177, which had misdated it (see *Letters and Papers*, vol.21, no.1233). I am most grateful to Peter Blayney for pointing out to me this later correction.

22. Arber, i. xix.
23. *Records of the Court of the Stationers' Company 1576 to 1602*, edited by W. W. Greg and E. Boswell (London: The Bibliographical Society, 1930), lx.
24. Graham Pollard, 'The Company of Stationers Before 1557', *The Library*, 4th ser. xviii (June 1937), 35.
25. Graham Pollard, 'The Early Constitution of the Stationers' Company', *The Library*, 4th ser. xviii (December 1937), 236.
26. Arber, i. 350, cited from *State Papers Domestic, Elizabeth*, vol.15, no.37. For other references to ffaulsete or Fawsett, see Arber i. 106, 164.
27. Arber i, 189-90.
28. Arber, i. 222-3.
29. Liber A, f.44^r, 26 March 1584. For the 1566 decree, see Arber, i. 322.
30. Arber, i. 556.
31. Greg and Boswell, *Records of the Court*, 59.
32. *Aspects and Problems*, 27. Given the allusion to it in 1591-2, presumably the Red Book was also the repository for the decrees of Star Chamber including those of 1586 and (if the book was still in use then) 1637.
33. Arber, i. 143.
34. Arber, i. 470. Greg's suggestion that the term 'White Book' may have been a generic term used to refer to any set of blank leaves for the recording of miscellaneous information, in this case lists of books received each year, is somewhat at odds with the reference to 'a particuler booke'.
35. Greg, *Aspects and Problems*, 29; citing Arber, i. 188.
36. Pollard, 'Early Constitution', 258; citing W. D. Macrae, *Annals of the Bodleian Library* (Oxford: The Clarendon Press, 1890), 44-5. Such an entry is no longer to be found among the Company records although some document containing it must have been still extant when Macrae wrote.
37. Arber, i. 451. In the wardens' entries immediately following this one, no further reference is made to 'the Clarkes booke', but given the known contents of its successor, Register B, also called the Clerk's book, it is a reasonable inference that it did include the binding of apprentices, admission of freemen and brothers, fines for the breaking of orders, and orders of the Court, as well as entries of copies from mid-1571 to mid-1576.
38. *Records of the Court*, ix. Sporadic allusions in Liber A to decisions of the Court 'holden this day' but not to be found in the Court Books themselves suggest that it might be misguided to think of any of the latter as 'minute books' in the modern sense.
39. Arber, i. 475.
40. Arber, i. 572.
41. W. A. Jackson (ed), *Records of the Court of the Stationers' Company 1602 to 1640* (London: The Bibliographical Society, 1957). From an early date it was probably usual for the Clerk to take rough notes during meetings of the court, although the earliest of such 'wast books' to survive is that for 1661-9. Comparison with the fair copy often reveals substantial omissions from the latter.
42. 'The Early Constitution of the Stationers' Company', 248.
43. *Aspects and Problems*, 26.
44. See Appendix.
45. Liber A, f.41^v.

46. Cyprian Blagden, 'The English Stock of the Stationers' Company. An Account of its Origins', *The Library* 5th ser.x (1955), 163-85.
47. Arber, ii. 753-69.
48. Arber, ii. 780-1.
49. Arber, ii. 770.
50. Arber, i. 777-8; reprinted from BL Lansdowne Ms 48, f.182.
51. Arber, i. 114-16.
52. Arber, ii. 771, 775.
53. Arber, ii. 422.
54. Arber, ii. 783-5.
55. Arber, ii. 786-9; Liber A, f. 46^v, dated 31 July 1584.
56. *Records of the Court*, 16.
57. Liber A, ff. 25^r-26^v.
58. *Records of the Court*, 24; Arber ii. 505.
59. Blagden, 'The English Stock of the Stationers' Company', 173-4.
60. Liber A, ff.2^v-3^r, 16^r.
61. Liber A, f.46^v; reprinted by Blagden, 'The English Stock of the Stationers' Company', 184-5.
62. Bodleian Library, Ms Pollard f.60, 11 March 1954. I am particularly grateful to Esther Potter for guiding to me to these papers and for her invaluable index to them.
63. Ms Pollard f.62, 9 June 1954. The document Pollard refers to in Liber A is at f.50^r-50^v; reprinted in S. T. Prideaux, *An Historical Sketch of Bookbinding* (London: Lawrence & Bullen, 1893; rprt. New York and London: Garland, 1989), Appendix IV: 'Early Documents relating to the Craft', 239-42.
64. Arber, v. li-lii; from Liber A, ff.51^r, 64^r.
65. W. W. Greg, *A Companion to Arber, being a Calendar of Documents in Edward Arber's Transcripts of the Registers of the Company of Stationers of London, 1554-1640, with a Text and Calendar of Supplementary Documents* (Oxford: Clarendon Press, 1967), 47.
66. Jackson, *Records of the Court*, 344.
67. Jackson, 349.
68. Jackson, 350.
69. Jackson, 361-2.
70. Jackson, 354-5.
71. Jackson, 371-4.
72. Jackson, 375-9.
73. For Cambridge, see Jackson, pp.371-4, 381-4, 396-8; and for Oxford and Cambridge, Jackson, pp.413-14, 433-4.
74. For Foxe, see Jackson, p.434; for Raleigh, Jackson, pp.355-7.
75. 'The Case betwixt the Printers of London and the Printers of Cambridge', Liber A, ff.186^r-187^v. Summarizing the Stationers' Company's objections to the charter granted to Cambridge on 10 February 1628, it opens: 'Thomas Bucke and Iohn Bucke Printers to the University of Cambridge have of late time Imprinted and do yet continue to Imprint divers and sundry Books which his Majesty and his Predecessors for good Considerations have Granted the sole Printing thereof unto the Company of Stationers and unto Bonham Norton and Iohn Bill his Majesties own Printers And the said Printers of Cambridge endeavour to justifie the Doing thereof . . . '. As Peter Blayney has pointed out to me, the final section of Liber A (ff.184-95 as they now stand) is from

a different and later stock of paper and was probably added to the original volume when it was rebound at the end of the seventeenth century.
76. Liber A, ff.138^r-138^v. It is reproduced by C. R. Rivington in Arber, v. liii-liv.
77. Arber, i. 593.
78. Lords Journals, iv. 182.
79. Liber A, f.164^r.
80. Arber, v. xliv-xlv; Liber A, f.184^v.
81. Greg, introduction to Greg and Boswell, *Records of the Court*, vii n. 3.
82. Greg, *Aspects and Problems*, 26.
83. Minutes of the Publications Committee, 66. I am much indebted here to Robin Myers for sending me copies of the relevant entries from the Society's minutes. Some of the discrete documents, and copies of Pollard's drafts, are duplicated in the Pollard Papers in the Bodleian.
84. Ms Pollard 414, f.51^v.
85. Also at Ms Pollard 414, f.51^v. At the end of this document, and also in an earlier version of 27 November 1958 at f.48, is a list of other possible topics for publication: the physical form of medieval manuscripts; international typefounding, 1500-1800; English newspapers after 1640; English marks of provenance on books and manuscripts; bookbinding after the blind stamped period; editions of English publishers' or printers' letter books or ledgers; the history of library arrangement; maps.
86. Minutes of the Publications Committee, 106. In his hopes of an active publications policy for the Society, Pollard envisaged an extension of its chronological and subject range to include all dates to 1900, all countries, a survey of trade documents and a vigorous search for those yet unlocated (Ms Pollard 414, item 6). At the same time he was realistic about the slim prospects of securing qualified editors with the free time to devote to such tasks. In his paper of 8 August 1958 he had reflected upon what was proving to be a passing era: 'The Society has been fortunate in having members (Duff, Greg, McKerrow, Ferguson et al.) who had both the leisure and the unexceptionable scholarship for producing the books which the Society has published.'
87. Walter Mitchell's typescript is currently in my possession but there is also a copy in the Bodleian Library at Ms Pollard 304. With the exception of that part edited by Jackson a copy also precedes the index to Liber A compiled by Michael Pearson: 'An Index to "Liber A", a Volume of the Records of the Stationers' Company of London'. Thesis presented for the Degree of Master of Arts, Victoria University of Wellington, 1980. A copy of this volume is on deposit at Stationers' Hall; a microfilm copy of it is also included in *The Records of the Stationers' Company, 1554-1920* (Chadwyck-Healey, 1987).
88. *Index to Liber A of the Records of the Worshipful Company of Stationers* (London: Privately Printed, 1902), 16pp.
89. Greg, introduction to *Records of the Court*, v; and Greg to Pollard, 27 February 1932, Ms Pollard 378, f.48.
90. McKerrow to Pollard, 21 December 1937, Ms Pollard 397, f.95.
91. Pollard to McKerrow, 22 December 1937, Ms Pollard 397, ff.96-7.
92. The material reprinted from Liber A by Jackson takes up 98 pages of his edition. It might not be an excessive charge on any new edition to include it and thus preserve the integrity of Liber A.
93. They are only lightly annotated: Jackson footnotes some *STC* references, gives some cross-references to Court Book C, the *Calendars of State Papers (Domestic)*, the *Analytical*

Index of Remembrancia, freedoms from C. R. Rivington's list at Arber, v. 685-8, Acts of the Privy Council, and to F. C. Dietz, *English Public Finance* (1932).
94. Greg to Pollard, 1 March 1931, Ms Pollard 378, f.47.
95. Greg to Pollard, 11 March 1954, Ms Pollard 59, f.60.

Appendix

Liber A, ff. 30ʳ and 30ᵛ

By the mayor
[*m.n.*] To the Wardens and companie of the stationars

Theis shalbe to aduertize yow that herew^th you shall receaue certen instruccions whiche we haue receaued from the righte honourable the lordes of hir maiesties moste honourable pryvie counsell touchinge the orderinge and trayninge of such harquebut shotte as are to be provided w^thin this Cytye whereof I charge and require you and in hir maiesties name Comaundinge you to haue speciall care and consideracion accordinglie and that yow wth as muche speede as convenientlie you maye doe certifie vnto me the saide mayor aswell the names and surnames of all suche persons as are appointed to provide for your saide Companie and specyallie of suche as are fytte to be captaines to trayne them, not failinge hereof as you will answere to the contrarye at your vttermoste perilles. yeven at the Guyldhall the xx^th of marche 1577.

Sebrighte.

Orders howe euery parson that
shalbe trayned shalbe taughte
to handle and vse his peece

ffirste that euerie harquebussher that is vtterlie voide of the knowledge of the vse of his peece to be instructed in manner and fourme folowinge.

1. Imprimis that euerye suche parson be instructed howe to handle and carrye his peece flaske and touchboxe.

2. Alsoe to instructe him what weighte of powder and shotte is meete for his peece.

3. Then to teache him how in handsome manner he shall charge his peece, and after how to laie yt to his cheke and beinge once acquaynted howe to charge then to teach him howe to carrye and shoote of his peece at random, and afterwarde to be taughte to shoote at a marke Certen, the same to be distante the vttermoste the levell of the peece.

4. Item after beinge at Twoe firste meetinges experymented howe to handle and charge his peece and to shoote at a marke at the laste meetinge they are to be furder trayned howe vpon a small staye eyther in marche or skyrmishe they muste redyly shoote & spedely charge and dyscharge their saide peeces.

5 Item that the peeces before their trayninge be visyted by the gentelmen to be good and meete for the purpose and not suche as are like to take or doe anye harme.

6 Item that good care be had and greate charge given that in the tyme of skyrmishe to excercise at the laste meetinge noe peece to be laden wth bullett or otherwise to be shotte of whereby anie parson maie be maymed or putt in hassarde of lief or lymmes. Twentye bulletes for the caliuer of the tower is iuste a pounde weighte and one pounde of powder will make xxv shotte allowinge iij quarters waighte of powder to euerye bullet and the ouerplus after that rate is v shotte more wch is for touche powder So that in their whole xx bulletes are to be made of the pounde and xxv shott to the pownde of powder whereof v allowed for touche powder.

        Tho: Sussex   Iaco: Croftes
        Ro: Lecester   Christo: Hatton
        Henr. Hunesdon   Franc: Walsingham
        Franc: Knowles   Tho: Wilson.

Liber A, fols 48^r, 48^v, 49^r

        Orders prescribed by the Wardens, to be observed
                by the prestemen of this Cumpanye

m^r Bishop } war.
m^r newbery }

j. ffyrste that nonne shall dyscharge any peece in the hall nor have any matche kyndled wth fire in the said hall.

2. That euery prestman shall followe the dyrection of the Wardens or their deputies for the Wearinge of his Armour and beinge so directed shall repaire to the Armorye and there shall receaue suche furniture as our Armorer shall thincke fitt for him.

3. Further that but one prestman shall at any time enter into the Armorye and the reste remayne in the hall vntill suche tyme as they shalbe called.

4. That euery prestman shall in all lawfull thinges be obedyent to the Wardens or their deputies in this service soe the same be not againste the direction of their Captaine.

5. That euery prestman shalbe contented wth suche Armoure as the Wardens or armorer shall thincke fitt and convenient for him from tyme to tyme.

6. That all the prestmen shall orderlie goe together from the said hall to suche place of service as shalbe appointed, and soe shall behaue themselues lovinglie and quietly together vntill their retourninge againe into the hall.

7. And finallie that euery prestman shall at thend of euery daies service repaire to the hall wth his Armoure and there in good order shall delyver yt to the Armorer, whoe shall there attend for that purpose.

1585   May

m^r Tottell m^r
m^r bishop   } wardens
m^r newbery   Armour provided by the wardens this yere

Item iij callivers	xxxiij s.
Item j morian	iij s.
Item ij flaskes & touchboxes	iiij s. viij d.
Item xxiij sweordes ⎫	viij li.
Item xx^{ti} daggers ⎭	
Item xx^{tie}iiij girdles	j li. xij s.
Item vi corslettes wth their furniture	viij li. viij s.
Item j firken of gunpowder	ij li. ix s.
Item iij halberdes	xij s.
Item iij pikes	xij s.

The names of the Trained men

Stephan peele	vincent williamson
Iohn Kid	humfrey lewes
henry brooke	Robert Baynes
Edw. Cowick	christofer heckford
Iohn Robertes	Edward dier
Robert ffrere	Thomas Lawe
Raffe waudell	Thomas Havilond
Iohn price	Edward wynnyf
Arthur Tomlin	David bedoo
Iohn lacye	marmaduke ponsonby
Thomas newton	Ambrose hacket
willm Rayman	Edw harslet
Iohn moore	
Thomas Cutler	
Edw dier [*duplicated entry*]	

The whole number of Stacioners according to my
L. maiors warrant deliuered vnder the
enseigne of m^r Captaine Vaughan

marmaduke pountsaby ⎫		Ambrose hacket ⎫	
Thomas Cutler ⎬ Halberdes		Edw. wynnyf ⎪	
Raffe waudell ⎭		christofer hacford ⎪	
		humfre lewis ⎪	
Stephan peele ⎫		wm Raymond ⎪	
henry brooke ⎪		Iohn lacy ⎪	
Thomas newton ⎪		Tho. lawe ⎬ Callyvers
Rob. Fryour ⎪		Io. Bradway ⎪	
Rob. Baynes ⎬ Pykes		david bedo ⎪	
Io. Kyd ⎪		Io. Apryce ⎪	
Iohn moore ⎪		Io. Robertes ⎪	
Edw. dier ⎪		Edw Cowick ⎪	
Tho. havilond ⎪		Arthur tomlin ⎪	
henry harslop ⎭		Vincent Williamson ⎭	

Members of the Stationers' Company who served in the Artillery Company before the Civil War; Ralphe Mabbe and his network[1]

JEAN TSUSHIMA

THE FRATERNITY or gild of St George, which was the forerunner of the Artillery Company, was set up and incorporated by Letters Patent on 25 August 1537.[2] It was based for its training in the Old Artillery Ground off Bishopsgate, a ground which it had to share with the Gunners of the Tower. It is not known why it was set up – it did not have to fulfil the same requirements as the Honourable Corps of Gentlemen-at-Arms founded by Henry VIII in 1509, which accompanied the king on his foreign ventures as the Bodyguard and whose members were required to prove that they were of gentle birth. The Artillery Company – the name dates from the post-Reformation and dissolution of the monasteries – was not a bodyguard, its members were required to be wealthy City merchants, freemen of a Company, with the exception of foreign merchants who were admitted without the necessity of being naturalized. The members of the Artillery Company were to practise with longbows, crossbows and 'handgonnes', the last item giving the clue to the need for members to be wealthy as they alone had the right to own firearms and keep them at home. Primitive though firearms were in the early sixteenth century, it was recognised by those in authority that they could be a dangerous threat if they got into the wrong hands. Rich merchants could be trusted to keep the peace – it was in their own interest to do so.

The history of the Company, apart from what can be researched in the State Papers Domestic and a few private documents, is a closed book up to the 1650s, from which date rough address books survive, with mention of the livery company of many members so that identification becomes possible. All the Company's Tudor and Stuart records were lost during the Civil War. The Company was reorganized in 1611 and a muster roll, known as the *Vellum Book* (1611-82) was opened.[3] Between 1611 and 1642, it is a bare list of some three thousand members but without addresses or livery company membership, and rarely military rank. So we have little idea of who they were except those in the *DNB* and prominent men, such as the Citizens and Haberdashers, Sir Hugh Hammersley, Lord Mayor (1627-8)[4] and Alderman Sir Richard Fenn,[5] the Regicide, Owen Rowe,[6] famous soldiers such as Major-General Philip Skippon, Sergeant-Major General of the Trained Bands,[7] and Captain Henry Waller who commanded the Company.[8]

In 1984 an HAC Biographical Dictionary Trust was founded and this paper must be regarded as work in progress for the period covered here. To open up this closed period of history a systematic search is being made for wills of members with unusual names and those of 'strangers'[9] and this has produced some surprising revelations about the composition of the Company's membership. We started with what was easy, the Company's benefactors at the back of the *Vellum Book*, but there are the inevitable problems with the common names and variant spellings in the index – the 19 Joneses, the 25 Browns, the 38 Clarks or Clerks, to say nothing of 74 Smiths or Smyths of whom only Alderman Humphrey Smith is easily identified. Even the rarer names can pose problems. Such was the case of Octavian Pullen or Pullein – the surname is rare enough, the Christian name even more so in this period; they proved to be father and son, both Citizens and Stationers, but which one belonged to the Artillery Company? Constructing a pedigree from the data found in their wills can sometimes sort out which is which as well as revealing intermarriages between members of the Artillery Company or between Stationers. Prominent merchants turn up in the State Papers and elsewhere; foreign merchants – who are never Stationers – are documented in their own church records and naturalization papers. There are nearly three thousand names in the muster rolls up to 1642 and trawling through them can be tedious work.

Odd names catch the eye and the unusual name of Ralph Mabbe (to whom most of this paper will be devoted) eventually led me to the search for Stationers in the muster roll. It did not take me long to find a number of them – Adam Islip, George Hurlock, Thomas Harper, Thomas Beale, Octavian Pullein (already mentioned), Luke Fawne, John Dawson, William and John, sons of Nicholas Oakes – all of whom were Stationers and members of the Artillery Company between 1612 and 1642. Adam Islip (obviously of a Puritan family) printed sermons for, or in association with, Mabbe. Their published works fall into four categories – military tactics and drill books; scientific works, usually gunnery and mathematics; sermons; translations and a small collection of miscellaneous works but – there were hardly any literary items. Publication reflected the dormant crises of the times; although some historians have described these years as the halcyon days of the Stuarts, they were, in reality, no such thing.[10]

Warfare was changing as armies became larger; siege warfare gave way to set battles, artillery became smaller and lighter as the large ordnance became too heavy to transport easily. Armies fought face to face, the outcome depending more on the cavalry charge and the 'thrust of pike', while musketeers had taken over the role of archers. This called for books on tactics, as well as drill books which were still necessary as men had to be trained to march and to fire a musket – an operation which took some five minutes. Unless strict drill order was kept a man was in danger of having his head broken by an 18-foot pike weighing at least 12 pounds or a musket weighing some 14 pounds. The popular idea of armies roaming the countryside looting and raping at will carrying such weapons and a quantity of heavy gear is wide of the mark, but if soldiers were to take the field as a disciplined army and not a useless rabble it meant careful drilling. Learning to wheel to left or right, open and close ranks and right-about-turn meant hours of drilling and the demand for drill books was therefore a steady one. The Artillery Company was renowned for the thoroughness of its drill and this was the reason it was entrusted with the training of the trained bands for more than two centuries.

The first drill book compiled for the Company was Thomas Trussell's *Souldier Pleading his owne Cause*, 1619, printed by Nicolas Oakes and sold by Thomas Walkley, author, bookseller and printer, all being members of the Artillery Company. It was a revision of an earlier, simpler manual printed by Adam Islip. The classic drill manual was Captain William Barriffe's *Military Discipline: Or the Young Artillery-Man*, 1st edition, 1635, printed by 'Thomas Harper for R. Mab', and dedicated to the Company (see fig.1). Barriffe, formerly a member of a Kentish militia[11] joined the Artillery Company in 1626. A second edition, dedicated to the Captains of the Artillery Company, appeared in 1639. Mabbe seems to have died before the third, revised and enlarged edition came out in 1643, printed by John Dawson for Andrew Crooke. The drill book remained in print until 1661 with three more editions printed by his widow, Gertrude Dawson.[12] It was, and remains to this day, the basic drill book of the Company of Pikemen and Musketeers of the Honourable Artillery Company, now the official bodyguard of the Lord Mayor.

Military drill books fairly poured from the press in this period; they were the 'in' topic of the day, fuelled by the constant war scares, the renewal of the Dutch War of Independence, the crisis of the Cleeves-Jülich

Fig.1. Title page and frontispiece portrait of William Barriff, *Military Discipline: or the yung artillery man*, 1635. Reproduced by permission of the British Library Board.

succession followed by the assassination of Henri IV, the start of the Thirty Years' War and the entry of the Swedish army into Germany, the miserable expedition to aid La Rochelle, as well as the constant hope that James I and later Charles I would make some sort of gesture towards the plight of the European Protestants, to keep up the war fever. Books on military matters did a roaring trade. In 1640, Captain Lewes Roberts of the Artillery Company, a rich Levant merchant, brought out *Warfare Epitomised*, 1640, printed by R. Oulton for Ralph Mabbe.[13] This was a justification for war, and considering the date of publication, it is surprising that a rich merchant should take such a stand; for only two years before Mabbe had published Roberts's *Merchants Mapp of Commerce*, a book of mercantile advice and information, printed by R. Oulton for Mabbe (see fig.2). It was dedicated to the members of the Levant Company, several of them Harveys, at least two of whom were members of the Artillery Company. It was a splendid book which was reprinted many times long after both Roberts and Mabbe were dead.

Mabbe's name was curiously familiar to me and I started hunting – in vain – for him in the usual trade or business records; then an early number, from 1922, of the *HAC Journal* chanced to give the clue – it had a seventeenth-century version of the Artillery Company arms on the cover and underneath the arms is 'Printed for Ralphe Mabb' (see fig.3). But where had Mabbe's arms sprung from – Goold Walker's history, *The Honourable Artillery Company 1537-1926*, gave no clue[14] and it was a year or two before I tracked it down. The discovery of Mabbe's name (spelt variously Mabbe, Mabb or Mab) in the Muster Roll caused me to look around for other booksellers or printers in the Artillery Company, which led me to the Stationers' Company's records.

About this time, 1994, I bought a copy of Captain John Bingham's *The Art of Embattailing an Army*, 1629, printed by John Beale and Thomas Brudenell for Ralphe Mab (see fig.4). Brudenell was not in the Muster Roll, but Beale was; he joined October 1613, a year after 'Sergeant Ralphe Mabb'. He was not, however, listed in Goold Walker's card index of Trained Band Officers in the HAC archive.[15] The dedication is interesting: 'To the Right Worshipful Sir Hugh Hamersly, Knight, one of the Aldermen and Coronels of the Honourable City of London, and President of the Martial Company, Exercising Armes in the Artillery Garden in London. To Captaine Henry Waller, now Captain of the Said Company and to all the Rest of the Worthy Captaines and Gentlemen of the said *Company*. Captaine I. B. wisheth such valour and experience, as may make them victorious against all sort of Enemies.' At the end of the book was

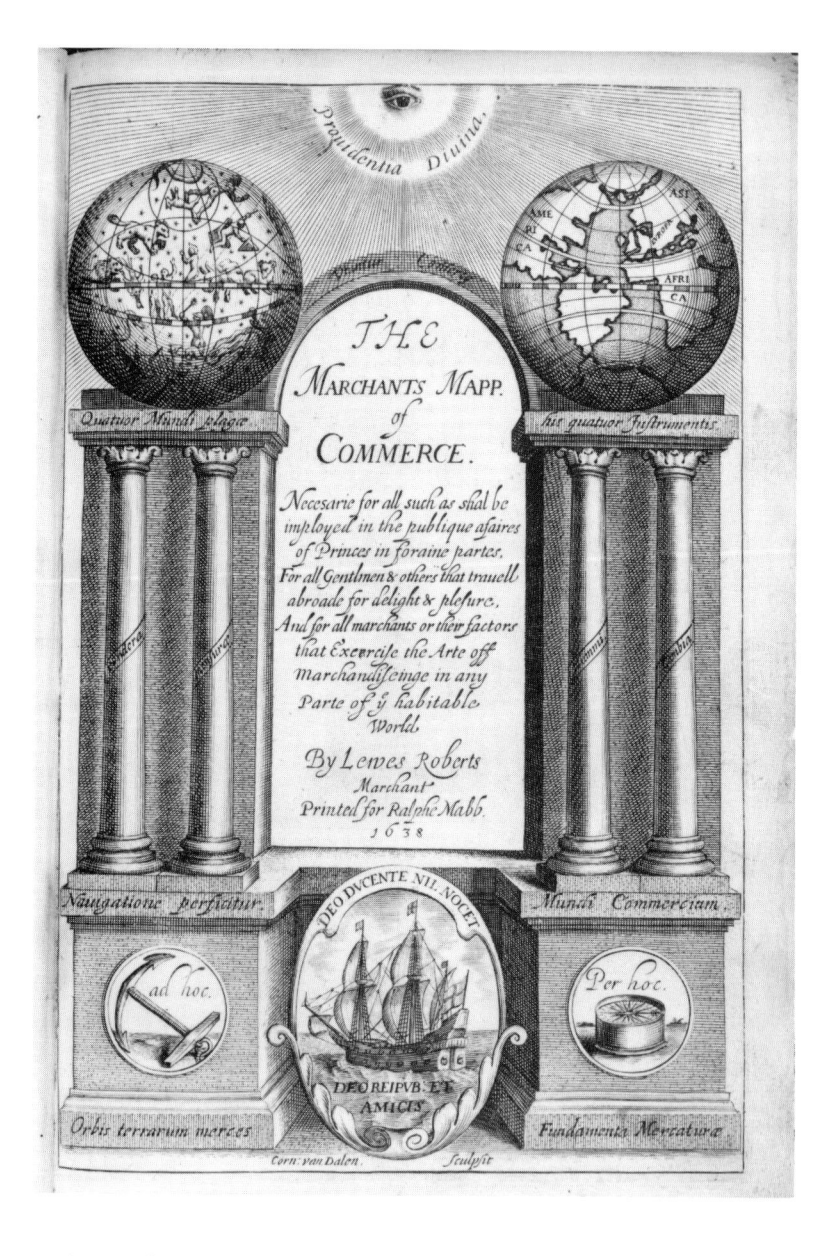

Fig.2. Title page of Lewes Roberts, *The Merchants Mapp of Commerce*, 1638. Reproduced by permission of the British Library Board.

THE ART OF EMBATTAILING
AN
ARMY.
OR,
THE SECOND PART OF
ÆLIANS TACTICKS.

WITH NOTES VPON EVERY CHAPTER.

By Capt. IOHN BINGHAM.

LONDON:
Printed by IOHN BEALE and THOMAS BRVDENELL for RALPH MAB.
1629.

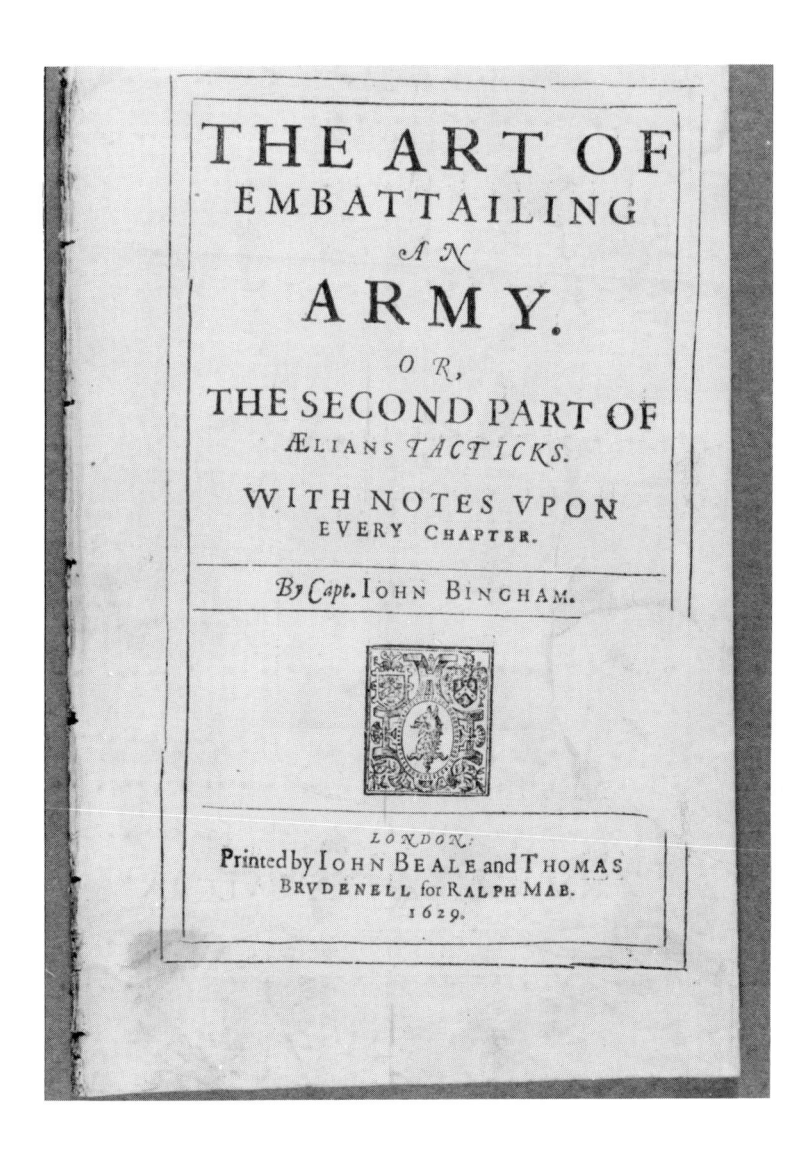

Fig.3. Colophon of *The art of embattailing*, 1629, with the arms of Ralphe Mabbe. *In the possession of Mrs Jean Tsushima.* Photograph by the author.

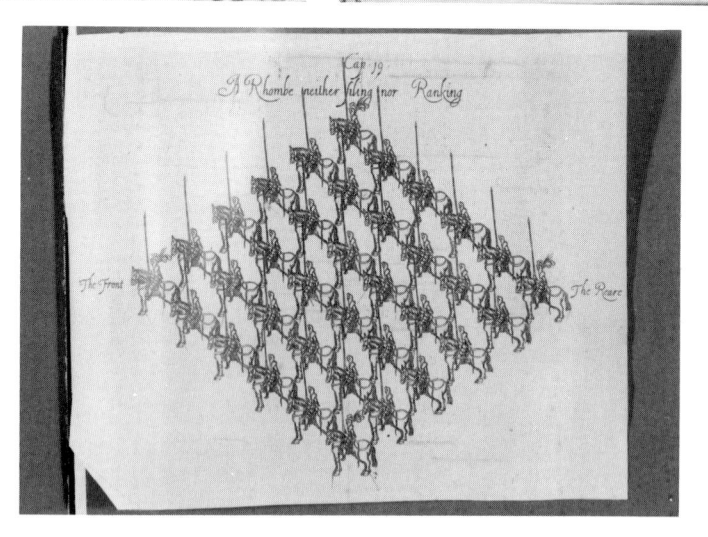

Fig. 4(a-d). Title page, dedication and plates of cavalry and pikemen formations from John Bingham, *The art of embattailing an army*, 1629. *In the possession of Jean Tsushima.* Photograph by the author.

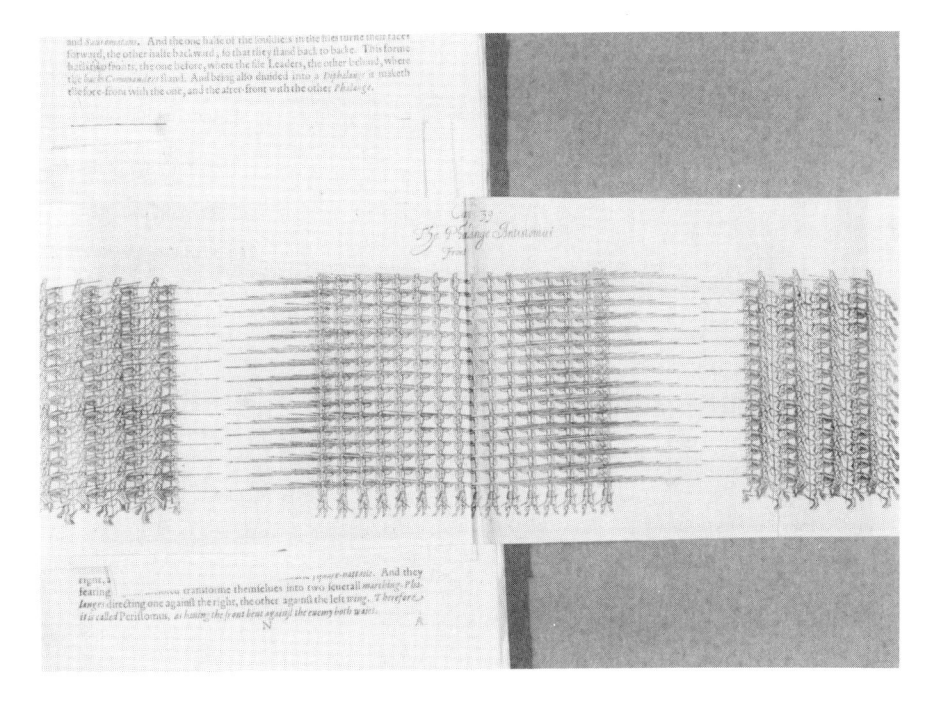

Fig.4(d)

the well-known coat of arms 'printed for Ralphe Mab'. It is no surprise that Mabbe had published Bingham's treatise on warfare; Captain John Bingham, a veteran of the Dutch wars, was President of the Artillery Company in the 1620s and was about to return to the Continent just as the Thirty Years' War moved into its last terrible phase.

It was not the first book that Mabbe had published for Bingham; in 1623 he had brought out Bingham's translation of *The Historie of Xenophon: containing the Ascent of Cyrus into the Higher Countries*, which included a comparison of 'the Roman manner of Warres' taken from the work of the sixteenth-century Flemish scholar, Justus Lipsius,[16] printed by John Haviland and dedicated to 'Colonel Sir Hugh Hammersley, and to all the Captains and Generous Citizens professing Armes there' in the Artillery Garden. Bingham was lavish in his praise of the men of the Artillery Company; the general impression is that the training was very thorough and that they were conscientious in turning up for drill. Little is known about Bingham, a professional soldier probably from the Irish family of that name, who spent most of his life abroad in the Low

Countries. His first known work, written while he was serving in Holland under his hero General Maurice of Nassau, Prince of Orange, but published in London by Laurence Lisle, was *The Tacticks of Aelian*, 'Englished by J. B.', 1616.

Throughout the 1620s and 1630s war was raging on the Continent and there was the fear that England would be drawn into it, while at home there was a battle between the Puritans and the episcopacy which Archbishop Laud was trying to impose on the country, with control of the press in part through the Stationers' Company.[17] So it is hardly surprising that Mabbe's list, in common with that of other booksellers in the Artillery Company, should concentrate on military books as well as publishing a number of books of sermons, often using military metaphors, particularly those preached before the 'Gentlemen of the Artillery Ground, being published at their earnest request'.[18] These he issued in editions of several hundreds. It is hard to understand the appeal of sermons nowadays but in the sixteenth and seventeenth century they were the very basis of spiritual life, eagerly read and well attended. They were even more popular than military books; every Artillery Company bookseller included some in his list and Ralphe Mabbe published more than 30 sermons, many of them reprinted over the years.

Mabbe is one of a number of extremely interesting Stationers in the sixteenth and early seventeenth century Artillery Company, and I shall devote the rest of this paper to recounting what I know of him to date – a fascinating story but very much work-in-progress at this stage. He was born into a wealthy family of goldsmiths in 1584, the eleventh of the thirteen children of John Mabbe, Citizen and Goldsmith, and his wife Martha Denham, daughter of another goldsmith, William Denham. They owned the Tabard Inn,[19] and Mabbe's son John bought land in Essex in the 1580s.[20] Ralph Mabbe's grandfather, John Mabbe, Citizen and Goldsmith, who died in 1582 leaving a very rich widow, Isabell, *née* Colley, was Chamberlain of London. Ralph's uncle, Stephen Mabbe, goldsmith, married Dionyssus, daughter of Affabel Partridge, Queen Elizabeth's goldsmith. The three families, Mabbe, Denham and Partridge, all lived in the area of Goldsmith's Hall and Cheapside.[21] Despite his affluent background, Ralph Mabbe could not, with four elder brothers, hope for an academic career. His elder brothers, John and James, both went to Oxford, John becoming Rector of Bulpham, Essex and James becoming Fellow of Magdalen in 1594 and Secretary to Sir John Digby, English Ambassador to Spain.[22] He translated a number of works from Spanish which were later published by his brother Ralph.

Ralph Mabbe was bound to William Leake, senior, Citizen and Stationer, in 1603 and freed by him in 1610.[23] He never took the livery and appears never to have obtained the City freedom. This could argue that after 1618, he left London and resided at one of the family country properties – so far mere speculation. In 1611 he settled in the parish of St Gregory by St Paul's occupying first the Angel (1611-13), then the Greyhound (1613-16).[24] He must have married before 1611, although the marriage details have not yet come to light, and two of his children were baptized at St Gregory by St Paul's, 1612 and 1613.[25]. He bound his first apprentice, Jacob Bloome on 8 April 1611 and freed him on 26 March 1618; a Jacob Bloome, probably the same man, joined the Artillery Company in 1624.[26] The same year, 1611, that he bound his first apprentice, Mabbe published his first book, the immensely popular *Display of Heraldrie* by John Gwillim, Rouge Croix Pursuivant, which went through six editions.[27] In the second edition, 1632, Mabbe added a list of *Terms of Hawking and Hunting*, drawn up by 'R. Mab'. Was there a closer connection between author and publisher? Leake's first apprentice was a John Guyllyam which may or may not be a coincidence although a Welsh name is not particularly unusual in London.[28]

In this work, the whole art and science of heraldry was systematized and illustrated for the first time; the illustrations, though clear, are not outstanding. It is unlike the other works published by Mabbe but not a strange choice for a man with goldsmith connections – goldsmiths regularly employed engravers to chase a client's arms on their work and needed a knowledge of heraldry. They would often consult the heralds, at the nearby College of Arms, for verification of details.

For the next seven years, until he moved in 1623, Mabbe published only sermons, apart from the almost obligatory epithalamium for the marriage of Princess Elizabeth to the young Palatinate Elector in 1613.[29] A few of them were funeral sermons for noblemen, but most were preached by popular Puritan divines, some still in office, others had been ejected for not following Archbishop Laud's instructions of 1622 that 'preachers should adhere strictly to their texts', or, in an afternoon sermon, confine themselves to some part of the catechism or to a text from the Creed, the ten commandments or the Lord's prayer.[30] We can presume, from Mabbe's choice of sermons, that he was a non-conformist sympathizer or, very likely, a Puritan. Some or his authors are obscure ministers but others are famous, some being members of the Artillery Company, their texts having direct links with the Company. Among Mabbe's list of obvious best sellers were the posthumous sermons of

Daniel Dyke (1570?-1614) who came of a family famous for its Puritan divines and scholars, two of them members of the Artillery Company.[31] Mabbe's list included such renowned contemporary Puritan preachers as Richard Sibbs (1577-1635),[32] William Gouge (1578-1653)[33] and George Hughes.[34]

Thomas Adams (*fl.*1612-53), vicar of Wingrave, Buckinghamshire (1614-36) who was the most prolific of all sermon writers of his time, held the preachership of St Gregory by St Paul's (1618-23).[35] Very likely Mabbe, who lived in the parish, knew him. He was in trouble with Laud, but appears not to have been silenced, although, in later years, he was forced to live a secluded and cautious life. Mabbe published more of Adams's sermons than those of any other preacher, including several of the major ones, preached in Wingrave before he came to London. Adam Islip also published some of Adams's sermons. Among a number of sermons preached to the Artillery Company and printed 'by earnest request of the men' is *The Souldiers honour* by Thomas Adams, 1617, printed by Adam Islip for Edward Blount (who was in trouble with the authorities and may or may not have been a member of the Company). Its language and imagery is robust and martial: 'We are all Souldiers, as wee are Christians, some more specially, as they are men. You beare spiritual Arms against the Enemies of your Salvation, and Material Arms against the enemies of your Countrey. In both you fight under the Colours of our great General Iesus Christ'; he goes on to quote Job 'who calls mans life a Warfare'.[36]

George Hughes's sermon on *The Saints losse and lamentation*, printed by John Beale for Ralphe Mabbe, 1632, was preached at the funeral of Captain Henry Waller, Captain of the London Trained Bands and the Artillery Company and Treasurer of the Company. Hughes was one of those suspended for refusing to comply with Laud's rubric. Another sermon preached to the Company was William Gouge's *The Dignity of Chivalrie*, printed by George Miller for Ralphe Mab, 1626. Its stirring text was 'The Lord is a Man of Warre'. No wonder, considering the bent of the Artillery Company's Stationer members, that the Artillery Garden earned the name of 'Nursery ground of Puritanism'.

Mabbe seems to have tried his hand at news-sheet publishing; there is an entry in the Stationers' Register, for 1 October 1627, that 'Ralphe Mabb Entred for his Copye under the handes of Master Weskherline and Master Knight Warden A Currant of Newes October 1 number 1'.[37] We may speculate whether this was his sole foray into news-sheet publishing, and whether it was the outcome of contacts in Europe. He published an Italian textbook, *New and easy directions for attaining the Thruscan Italian tongue, by Giovanni Torriano, sold by the Professor at his lodgings in Abchurch Street adjoyning Lumbard Street*, 1639. Ralphe Mabbe also published a novel translated from the Spanish by Mabbe's elder brother, James, who was the translator of a number of Spanish works still in print today. It is a surprise to find the staid Mabbe publishing his brother's translation of such a novel as *The Spanish Bawd*, 1631. His brother's works were definitely risky for Mabbe to publish, although Islip undertook publication of *Devout contemplations expressed in two and fortie sermons* by 'Christovale de Fonseca... englished by JM of Magdalen College, Oxford. for A. Islip, 1628-9'.[38] Edward Blount brought out the most controversial of all James Mabbe's translated works – *Christian policies; or, the Christian Commonwealth*. The names of the author, Fr Juan de Santa Maria, and of the translator are written in the British Library's copy. It has a grovelling dedication by Blount to James Hay, Earl of Carlisle, one of the Lords of the Privy Council. The Spanish dedication is to the King of Spain. It is described as being 'for the Good of Kings and Princes, and such as are in authorities under them and trusted with State Affaires'. It was immediately banned in Spain but secretly printed by various provincial presses there.[39] No doubt Mabbe thought it best to distance himself from such a work coming out of Catholic Spain; perhaps James Mabbe himself, an Anglican and Prebendary of Wells, also thought his brother should keep his distance on this occasion. On another occasion James Mabbe took the precaution of using a punning *nom de plume* 'Don Diego Puede-Ser', Spanish for 'perhaps', 'maybe'.[40] An aspect of the Civil War that is little stressed these days is that, even before the conflict broke out, the violence of religious and political passions were tearing families apart and the translating of Catholic polemical books could have been enough to split the Mabbe family. On the other hand, the differences between Anglican and Puritan were probably enough to do that.

The last of the four categories I mentioned as forming the publication staple of Stationer members of the Artillery Company was gunnery and mathematics. By the late 1630s the study of mathematics was obligatory for gunners and serious soldiers, both from its uses in surveying the ground and in the study of artillery. One bookseller member of the Artillery Company who published in this area was George Hurlock,[41] who published *The Complete Cannoniere: or, The Gunners Guide...with divers excellent Conclusions, both Arithmeticall and Geometricall belonging thereupon: as also sundry serviceable Fireworks, both for Sea and Land service. A study delightfull and very usefull for men of the best Quality, and imbrac'd by the greatest Princes*, 1639 (see fig.5). The author was John Roberts, who

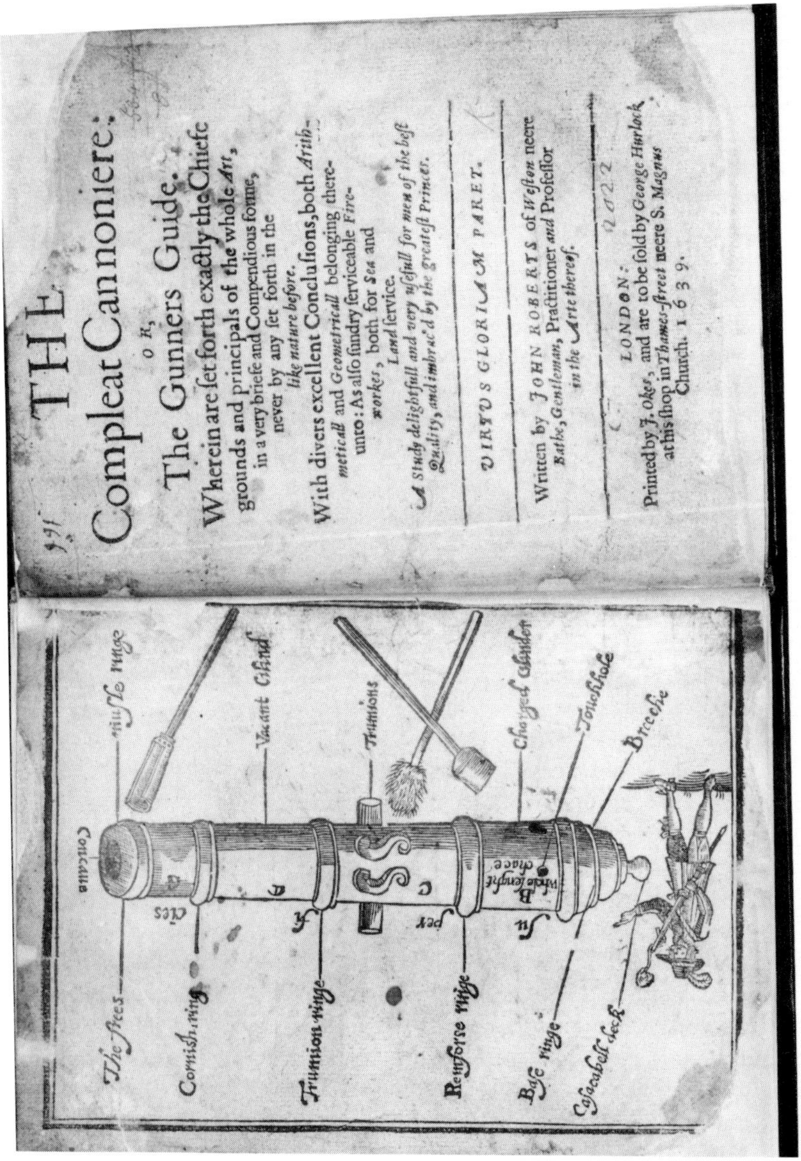

Fig. 5. Title page and illustration from John Roberts, *The Compleat Connoniere*, 1639. Reproduced by permission of the British Library Board.

had served in the Yarmouth Trained Bands and was an experienced gunner. To most people today fireworks mean pretty entertainment on a summer's evening but to the artillery man 'fireworks' were the study of gunpowder and its wartime uses.

As war approached, first with Scotland and then the Civil War, little handbooks – somewhat crude but fitting the pocket of a buff coat – written by some aspiring young soldier or veteran of the Continental wars, began to appear. Thomas Harper published some of these best-selling little booklets, such as *Warlike Directions of the Souldiers Practice. Set forth for the benefit of all such as are, or will be Scholars of Martiall Discipline by a practitioner of the same Art. T. F.* 1643. Printed by Thomas Harper and are to be sold at his House in Little Britain.[42]

Mabbe published one magnificent work on mathematics and 'fireworks'; this was *Pyrotechnia. Or, A Discourse of Artificiall Fireworks...whereunto is annexed a short Treatise of Geometrie*, Printed by Thomas Harper for Ralph Mab, 1635 (see fig.6). The author was 'John Babbington, Gunner and Student in the Mathematics'. Part of *Pyrotechnia* is devoted to the effects that can be created in masques and plays with clever machinery, similar to the three-day firework displays at the wedding of Princess Elizabeth and Frederick of the Palatinate which included dragons flying through the air. But it is also a serious work on gunnery and the author describes a shell which can be regarded as the forerunner of the shrapnel shell.

There are very few references to Mabbe in the Stationers' Company records – he entered some books in the registers and he bound four apprentices, Jacob Bloome, Ives Bassingbourne, Joseph Manley and Edward Packston at the Hall. He was chosen auditor in 1629 and 1635, which seems to argue some status in the Company. I had given up hope of finding out anything more about him when I happened upon his name in the State Papers Domestic, Charles I. He was in real trouble, together with John Dawson and Thomas Shelton who were all up in the Court of High Commission.[43] On 30 April 1640, he and John Dawson were to be 'attached' (that is imprisoned or fined) 'unless they give in their answers by next court day'. Unfortunately it not clear what for, as the printed accounts give no cause and we can only speculate that they were caught printing Puritan forbidden books. They had certainly published *Threnikos*, a collection of 47 funeral sermons by four well-known Puritan preachers and this would have been enough to get a Stationer into prison. The discovery that Shelton was the inventor of a system of shorthand put things in a different light because shorthand of all kinds was much in

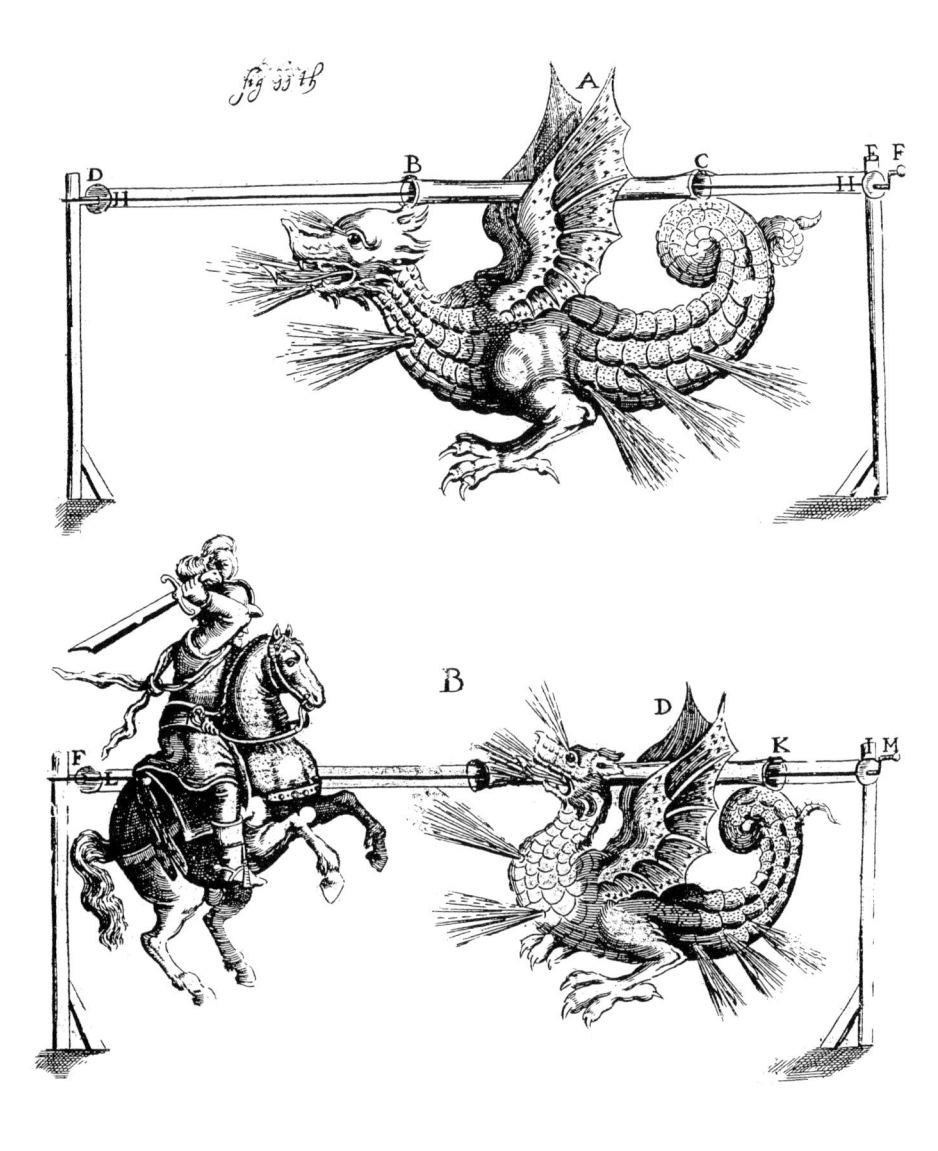

Fig.6. Illustration from John Babbington, *Pyrotechnia*, 1635. *In the possession of Mrs Jean Tsushima.* Photograph by the author.

vogue at this period and used for taking down sermons (particularly forbidden Puritan sermons) or political speeches which could later be printed clandestinely.[44] What the three were up to we may never know, but Mabbe and Dawson were in court five times throughout the summer of 1640.[45] They were by no means the only Stationers to be in trouble; between January and July 1640 fourteen printers or booksellers appeared in the Court of High Commission, but Mabbe and Dawson were examined more often than any of the others.[46] By 25 June Mabbe was threatened with attachment, 'to be decreed if he give not his answer within a fortnight'. There were no more entries so he may have been let off with a fine. He was able to print another book in the autumn, his last under Laud's regime.[47] In July of next year, 1641, the Star Chamber and Court of High Commission were both abolished. John Pym made several great speeches to the House of Lords attacking both Laud and Stafford, which were translated into Dutch and appeared in print in Amsterdam a few days later. Keen interest was shown by the Dutch in the English political speeches and publications, and there was tough competition to be first with a translation. What is particularly interesting is the imprint of both the Dutch and English versions – *The Speech or Declaration of John Pymm Esq...against William Laud* printed for Ralph Mabb of the Artillery Company. Did Mabbe have Dutch connections? He used at least three Dutch or Flemish engravers, but his involvement remains a mystery for the time being.[48]

Acknowledgements

I would like to thank Robin Myers for inviting me to give a paper at the 1996 conference at Stationers' Hall and for her continuous help with the quest for references. I must thank Ann J. King who acts as my 'eyes' and transcribed all the Mabbe wills. I would also like to thank Dr Elisabeth Leedham-Green and Michael Turner for help in tracing elusive material, and Dr Sonia Anderson for kindly letting me read and benefit from her new life of Lewes Roberts. Also heartfelt thanks to Chrissie Rowlands and her colleague in the photographic section of the British Library, for their constant help with my copying requirements, often at very short notice. I would like to thank Mr Jaap Harskamp of the Dutch Section of the British Library and Professor Paul Hoftijzer of Leiden University for guidance on Anglo-Dutch publishing and printing of this era.

References

1. This is an abstract from a forthcoming monograph to be included in *HAC Biographical Dictionary* (1537-1914), to be published by the HAC Biographical Dictionary Trust.
2. The Artillery Company had over 20 different appellations during this period; the term Trained Bands is the same as Militia from 1600, both terms appearing throughout this paper.
3. *The Vellum Book Muster Roll* is said to date from 1611 but the present volume, replacing one that was lost, was no doubt rewritten in 1635 and it is very likely that it was rewritten yet again. It is full of gross errors in the spelling of names, and the 1890 printed version contains a few more – it must be used with caution.
4. Sir Hugh Hammersley (1565-1636), twice Master of the Haberdashers' Company (1619/20, and 1627/8); Governor of Christ's Hospital, of the Russia Merchants', East India, Levant and Virginia Companies; Sheriff of the City of London (1618) and Lord Mayor (1627/8).
5. Sir Richard Venn, or Fenn (d.1639); Haberdashers' Company: Alderman (1626/7); Lord Mayor (1636/7); Colonel of the Trained Bands (1631-9); President of the Artillery Company (1633/4).
6. Owen Rowe (1593?-1661); Haberdashers' Company; officer in the Green Regiment of the Trained Bands; joined the Artillery Company (1619); a regicide; died in the Tower. See *DNB*.
7. Major-General Philip Skippon (d.1660); a professional soldier who served under Vere in the Low Countries; Parliamentary soldier; Commander of the Artillery Company (1639); Sergeant-Major-General of the City Trained Bands.
8. Captain Henry Waller (d.1632); Captain of the Trained Bands; joined the Artillery Company (1611); commanded the Company.
9. Stranger was the usual term to denote overseas *emigrés*, usually from the Low Countries, North France and the German States; this was to differentiate them from 'foreigners' who were usually people who came into the city or town from outside. The term aliens was also used for strangers. They were called strangers even if denized or naturalized, though this was usually mentioned. In theory children born of strangers in England were English by birth, but this was a matter for dispute in the case of rich families because double tax was levied on strangers.
10. Barbara Donagan, 'Halcyon Days and the Literature of War', *Past and Present* no.141, gives a very good review of the horrors of war in Germany against which England did seem a charmed land of peace and plenty; but life in England was bad enough for thousands to emigrate to New England, and they were not all fanatic Puritans at all; England's horrors of war arrived in 1642. See Charles Charlton, *Going to the Wars*, 1992.
11. Very little is known about William Barriffe in spite of the important role he played in training men and cavalry; what little we do know is from his own notes in the various editions of his great work; he joined the Artillery Company in March, 1626/7, and served in Hampden's Regiment in the Civil War.
12. The deaths and successions of the Dawson family are found in Plomer's *Dictionary of. . .Booksellers and Printers. . .1641-1667.*
13. Captain Lewes Roberts (1596-1640) was a Director of the Levant Company, and a great merchant. His *DNB* entry is being revised by Dr Sonia Anderson.

14. *The Honourable Artillery Company 1537-1926*, by Major G. Goold Walker, DSO, MC, FSA, FHS, Secretary to the HAC (1922-47); 2nd edition, revised and enlarged, 1954; 3rd edition revised and enlarged, 1987.
15. Though a useful tool, Goold Walker's index is not entirely accurate or exhaustive and must be used with caution.
16. Justus Lipsius (1547-1606), Flemish scholar, an authority on Roman literature and history; his works were translated and published in England by Burbie, Bishop, Kingston, Ponsonby and Legate.
17. I would take issue with Sheila Lambert, 'State control of the press in theory and practice; the role of the Stationers' Company before 1640', *Censorship and the Control of Print*, ed R. Myers and M. Harris, 1992; Lambert maintains that the Star Chamber decrees were more to protect the Stationers than to block subversive printing, Archbishop Laud appears as quite a decent chap, there is no mention of the fate of Prynne, Bastwick and Burton.
18. See Appendix for list of Mabbe's publications.
19. From the will of Isabell Mabbe (PCC 101 Lewyn: 1598).
20. The Manor of Gibcracke, messuage in Sandon, Manor of Little Yeldham Hall during 1580s. They were sold before his death, perhaps at his death. *Feet of Fines for Essex 1581-1603*, vol.VI in the series, edited by Dr F. G. Emmison (1993), and Gary M. Bell, *A Handlist of British Diplomatic Representatives 1509-1688* [1990].
21. Family details are taken from the printed registers of St Mathews, Friday Street, and the funeral certificate (for John Mabbe senior) issued by the College of Arms [I.12/f.55]. I would like to thank Robert Yorke, the Archivist, for bringing this valuable document to my notice.
22. Details from Foster's *Alumni Oxoniensis*, and Gary M. Bell (cited 20 above).
23. D. F. McKenzie, *Stationers' Company Apprentices 1605-1640*, 1978.
24. P. W. M. Blayney, *The Bookshops in St Paul's Churchyard*, Bibliographical Society 1992, pp.24 & 28.
25. The registers of St Gregory by St Pauls record Katherine, baptized 21 May 1612 and Thomas, baptized 21 December 1613.
26. McKenzie, *Stationers' Company Apprentices*.
27. John Gwillim or Guillim, Rough Croix Pursuivant at Arms (1565-1621). See *DNB* and H. Stanford London, FSA, 'The complete list of the Officers at Arms', in entry on the College of Arms in *The Survey of London*, vol.16. Both contain inadequate accounts of Gwillim.
28. McKenzie, *Stationers' Company Apprentices*.
29. Princess Elizabeth and Frederick, Elector of the Palatinate were married on St Valentine's Day, 1613.
30. In 1622 'instructions' were issued that preachers were to adhere strictly to their texts, and that the afternoon sermon should be confined to some part of the catechism or to a text from the Creed, the Commandments or the Lord's prayer. 'Further restrictions were passed in 1626 when writing or preaching about controversial matters in religion', Godfrey Davies, *The Early Stuarts, 1603-1660*, p.74. Many Puritan ministers lost their livings as a result of being unable to comply with this edict, and were referred to as 'silenced'; their only hope was a lectureship, usually in London, or a living in a parish protected by a powerful and sympathetic magnate; the Earls of Bedford came to the rescue in several hard cases.

31. Daniel Dyke, BD, (1570?-1614); his father was a 'silenced' non-conformist minister; he was educated at Cambridge and became a Fellow of Sidney Sussex College in 1606; he was suspended for non-conformity by the Bishop of London; he was in religious trouble for the rest of his life; a man of blameless character, famous for his preaching; some of his sermons were published after his death. See *DNB*.
32. Richard Sibbs, DD (1577-1635), Puritan divine, educated at Cambridge; in 1615 he was deprived of both offices on account of his Puritanism; luckily he was chosen preacher at Gray's Inn; he became Master of St Catherine's Hall, Cambridge in 1626; he was famous for his preaching, and was revered even by those who were not Puritans; many of his sermons were published. See *DNB*.
33. William Gouge, DD (1578-1653), Puritan divine, he went from Eton as a scholar to King's College, Cambridge; MA, 1602; he lectured in logic and philosophy, and taught Hebrew; he was one of the 12 trustees of a society for buying up impropriations in order to build up a Puritan ministry but this was later deemed illegal by the Court of Exchequer; he was later imprisoned for editing Sir Henry Finch's *The World's Great Restauration*. See *DNB*.
34. George Hughes (1603-1667), Puritan divine, Corpus Christi College, Oxford (1619); Fellow of Pembroke College, Oxford (1625); in 1631 he was chosen lecturer at All Hallows, Bread Street, and was very popular; suspended by Laud, he sought the protection of Lord Brooke at Warwick Castle, and later the Earl of Bedford gave him a safe living at Tavistock. See *DNB*.
35. Thomas Adams (*fl.*1612-53); very little is known about his early life, but he was preaching in Bedfordshire by 1612; he became vicar of Wingrave in 1614, and held the lectureship of St Gregory by St Pauls (1613-23); he preached at Paul's Cross and Whitehall; he was chaplain to Sir Henrie Montague, Lord Chief Justice; he had many friends in high places who must have defended him, though his vehement attack on popery in later life annoyed Laud.
36. Thomas Adams, *The Souldiers Honour*, 1617.
37. Edward Arber, *A Transcript of the Register of the Company of Stationers of London, 1554-1640*, vol.iv, 1894.
38. Christovale de Fonseca, *Devout contemplations expressed in two and fortie sermons*, written in Spanish, *Englished by JM* [i.e. James Mabbe] of Magdalen College, Oxford, *for A. Islip*, 1628/9.
39. I take my information from A. F. Allison, *English translation from the Spanish and Portuguese to the year 1700*, 1974.
40. James Mabbe's punning *nom de plume* of Diego Puede-Ser raises the question of whether the name was pronounced as two syllables; this seems unlikely as in all genealogical entries, from John Mabbe senior on, the name is variously spelt Mab, Mabb, Mabbe, and never either Mabbs (though it is erroneously spelt so in texts) and never Mabbey. It is an unusual name, occurring in Sussex and Cornwall; in Breton it means 'son' which suggests that the family were originally Breton and migrated to Wales or Cornwall, as was common; Professor Reaney suggests that it is a diminutive of Mabel, a suggestion dismissed by Professor Prys Morgan; it is possible that the London Mabbe added a final e to smarten it up and make two syllables as Stow scornfully records was done by certain Jacks in the Tudor period who turned their names into Jaques to be French and classy.
41. A member in 1631. His main scientific thrust was towards books on navigation and seamanship.

42. *Warlike Directions in the SOULDIERS PRACTICE, set forth for the benefit of all such as are, or will be Scholars of Martiall DISCIPLINE. By a Practitioner of the same Art. T. F. 1643*, printed by Thomas Harper, and are to be sold at his House in Little Britain. T.F. was Thomas Fisher, an old veteran of the Dutch Wars.
43. A Thomas Shelton, of unknown origin, translated *Don Quixote*; he ended up, with a knowledge of Spanish and Italian, in Ireland in the service of various Irish nobles who were in correspondence with foreign powers; it is unknown just how unlawful their activities were, but it is suspected; Shelton was probably a recusant; he was in Brussels at some point where it is thought he acquired his copy of Cervantes's *Quixote*, which had recently appeared; he did other translations and some of these have been suspected to have been James Mabbe's; Edward Blount was involved with the printing of his works, including a sequel which may have been written by Shelton; it is not known where or when he died. See *DNB*.

   Thomas Shelton 2, was born in Norfolk in 1601; he began life as a writing master and perfected a *System of Short or Quick Writing*, which he published and it became very popular; it was of great value in taking down sermons and speeches; he later evolved another system called *Tachygraphy*, which was also published; he was a very keen Puritan, and no doubt was taking down sermons in shorthand; he is a very important figure in the history of shorthand writing. See biography of Shelton by Alex. T. Wright, 1896 and *DNB*.
44. It was the system used by Pepys.
45. Mabbe was usually singled out as if he were regarded as the trouble-maker.
46. The following printers and booksellers appeared in the Court of High Commission *Cat.S.P.Dom.Ch I 1640* Jan-July; Daniel Fere, John Beale, Stephen Bulkley, Henry Occold, Laurence Sadler, Christopher Bee, Robert Bales, Francis Grove, Richard Harper. Edward Allen, 'gent' appears with Nicholas Johnson of Canterbury, bookseller, Richard Burton and Edward Anderton. Is he the Edward Allen, Stationer of London?
47. This was another copy of *Threnoikos*, each sermon stating that they were printed in 1639, but the title page to the whole collection is 1640.
48. Pym's other speeches were printed by Walkley, Constable and H. Perry, which seems to suggest that Mabbe was no longer around after November 1641.

Appendix
Ralph Mabbe: Printer and Publisher

The following list of Mabbe's publications, 1610-41, is taken, with one exception, from the British Library's copies of the books themselves, giving, in original spelling, author, short title, printer, and STC number. The exception is a book of which only one copy, in the New York Public Library, is known, and that I saw on microfilm. Brevity has been of the essence because readers can use the STC for full title page and format details and other locations. I have used Upper Case for author, Upper and Lower for the subject of an anonymous or composite work.

Readers will note that Mabbe published almost annually and that in years in which nothing was issued, the following or preceding year's list was longer. The exception to this was 1625, a plague year which made a terrific gap in public life in London, and when, no doubt, plenty of printers' apprentices and helpers died, which would have affected the trade badly.

The purpose of giving this list is to shew which authors Mabbe published or sold, in the hope of finding something of his religious and political opinions. The names of printers and assignees may also help to show his network; some of the authors were Artillery Company members, others Puritan divines who preached to them, and some of the printers, though this is more difficult to establish, may also have been members of the Artillery Company. I get the impression that they were a pretty Puritan band of men.

Date	Author	Title	Printer	STC reference
1610	GUILLIM, John	A display of Heraldrie	(W. Hall)	12500
1611	GUILLIM, John	another edition	W. Hall	12501
	SELLER, John	A sermon against halting between two opinions	T. Creed	22182 a.
	TOOKER, William	Duellum sive singulare certamen cum M Becano jesuita, futiliter refutante Apologiam et monitoriam praefationem	N Butter & R Mab. G Eld	24119

Date	Author	Title	Printer	STC reference
1612	APPELIUS, Joannes	A true relation of the right christianly departure, or death, of Philippus Lodovicus, earle of Hanaw. f. N Bourne sold by R Mab.	T. Snodham	712
	TAYLOR, Thomas	A sermon: Japhets first publique perswasion into Sems tents, or Peters sermon. (for Univ. of Cambridge)	C. Legge	23830.5
	WEBBE, George	A catechism: A briefe exposition of the principles of the christian religion.	T. Snodham	25158
	WEBBE, George	A sermon: The pathway to honor.	W. S(tansby)	25163
1613	ADAMS, Thomas	A sermon: The white devil, or the hypocrite uncased	M. Broadwood	131
	DUNSTER, John	Prodromus, Or the literall destruction of Jerusalem as it is described in 79 psalme.	T. S(nodham)	7355
	GIBSON, Abraham	A sermon: The lands mourning for vaine swearing, preached in Pauls Crosse.	T. S(nodham)	11829
	GIBSON, Abraham	second edition		11830
	WEBBE, George	A sermon: The bride Royall, or the spirituall marriage. Delivered by way of congratulation upon the marriage between the palsegrave and the ladie Elizabeth.	W. Stansby	25157
1614	ADAMS, Thomas	A discourse: Diseases of the soul.	G. Purslowe for J Budge	109
	ADAMS, Thomas	Four sermons: The devills Banket.	W. Stansby	110.5
	DYKE, Daniel	The mystery of selfe-deceiving. Or a discourse of the deceitfullnesse of mans heart.	E. Griffin	7398
	MERITON, George	Two sermons: The Christian mans assuring house. And a sinners conversion.	E. Griffin	17837
1615	ADAMS, Thomas	Two sermons: Englands sicknes, comparatively compared with Israels.	E. Griffin	114

Date	Author	Title	Printer	STC reference
	BOUND, Nathaniel	Two sermons: Saint Pauls trumpet sounding an alarme to judgement.	E. Griffin	3435.7
	DYKE, Daniel	further editions of 7398: 7399: 7400: 7401		
	ELTON, Edward	Sundry sermons: An exposition of the epistle to the Colossians.	E. Griffin	7612
	FEREBE, George	Funeral sermon: Lifes farewell. Or a funeral sermon after the funeral of John Drew, gentleman.	E. Griffin	10818
	FORSYTHE, James	A sermon: The bitter waters of Babylon.	E. Griffin	11191
	WEBBE, George	Six sermons: The practice of quietnes.	E. Griffin	25165
1616	DOWNAME, John	The plea of the poore. Or a treatise on beneficence and almes-deeds.	E. Griffin	7146
	DYKE, Daniel	another edition of 7399.	E. Griffin for R M a. N. Butter	7401
	DYKE, Daniel	Two treatises: The one of repentence. The other of Christs temptation. Published by J(ohn) Dyke	E. Griffin	7408.2
	ELTON, Edward	A form of catechizing set down by questions and answers.	E. Griffin	7615
	GIBSON, Samuel	A sermon: The only rule to walk by.	G. Purslowe	11837
	HOPKINS, Thomas	Two sermons: upon the xii chapters of Hebrews.	ass. R.M.	13772.5
	RAWLINSON, John	A sermon: The unmasking of a hypocrite.	E. Griffin	20776
	WEBBE, George	second edition of 25165 ass by R Mab.		
1616	WHALLEY, John	A sermon: Gods plentie, feeding true pietie, preached at Pauls Cross.	W. Stansby	25294
1617	ELTON, Edward	further editions of 7615:		7615.5 & 7615.7
1618 1619	ELTON, Edward	another edition of 7612 disputes over items 7142 and 7145.		7613
1622	TAYLOR, Thomas	A sermon: Japhet's first publique perswasion		23830.5

Date	Author	Title	Printer	STC reference
1623	BINGHAM, JOHN	Translation of Xenophon "Anabasis" by Captain John Bingham	J. Haviland	26064
	------	Funeral elegies upon the death of John Stanhope, son of 1st Earl of Chesterfield.	G. Purslowe	23225
1625 PLAGUE YEAR				
1625	GOUGE, William	A srmon preached to the Artillery Company, The dignitie of chivalrie.	G. Miller	12112
1627	Christian	The character of a christian: as hee is distinguished from all hypocrites and hereticks.	G. Purslowe	5151
	GOFFE, Thomas	A sermon: Deliverance from the grave.	G. Purslowe	11978
	WHITE, Christopher	Three sermons: Of oathes; their object, forme, and bond: perjurie, and papall dispensations.	G Purslowe	25377
1629	Aelianus / BINGHAM, John	The art of embattailing an army, Or the second part Aelians Tacticks. Englished by John Bingham.	J. Beale a. T Brudenell f. R Mab.	162
	BURRELL, Percival	A sermon: Sutton's synagogue or, the English centurion: shewing the unparrallelled bounty of protestant piety.	T. C(otes)	4126
		another version.		4126.5
	DAVENPORT, John	A sermon for the gentlemen of the Artillery Garden: A royall edict for military execises.	Eliza Allde	6313
	STRUTHER, William	Christian observations and resolutions.	?J. Dawson	23367.5
		another version.		23368
1631	AELIANUS / BINGHAM, John	another edition		163
	CELESTINA	The Spanish Bawd translated by James Mabbe. second edition.	J. B(eale)	4911.2
	HENSHAW, Joseph Bp.	Horae succisivae, or, spare-houres of meditations. The second edition, corrected and much enlarged.	R. Badger	13167
		Another edition.		13167.5

Date	Author	Title	Printer	STC reference
1632	GUILLIM, John.	A display of herladrie second edition. ass. to Jacob Bloome.	R. Badger	12502
	HENSHAW, Joseph, Bp.	Horae succisivae: third edition.	J. B(eale)	13168
	HUGHES, George	A funeral sermon: The saints losse and lamentation. A sermon preched at the funerall of capataine Henry Waller.	J. B(eale)	13913
1634	BATE, John	Mechanician: The mysteryes of nature and art.	T. Harper	1577
		another edition, variant.		1577.5
	Hocus-Pocus	Hocus-Pocus junior. The anatomie of legerdemain. Unto each trick is added the figure, where it is needful for instruction.	T. H(arper)	13542.5
1635	AUSTIN, William	Devotional Augustinianae flamma. Set forth by his wife Mrs A Austin.	J. L(egat)	972
	BABBINGTON, John	Pyrotechnia or, a discourse of artificiall fire-works. Whereunto is annexed a short treatise on geometrie.	T. Harper	1099
	BABBINGTON, John	A short treatise on geometrie, to which is adjoyned certain tables.	T. Harper	1100
	BARRIFFE, William	Military duscipline, or, the yong artillery man.	T. Harper	1506
	BATE, John	Mechanician. Another edition with many additions.	T. H(arper)	1578
	GUILLIM, John	A display of heraldrie assd. to R Mabb		12503
	HENSHAW, Joseph	Horae successivae. Fourth edition	T. H(arper)	13169
	Hocus-Pocus	Hocus-pocus, second edition with many additions.	T. H(arper)	13543
1637	AUSTIN, William	Devotionis Augustinianae flamma, Mabbe's share ass'd to R. Meighen		973
	AUSTIN, William	Haec homo, wherein the excellency of the creation of woman is described.	R. Olton	974

Date	Author	Title	Printer	STC reference
	ELTON, Edward	An expostion to the Colossians. revised third edition. Ass'd by Mab to J Bloome	W	7614
1638	ANDREWS, Lancelot Bp.	A sermone: The true Israelite, or, the sincere christian SOLD BY C Greene,	R. Olton	630.5
	ANDREWS, Lancelot	Another edition SOLD BY John Jackson	R. Oulton	631
	AUSTIN, William	Haec homo. another edition.	R. Olton	975
	Calabria	Dreadfull newes: or, a true relation of the great, violent and late earthquake . . . at Callabria in Naples.	J. Okes	4349.5
	Hocus-pocus	Hocus-Pocus: the third edition. SOLD by F Grove.	J. D(awson)	13544
	Calabria	A true and terrible narration of an eathquake in Calabria, under Martin Parker. SOLD by F Grove.	T. Cotes	19273
	ROBERTS, Lewes	The merchants mappe of commerce.	R. O(ulton), E C P, T Harper a. F Kingston.	21094
	SIBBES, Richard	The riches of mercie in two treatises: 1. Lydia's conversion. 2. A rescue from death.	J. D(awson) f. F Eglesfeild. R. Mabbe ent.	22501
1639	AUSTIN, William	Haec homo. another edition SOLD by N Fussell. another issue SOLD by Ph. Nevil.	R. O(ulton) assd C G(reene)	976 976.5
	BARRIFFE, William	Mars His Triumph, or, a description of an exercise performed by certain gentlemen of the Artillery Garden, London.	J. L(egat)	1506
	BARRIFFE, William	Military discipline, second edition, newly revised and much enlarged.	R. O(ulton)	1507
	RAMSDEN, Henry	Sermons: A gleaning in Gods harvest. Foure choyce handfuls. Edited. SOLD by T Slater	(J. Goodwine) J. D(awson) for J Dawson a. R. Mabb.	22660
	SIBBES, Richard	A breathing after God. Or a christians desire of Gods presence.	J. Dawson	22477

Date	Author	Title	Printer	STC reference
	Threnoikos	The house of mourning. Delivered in XLVII sermons preached at funeralls. By D Featly, M Day, R. Sibbs. T Taylor. SOLD by P. Nevill.	J. Dawson	24208
	TORRIANO, Giovanni	New and easie directions to attaining the Thruscan Italian tongue. With a nomenclator, or little dictionarie. SOLD by the professour at his lodging in Abchurch lane, adjoyning to Lumbard -street.	R. O(ulton)	24138
1640	CERVANTES, Saavedra, Miguel de	Exemplarie novells; in sixe books. Turned into English by don Diego Puede-Ser [James Mabbe] SOLD by L Blaicklocke	J. Dawson	4914
	HENSHAW, Joseph Bp.	Horae successivae: fifth edition.	T. Payne	13170
	KEM, Samuel	A sermon: The new fort of true honour, ade inpregnable.	R. Oulton	14922
	ROBERTS, Lewes	Warre-fare epitomized, in a century, of military observations.	R. Oulton	21095
	SIBBES, Richard	The spiritual favorite at the throne of grace.	T. Paine	22512
	Threnoikos	Threnoikos: another issue. SOLD by J Bellamie, a. R Smith	J. Dawson	24049
		another variant.		24049.3 not in STC
1641	PYMM, John, MP.	The SPEECH or DECLARATION of JOHN PYMM, Esq to the Lords of the upper House, upon the delivery of articles of the Commons assembled in Parliament, against WILLIAM LAUD. London, Printed for Ralph Mabb 1641. [no printer's name].		

*The Mechanicks of Difference:
a study in Stationers' Company Discourse
in the seventeenth century*[1]

IAN GADD

BEFORE THE 1640S the Stationers' Company had seldom expressed its corporate views in print; but in April 1643, it published *The Humble Remonstrance of the Company of Stationers*, a document extraordinary in argument, language and style. At first glance it seems to be a typical corporate petition, its grievances at once familiar to all livery companies of the period – the need for better regulation, restriction of centres of production and of numbers entering the trade, defence of privileges (private and corporate), exclusion of 'strangers' and the unfree, checks on poor quality workmanship and so on. The importance of the *Remonstrance* has hitherto been overlooked – Greg dismissed it as a petition 'praying that speedy course be taken for a perfect regulation of the press', while Blagden only mentioned it in passing in his *History* of the Company. A closer reading shows it to be very different from what it seems at a superficial reading – a key document for the understanding of the next half century of the Company's history as it struggled for its very existence against other kinds of book trade organization.[2]

In the *Remonstrance*, the Stationers portrayed themselves as 'different', socially and culturally superior to mere 'mechanicks' – a term which was to acquire various layers of meaning above and beyond Shakespeare's 'rude mechanicals' of *A Midsummer Night's Dream*.[3] I shall examine three later seventeenth-century documents, the first a petition, the second a polemic and the third a printing manual, all of which made use of 'mechanick' in a variety of ways, their arguments turning on the controversial interpretation of the role of the book trade 'mechanick', whether artisan or artist. Each in turn redefined 'mechanick' in an attempt to resolve the essential opposition of cultural and mechanical, between text and producer. I shall conclude by investigating the idea of corporate discourse as a way of evaluating the corporate world of the seventeenth-century London book trade.

The Humble Remonstrance

Henry Parker, 'Secretary first to the Parliamentary Army and then to the House of Commons', 'sometime Lincoln's Inn Barrister', a prolific political-pamphlet writer of the early 1640s, was almost certainly the author or ghost writer.[4] George Thomason scribbled 'by Henry Parker Esq.' on his copy of the *Remonstrance*. It was usual, at this date, to employ a notary or scrivener to draft a petition in the best possible way, framing it in the most appropriate language and Parker's drafting of the petition does not therefore invalidate it as a *corporate* text.[5] Parker, a parliamentary activist and a rising star, was a sound choice of author for the Stationers, who were not the only company to have employed him in this way.[6] Whether or not it was his skilful drafting which achieved the results, the fact is that within weeks Parliament had passed an Ordinance on the Regulation of Printing.

There remains the question whether the *Remonstrance* does, in that case, represent the Company's authentic voice. Part of the difficulty is to decide, when we know nothing about the process of its composition, how much the ideas expressed were the Company's and how much was put in at Parker's suggestion. There is no mention of Parker's name in the Court minutes nor of a commission or a fee but this does not mean that the petition was in any way unofficial or unauthorized. As the dates suggest some possible collaboration, the *Remonstrance* can be cautiously assumed to represent the values and views of the mid-seventeenth-century Stationers.[7]

The central message of the *Remonstrance* is strongly enforced regulation of the book trade – 'It is not meere Printing but well ordered Printing that merits so much favour and respect.'[8] This, the Company argues, was all the more important with the abolition of the Star Chamber and the Court of High Commission two years earlier, which had provided backing for the Company's own regulatory machinery. Thus, the *Remonstrance* can be seen as a renegotiation of the Company's traditional relationship with authority, now Parliament rather than the Privy Council; as Blagden notes, with the passing of the Ordinance in June, 'The Government and the Stationers were once more in partnership on much the same terms as in [the Star Chamber Decree of] 1637'.[9]

The main part of the *Remonstrance* deals with the privations of the Stationers caused by 'irregular printing' stemming from lack of regulation. The petitioners are careful to differentiate between the hardship to individuals and to the Company as a corporate entity. They note that:

The late decay of the Stationers (chiefly brought upon them by want of due and Politick regulation), has been an occasion of emboldning Printers to run into enormous [sic] disorders, and in the like manner the same disorders have been a further occasion of bringing a decay upon the Company.[10]

The Company is a 'feeld overpestred with too much stock', the 'great multitude of Presses and Apprentices' encourages 'trespasses' and invites 'Strangers, as Drapers, Carmen, and others to...set up Presses in divers obscure corners of the City, and Suburbs.' They complain that the current outburst of pamphlet literature has lowered standards of workmanship and flooded the market to the detriment of high-class, more costly printing ventures. The system of granting monopolies to individuals in certain titles and classes of book has also undermined the Company's 'modest limited power' to enforce proprietary rights.[11] They enumerate the evils: 'Community...brings in confusion...will hinder many men from Printing at all...destroyes that commerce amongst Stationers... discourages...Authors of Books...[and] will [be] injustice.'[12] Community is here used in a legal sense, meaning the holding of rights in common, a somewhat double-edged expression in a corporate petition.[13] The conclusions are damning – if its grievances are ignored, the Company will no longer 'remain incorporate...but must immediately moulder away, and dissolve without some redresse of this irregularity.'[14]

In contrast to the plaintive laments of much of the petition – which should not be taken altogether at face value – the opening paragraphs of the *Remonstrance* read very differently, with their reference to press regulation and its effects in eight other countries to prove how important effective regulation was – 'the publicke good was very much concerned in that Art and...no act did more depend upon the publicke Care'.[15] In an extraordinarily bold assertion considering the prevalent anti-popery feeling, inflamed by the Civil War, the Company argues that:

We must in this give Papists their due; for as well where the Inquisition predominates, as not, regulation is more strict by far, then [sic] it is amongst Protestants; we are not so wise in our Generation, nor take so much care to preserve the true Religion as they do the false from alteration and for that cause not onely their Church is the more fortified, but the Art of Printing thrives, and the Artists grow rich also beyond any examples amongst us.[16]

The implication is clear; while well-regulated printing can help to suppress dangerous radicalism, poorly regulated printing only encourages it. There is a threat in the equation – if Parliament does not provide regulatory powers, it must suffer the consequences. It is a threat reinforced by the opening line of the petition: 'That the Mystery and Art of Printing is of Publicke and Great Importance, and ought to be held worthy of extraordinary regard; and consideration, in all well-govern'd States'. The tone is not in keeping with the formulaic humility of the supplicant, which reinforces the view that the document is much more remarkable than it seems at first sight.

What makes the *Remonstrance* so interesting is the way it attempts to put forward a view of printing as crucial to culture: 'For as Learning must needs make us favour Printing, so Printing is a great means to advance Learning amongst us'.[17] Put another way, the Stationers argue that printing is essential to the cultural hegemony of the state ('The first and greatest end of order in the Presse, is the advancement of wholesome knowledge') and therefore the Company and its members deserve special treatment.[18]

This argument seems misplaced in a document which is primarily concerned with the economics of printing; in that way the *Remonstrance* is typical of corporate petitions of the period. Rather than making it more forceful, the cultural and economic arguments seem out of place; the Company's belief in the cultural importance of printing has nothing to do with the realities of the market-place, which is the main thrust of the petition.[19] In short, the petitioners argue that by virtue of their wares – books – they are essentially *different* from other London companies and trades, and should be so treated – a key sense of difference which is a central theme of studies of the Company, the book trade and books themselves up to the present day.[20]

The Stationers' ambivalence over the precise nature of their 'difference' is seen in its reference to the practice of Catholic countries where, 'the Art of Printing thrives, and the Artists grow rich also beyond any example amongst us.' They are not, it goes without saying, using the word *artist* in the modern sense – a meaning which did not emerge until the eighteenth century.[21] They are using it to mean craftsman or artisan (as in the 'Mystery and Art of Printing'); but *artist* also had another usage in this period as one skilled in the liberal arts, giving the word a significant overtone in a document which sought to identify printing with learning, arguing their case on the dichotomy of craft and culture.[22] The Apothecaries invoked this distinction when, in 1630, they protested against a Common Council ruling regarding their corporate ranking among the London livery companies: 'His Majesty never intended that they should be cast to the twenty-eighth company. . .considering their arte which is not Mechanick but Liberall'.[23]

Further playing down the artisan association of the word, *artist*, the alliance of printing and learning is emphasized with reference to the French attitude to 'this ingenious Craft':

> ...*France* especially is famous for the value she sets upon that Profession and Trade of men (whom we in *England* incorporate by the name of Stationers) for they are privileged above meer Mechanicks, and honoured with a habitation, as it were, in the Suburbs of Literature it self.[24]

The French, the Company argues, italicizing the word to enforce their point, treat their printers with a respect which is lacking over here, and they conclude the sentence with a series of resonant words – *privileged, honoured, literature*; they treat *their* printers as the servants of literature, those who dwell in the 'Suburbs' (another word with overtones) or outlying regions of the city of learning.[25] In using this analogy with the French, the Company is seeking both to raise its public image and to claim an important – albeit not central – role in the propagation of a literary culture, once again strengthening the close ties of printing, learning and cultural leadership.

Yet the argument to a certain extent cuts the ground from under its own feet. By its use of socio-economic language, its use of the example of the French printers as privileged above 'meer Mechanicks', artisans and nothing more, its insistence on its privileged position in the cultural hierarchy, it is in danger of disowning the printers, type-founders and bookbinders who made up about a third of the membership, and so denying the mixture of occupations in the Company itself.[26]

The word *mechanick* must have been used advisedly both by Parker in drafting and the Stationers in directing the wording of the *Remonstrance*. By the mid-seventeenth century it had acquired layers of meaning in addition to that of artisan, and was much used in all its variety by critics of the Stationers' Company for the next 40 years.

The Mechanics of 'Mechanicks'

Recent historical scholarship has analysed early modern attitudes to social stratification and the language of social description, although, with the exception of Raymond Williams, the changing meaning of the word *mechanick* has not been investigated by modern scholars.[27] By the eighteenth century it was applied to the labouring classes – Robinson Crusoe's father spoke of 'the Labour and Sufferings of the Mechanick part of Mankind', while James Nelson, a London apothecary in the mid-eighteenth century, equated 'mechanicks' with 'common trades' as distinct from 'the genteel Trades'.[28] By the end of the century it had come, by descent through 'industrious' sort, 'labouring' sort, to a nineteenth-century meaning of plain working class.[29] At the same time, the precise mechanics of *mechanick* have never been explained, probably because sixteenth-century social historians such as Sir Thomas Smith and William Harrison tended to think it beneath them to take note of the lower classes.[30] They noted, in passing, the distinction between merchant and craftsman in order to appease the commercial elite rather than to differentiate the lesser merchants and shopkeepers from the artisans.[31]

It is difficult to date the beginning of the derogative use of *mechanick* from the Greek *mekhanikos*, nowadays most used in the meaning of 'mechanic', 'mechanical' and 'machine'. I cannot find that *mechanick* was explicitly used in English in the sixteenth or seventeenth century to mean, as it did in Greek, 'unfit for citizenship'. Its older meanings are confined to translations of Aristotle's *Politics* and Xenophon's *Economics*, where it is used for the Greek *banausikos*, another word meaning craftsman or artisan.[32] Ralph Robynson, in his 1551 translation of More's *Utopia* in Latin, does not distinguish between More's use of Latin *opifex* and, more rarely, *mechanicus*, translating both as *handycraftes man* or *artyfycer*.[33] The sixteenth-century translator of Xenophon, 'Gentian Heruet' used the word *handycraftes* and 'I.D.'s translation of Aristotle also used *artificer* as an alternative, and his occasional use of *mechanical* was in the meaning of *base, servile, mercenary, vile*.[34] The influence of classical texts – *The Politics* and *The Economics* were first translated into English in the sixteenth century, *The Economics* going through five editions – was beginning to affect even those who knew no Latin or Greek, perhaps filtering through from the teaching of Aristotle in the universities.[35] Yet while the word *mechanick* as used in the sixteenth century seems not have been derived directly from the classical heritage, it did retain a derogative sense as 'good for little except pursuing their mechanical trades'. Xenophon, Plato and Aristotle all emphasize this aspect:

The crafts that are called mechanical are disparaged and quite rightly carry a bad reputation in the cities. For they ruin the body. . .and consequently undermine the strength of the soul too. . .That is why in some cities. . .no citizen is allowed to practice a mechanical craft.[36]

Their bodies [i.e. those of craftsmen] are deformed by their craft-work and production, and in the same way their souls are warped and stunted by the mechanical nature of their work. . .[37]

The citizens must not live the life of mechanics or shopkeepers, which is ignoble and inimical to goodness. . .The class of mechanics has no share in the city. . .[38]

The Leathersellers seem to be using it in this way when, in 1619, the Glovers tried to break away from them:

[This] will be a President to all the Mechanick trades about London to attempt the like, which wilbe such a Rent and innovation in the city as we may see the beginning, but can hardlie discern what will be the end thereof.[39]

I have not come across *mechanick* used in this way by any other London company.

Thus some sort of distinction continued to be made between the use of *mechanick* meaning, simply, urban craftsman and the derogative sense, apparently derived from Greek usage, of vulgar and base men, the two meanings gradually shading into one another.[40] Of more importance to the sixteenth- and seventeenth-century citizen who may have felt his social status depended on how the word was used, was that there was no common usage of the word to mean a particular type of craftsman or whether being a master craftsman (or artisan) or practising a particular trade was more socially acceptable or respectable than another. Where the *mechanick* stood in the social scale was becoming particularly difficult to determine at the time when the gentry were growing more and more hesitant about binding their sons in London companies; as Christopher Brooks puts it: 'the term "mechanical" obviously applied to handicraftsmen, but it also came to be associated with any occupation, including that of attorney or surgeon, in which training was by apprenticeship'.[41]

In contrast to its derogative usage, another important and distinct meaning of the word crept in at the beginning of the seventeenth century, connected with the world of mathematics and science. The word *scientist* was first used in 1840 (according to the Oxford English Dictionary) and Francis Bacon coined 'mechanic' for this Renaissance phenomenon. He distinguished between the liberal (classical learning) and the mechanical arts (both practical science and manual crafts) and placed printing among the latter.[42] While the seventeenth-century scientists, as far as they existed in any modern sense, may have been happy to indulge in the 'mechanics' of practical science, the mechanical arts were placed lower than the liberal arts which once again reinforced the non-genteel nature of mechanick in the spheres of both learning and citizenship.

The Mechanicks of Difference: a Brief Discourse of Printers and Printing

The events of the 1640s and 1650s, when many London companies, the Stationers' Company among them, were riven by internal constitutional and structural conflict, have a bearing on an understanding of the use of *mechanick* in corporate discourse, as the lines, real or imagined, in the internecine struggles were drawn between the merchant livery and the 'mechanical' yeomanry.[43] In 1663, twenty years after the *Remonstrance*, an anonymous 24-page pamphlet, *A Brief Discourse concerning Printing and Printers*, appeared purporting to be 'printed for a Society of Printers'.[44] Cyprian Blagden, in his article on the agitation of the 'company' of printers in the 1660s notes, with reference to this pamphlet, that this devolutionary desire dated back to 1651.[45]

The *Brief Discourse* can be interpreted as a reply to the *Remonstrance*; it concludes by quoting several lines from it, including the key *mechanick* passage.[46] Central to its argument, as in the *Remonstrance*, is a well-regulated press, and it too emphasizes the benefits of regulation. It not only concurs in the argument for the cultural importance of printing, but enlarges upon it, citing a range of authors in support;[47] but, unlike the *Remonstrance*, it bases its arguments on an historical precedent, showing how the ecclesiastical veneration of printing has declined, which the *Discourse* explicitly blames on the increase in the numbers of booksellers in the Company:

At first they were but as an Appendix to the Printers, and (as cyphers) stood but to make up a number; now they are grown so bulkie and numerous. . .and so considerable thereof. . .that there is hardly one Printer to ten others than have a share in the Government of the Company.[48]

The problem was aggravated because the number of printers within the Company was restricted so that the booksellers, who had no limitation imposed on them, increased at a much faster rate; this, argues the pamphlet, is 'no small argument of the absurdity and unnaturalness of their Concorporation; since in all sound bodies, the natural growth is in all members proportionable; and where it is otherwise, it is esteemed monstrous'. Not permitting the printers to run their own affairs as printers (rather than as Stationers) has affected the quality of English printing itself for 'we print not so well here as they beyond the Seas'.[49] The inescapable conclusion is that the printers should be able to regulate themselves free of interference from the Stationers – by implication as a separate (less monstrous) company.

Even more interesting is the re-interpretation of the word *mechanick* as it had been used in the *Remonstrance*. The following quotation shows how aware the printers are of the overtones of the term, something which escapes the author of the *Remonstrance*:

And whereas it was urged once before the Lords, that Printers were the Mechanick part of the Company, and so unfit to rule; let the import of the word be considered, and it will be found to bear no such slight significance as that Gentleman was pleased to put upon it. For besides that a considerable branch of the noble Science Mathematical (*viz*, the Art of moving great weights) goes under that denomination; if it be taken for Manual Arts, or handy-crafts, yet it is to be understood of such as require ingenuity of the minde, as well as labour of the hand; as the learned *Scapula* observes upon the word. . .[*mekhanikos*].

But let them be supposed to be Mechanicks in his sense, that is, such as are below the grandeur of Shop-keepers; must they not therefore have the management of their own Affairs? [. . .]

Nor should Mechanicks or Handy-Crafts be so lightly esteemed, when the Law hath so great a regard for them, and make so manifold Provision for their improvement, and the encouragement of Manufactors. . .

Neither was this care taken of them without good reason, since they are essentially necessary, whereas Shop-keepers are but accidental, like suckers springing out of the root of the former. For without the Clothier, where were the Draper? without the Hat-maker, where were the Haberdasher? and without the Printer, where were the Book-seller? Yea, having the Clothier, what need (necessarily) is there of the Draper? having the Hat-maker, what necessity of the Haberdasher? and having the Printer, no fear of wanting Books, though there were no Book-seller.[50]

Here the printers seek to put a political interpretation on the term *mechanick*, in contrast to the Aristotelian view of *mechanicks* as non-citizens. In the printers' view, they are fully able to govern themselves and are, besides, more important to the economic structure than any middle-class shop-keeper. They have no doubts about their true civic place: 'whereas formerly. . .they were Aldermens fellows. . .'[51] The immediate aim is to highlight their ruined plight but they are also at pains to show how printers should hold high civic office in keeping with the cultural importance of printing itself. In effect, they use the terms of the *Remonstrance*, going further and giving much more detail about the cultural benefits of printing as well as of the origins and nature of the privations of the printers, their arguments turning on the 'difference' of the book trade. At the same time they try to change the social structure which the Stationers had put forward in the *Remonstrance*, and to overturn the traditional ascendancy of bookseller over printer by re-interpreting *mechanick* and appropriating keywords which the Stationers had used to assert their own superiority. Yet, because they accept the old corporate framework of the *Remonstrance*, they are forced to argue for a break-away company of printers which the Stationers' Company was ultimately able to suppress. The printers' definition of *mechanicks* as 'the Art of moving great weights' is therefore ironic.[52]

The Mechanicks of Difference: the Original and Growth of Printing

Richard Atkyns's pamphlet, *The Original and Growth of Printing*, 1664, an expanded version of his 1660 broadside of the same name, again takes the regulation of printing as its central theme.[53] Atkyns came from outside the trade, a self-styled gentleman who inherited the law patent through marriage.[54] He follows the same line of argument as the *Remonstrance* and the *Discourse*, extolling the cultural benefits of printing, an art 'of so Divine a Nature'.[55] Atkyns, who had fought in the Civil War, uses explosive images to describe the consequences of weak regulation of the trade – 'In the Statute of *21 Jac.*, Printing keeps very able Company as *Salt-Peter, Gun-Powder, Ordnance,* &c', the paper-pellets of books were 'as dangerous as Bullets'.[56] He opens with an account of the origin of printing having been introduced into England in 1468, the printer smuggled into Oxford by Archbishop Bourchier. This extraordinary fable forms the basis of his argument.[57] The *Remonstrance* makes no reference to the origin of printing; the *Discourse* mentions Caxton by the way but does not wish to 'insist here, upon the time when, place where, and manner how *Printing* was invented'.[58] Atkyns cites the complaints of the *Discourse* as evidence of the bookseller's abuses.[59] He makes much use of the word *mechanick*, spending a considerable time redefining it as the main line of his attack on the Company which has reduced the noble art of printing to a 'mechanick trade':

Thus was this excellent and desireable ART, within less than one hundred years, so totally vitiated, that whereas they were before the King's Printers and Servants, they now grew so poor, so numerous, and contemptible, by being Concorporated, that they turn'd this famous ART into a Mechanick Trade for a Livelyhood.
. . .I must crave leave to give you the significance of the Word *Mechanick*, the rather, because the several sorts of Trades, of which the Company of *Stationers* are Composed (and more particularly the *Book-Sellers* who say they are of no Manufacture) do peremptorily deny themselves to be *Mechanicks*.
The Word *Mechanicus*, which signifies a Handicrafts-man, doth in the strict Sense comprehend *Printers, Founders of Letters,* and *Book-Binders*; And I believe, in the large Sense, all Trades-men whatsoever. But if that be deficient, let us go to the Original Greek Word. . .[*mekhane*], which signfies, a *Cunning Contrivance* of the Head, as well as Hand; and this will certainly take in all Trades, for as much as there is *Cunning* in all Trades: But if it should miss any, yet it cannot fail of the *Company of Stationers*, because they are denominated a *Mystery*, and there the strict signification of the Word comes in again. . .'[60]

Thus Atkyns points out the flaw in the arguments used both by the *Remonstrance* and by the *Discourse* in its attempt to support devolution, namely that *mechanicks* would always be part of a corporately organized book trade, which was no different from any other trade even if books were different from other wares. The *mechanick* is, no less than the rest of the book trade, a social upstart who 'is willing to disguise his want of Gentility, that when he arrives to a Considerable Estate he is very forward to purchase Honour'.[61] From this he concludes that printing should remain the sole prerogative of the crown, regulated through a number of carefully selected patentees, such as himself. He claims not to be aiming to abolish the Stationers' Company although his belief that a 'Corporation being in itself a *Petit-State*, is inconsistent with *Monarchy*' left little room for the operation of any corporate book trade organization (such as the Stationers) in the cultural hegemony of the post-Restoration years.[62]

The Mechanicks of Difference: Mechanick Exercises

Any study of the seventeenth-century use of *mechanick* must conclude with Joseph Moxon's key, pioneering *Mechanick Exercises*, 1683-4.[63] Moxon is venerated by scholars of the London book trade – his manual was the first and remains one of the best accounts of the craft of printing. With reference to Part I of the *Mechanick Exercises*, 1677-80, one modern editor called Moxon the 'first English philosopher. . .of the crafts.'[64] But his detailed description of the art of printing and of the other crafts violated the central tenet of seventeenth-century corporate culture, that of the sanctity of trade secrets.[65] But then Moxon was not a practitioner of the crafts he described, but a surveyor and, it goes without saying, he did not enter his work at Stationers' Hall, and as the London printers would not have dared to betray the secrets of their trade he had little to fear from piracy.[66]

In his first number of *Mechanick Exercises*, 1677, Moxon declines to 'dive into the Original of Mechanicks' maintaining that it 'is impossible, therefore I shall not offer at it.'[67] It is the origin of the activity, rather than the derivation of the word that he means here, but, by beginning his work with an account of smithing, he is unconsciously emphasizing (something that both Atkyns and the authors of the *Discourse* are at pains to avoid) the Greek term *banausic* which derives from the furnace and forge. Moxon's refusal to define the term seems all the more pointed considering that he gives over much of the preface to explaining the use in his subtitle of 'handy-works' instead of 'handi-crafts' and that he is at pains to include glossaries of trade terms throughout the work.[68] Although he uses *mechanick* in the Baconian sense, he is conscious that 'mechanicks' might 'be by some accounted ignoble and scandalous', although 'it is very well known, that many Gentlemen of this Nation of good Rank and high Quality are conversant in Handy-Works: And other Nations exceed us in numbers of such.'[69] He seems to be aiming his *Exercises* at a gentry readership, including members of the Royal Society to which he was later elected.[70]

Moxon prefaces the printing volume by giving the same account as Atkyns's of the first English printing having been at Oxford, a more respectable location for its origin than the London world of commerce; he continues with a few paragraphs on the cultural importance of printing but his concept of it is as a form of learning, a 'Science, nay Science of Sciences'. 'Printer' is a 'vulgarly accounted term' and he preferred 'typographer', with its overtones of the universal Renaissance man. By uniting the 'mechanical' ingenuity of hand with that of mind, Moxon dignifies the term *mechanick* and puts printing on the same level as the other *banausic* crafts or manual skills without making it 'different', allowing gentlemen to be 'mechanicks', in marked contrast to the thesis of Atkyns and the petitioners of the *Remonstrance* and the *Discourse*. His manual, produced mechanically by a mechanick who was outside the Stationers' Company, for the use of gentlemen-mechanicks, is proof that the term could be used to strike at the very cultural hegemony of which the Company had claimed, in 1643, to be part.[71]

Twelve years after Moxon published the *Mechanick Exercises*, printing presses were allowed to set up in the provinces. We may speculate whether Moxon's work had any direct influence on the craft of printing and whether any trade printer used his work as a guide, or gave support to those who operated outside the Company after the lapsing of the Printing Act in 1695.[72]

Conclusion
Throughout the sixteenth and seventeenth centuries the Stationers' Company dominated the London trade. D. F. McKenzie has commented on the 'roles of institutions, and their own complex structures, in affecting the forms of social discourse, past and present'.[73] This paper has sought to show that while institutions can affect discourse, discourse can have a strong impact on institutions in its turn. The place of the *mechanick* was not confined to the book trade; it remained a powerful term with social and economic significance, one which could be reappropriated, redeployed and refashioned by those whose identities might be shaped by its

fluctutating meaning. By using the term in 1643, the Stationers refashioned their corporate image, and opened a discursive struggle with a series of later texts, all attempting to fix their own conception of the meaning of *mechanick* and thus altering our understanding of the London book trade and its organization.

As Keith Wrightson has said:

Social identities and alignments, like medical conditions, may be defined by experts, but they are discovered by lay people in the immediacy of their own experience.[74]

References

1. This is an expanded version of the paper I delivered at Stationers' Hall on 30 November 1996. I would like to thank: the Pirie-Reid Board, Oxford, for funding the doctoral research from which this paper developed; Martin Moonie, Somerville College, for his mercilessly candid criticism, and for suggesting the title; and several of the conference delegates who offered ideas and comments which I have tried to incorporate in the revision of this paper. My approach and methodology in this paper have been strongly influenced by D. F. McKenzie, who I would also like to thank for his continuing support in my doctoral work. I would also like to thank Robin Myers for her patient efforts in helping me prepare this paper for the press.
2. *To the High Court of Parliament: The Humble Remonstrance of the Company of Stationers* (London: [1643]) (Wing P425); *A Companion to Arber*, ed. by W. W. Greg (Oxford: Clarendon Press, 1967), p.109; Cyprian Blagden, *The Stationers' Company: A History 1403-1959* (London: George Allen & Unwin Ltd, 1960), p.146. Wing notes at least two other copies, one in New York, the other in the Bodleian Library. The Oxford copy (shelfmark 4 X 49 (34) JUR) has one minor but seemingly contemporary marginal emendation – see note 12. The pamphlet is reprinted in its entirety in *A Transcript of the Registers of the Company of Stationers 1554-1640 AD*, ed. by Edward Arber, 5 vols (London & Birmingham, 1875-94; repr. Gloucester, Mass.: Peter Smith, 1967), I (1875) 584-88. References to the *Remonstrance* have been given both with respect to the original pamphlet, and to the Arber reprint. Of the ten items listed, for example, in Pollard and Redgrave's *Short-Title Catalogue. . .1475-1640* as published on behalf of the London book trade, none of them can be obviously described as representing the views of the Company. London companies seem only occasionally to have published corporate petitions in this period. See STC 16768.2-16787.14, especially 16768.6-16768.10 and 16786.2-16786.12.
3. '. . .*mechanical*. . .was used from [the fifteenth century] to describe various mechanical arts and crafts; in fact the main range of non-agricultural productive work. For social reasons *mechanical* then acquired a derogatory class sense, to indicate people engaged in these kinds of work and their supposed characteristics. . . From [the early seventeenth century] there was a persistent use of *mechanical* in the sense of routine, unthinking activity. . . But in the earliest uses the social prejudice seems to be at least as strong. . . The complexity of the word, whenever it is used beyond the descriptive sense directly related to machines, has remained difficult, even where some of the early associations

and fusions have, as such, been discarded. Both the real sources of these senses of the word, and the various implied oppositions, need continual examination' (Raymond Williams, *Keywords: A Vocabulary of Culture and Society* (London: Fontana, 1976), pp.167-9).
4. The phrases are from Christopher Brooks, 'Professions, Ideology and the Middling Sort in the Late Sixteenth and Early Seventeenth Centuries', in *The Middling Sort of People: Culture, Society and Politics in England, 1550-1800*, ed. by Jonathan Barry and Christopher Brooks (London: Macmillan, 1994), pp.113-40 (p.137) and Blagden, p.146.
5. Ian Archer has shown in his work on the London companies in the late sixteenth century that companies could be extremely sophisticated and wide-ranging in the techniques they used to lobby authority. See Ian Archer, 'The London lobbies in the later sixteenth century', *Historical Journal*, 31, no.1 (1988), pp.17-44.
6. Parker's authorship has also been attributed to another pamphlet of twelve months later: *The Vintners answer to some scandalous pamphlets* (London, 1642) (Wing P431).
7. For example, the references to 'the third and fourth of *Edw.* sixth; and the third of King James' (*Remonstrance*, sig. Av, Arber I.585) are in fact precise references to statutes against popish books (3 & 4 Edw. 6, c.10 and 3 Jac. 1, c.5), rather than, as they may seem on the face of it, misdatings of the charter of incorporation and grants of English Stock – a sensible bias given the Parliamentary, rather than royal, audience. Natalie Zemon Davis's work on early-modern French pardoners' petitions has shown that the 'authentic' voice of the supplicant can still be picked out from a text that was in fact technically written by a notary. Obviously, the precise details of her argument are not directly applicable here, but her general point that it was in the interests of both supplicant and notary to allow the supplicant's voice to dominate remains pertinent. See her *Fiction in the Archives: Pardon Tales and their Tellers in sixteenth-century France* (Cambridge: Polity Press, 1987), especially, pp.15-25.
8. *Remonstrance*, sig. Ar, Arber I.584.
9. *Remonstrance*, sig. A2r, Arber I.585; Blagden, p.146.
10. *Remonstrance*, sig. Av, Arber I.585 (Arber mis-transcribes 'have' as 'haue'). This separation, reinforcing the validity of a separate corporate identity, may have been necessary to justify the document's corporate authorship, but was predicated on a dangerous alienation of the Company itself from its membership.
11. *Remonstrance*, sig. A2v-3r, Arber I.586.
12. *Remonstrance*, sig. A3v-4r, Arber I.587. I have interpolated 'be' here, rather than Arber's somewhat more grammatical suggestion, 'cause', on the basis of a marginal emendation in the Bodleian Library copy – see note 2.
13. *OED*, s.v. 'community', I.1.a-b.
14. *Remonstrance*, sig. A4v, Arber I.588.
15. *Remonstrance*, sig. Ar-v, Arber I.584. The countries cited are: China, France, 'Muscovy', Turkey, Greece, Germany, the United Provinces and Poland.
16. *Remonstrance*, sig. Av, Arber I.584-85. For studies of the heightened fear of Popery in the civil war period, see Robin Clifton, 'The popular fear of Catholics during the English Revolution', *Past and Present*, 52 (1971), 23-55, and Clifton, 'Fear of Popery', in *The Origins of the English Civil War*, ed. by Conrad Russell (London: Macmillan, 1973; repr. 1978), pp.144-67.
17. *Remonstrance*, sig. Ar, Arber I.584.
18. *Remonstrance*, sig. Av, Arber I.585.
19. See note 35.

20. The *Remonstrance* was quite explicit about the 'difference' of books as '(except the sacred Bible) [they] are not of such generall use and necessity, as some staple Commodities are. . . .' (*Remonstrance*, sig. A3r, Arber I.587). For a modern investigation of whether books, and by extension the book trade, are indeed different, see Alison Baverstock, *Are Books Different? Marketing in the Book-Trade* (London: Kogan Page, 1993).
21. See Alvin Kernan, *Samuel Johnson & the Impact of Print* (Princeton: Princeton University Press, 1987), *passim*.
22. *OED*, s.v. 'artist', I ('skilled in "liberal" or learned arts'), II.5 ('A follower of a manual art') & III.8.c. ('One who practises the arts of design'). It should be noted that the particular Papist characteristic that so excited the envy of the Stationers here was wealth.
23. Quoted in Michael C. Burrage and David Corry, 'At Sixes and Sevens: Occupational status in the City of London from the fourteenth to the seventeenth century', *American Sociological Review*, 46 (1981), pp.375-93 (p.385).
24. *Remonstrance*, sig. Ar, Arber I.584.
25. It is outside the scope of this paper to speculate on what exactly the Stationers meant by the word 'suburb'. A neutral sense is possible, although the London suburbs were notorious for vice and crime throughout this period – an inappropriate association with 'privilege' and 'honour'. There is the possibility that, as 1643 was the year of major suburban fortifications in London, this is an image of defence but, if so, it is the only martial image in the whole document.
26. This is a rough calculation based on the numbers of printers' apprentices and non-printers' apprentices freed 1605-40, computed from *Stationers' Company Apprentices 1605-40*, ed. by D. F. McKenzie (Charlottesville, Virginia: Bibliographical Society of the University of Virginia, 1961). Ironically, the Company seemed aware of this paradox: any committee of Stationers authorized by Parliament would not claim powers beyond 'such limits as other Companies are confined to' (*Remonstrance*, sig. A2v, Arber I.586). We must also bear in mind that 'mere' at this time meant 'purely' or 'entirely' – *OED*, s.v. 'mere'. I am grateful to Robin Myers for this point.
27. David Cressy, 'Describing the Social Order of Elizabethan and Stuart England', *Literature and History*, no.3 (1976), pp.29-44; Keith Wrightson, 'The Social Order of Early Modern England: Three Approaches', in *The World We Have Gained: Histories of Population and Social Structure*, ed. by Lloyd Bonfield, Richard M. Smith and Keith Wrightson (Oxford: Basil Blackwell, 1986), pp.177-202; *Language, History and Class*, ed. by Penelope J. Corfield (Oxford: Basil Blackwell, 1991); *The Middling Sort of People*.
28. Daniel Defoe, *The life and strange surprizing adventures of Robinson Crusoe*, ed. by J. Donald Crowley (Oxford: Oxford University Press, 1976), p.4; Penelope J. Corfield, 'Class by name and number in eighteenth-century Britain', in *Language, History and Class*, pp.101-30 (pp.101-2).
29. This genealogy is traced by Geoffrey Crossick in his 'From gentlemen to the residuum: languages of social description in Victorian Britain', in *Language, History and Class*, pp.150-78 (pp.167-8).
30. Sir Thomas Smith, *De Republica Anglorum* (1583); William Harrison, *The Description of England* (1577, 1587), part of Holinshed's *Chronicle*.
31. Cressy, *passim*.
32. I owe much of my knowledge of the classical use of *banausikos* to Susan Sauvé Meyer, 'Plato's Rude Mechanicals: Ordinary Morality in the Republic', unpublished paper

(University of Pennsylvania, 1996). I wish to thank Dr Meyer for her generosity in providing me with a copy of this paper. See also Alison Burford, *Craftsmen in Greek and Roman Society* (London: Thames & Hudson, 1972), pp.28-9. 'Banausic' was eventually imported into the English language in the nineteenth century: see *OED*, s.v. 'banausic'.

33. See Thomas More, *The Utopia of Sir Thomas More: in Latin from the edition of March 1518 and in English from the first edition of Ralph Robynson's translation of 1551*, ed. by J. H. Lupton (Oxford: Clarendon Press, 1895), pp.50, 141, 148. An 1899 edition of *Utopia* preferred 'mechanic', but the current Cambridge University Press edition gives either 'craftsman' or the rather more bland 'town workmen'. See Thomas More, 'Utopia', in *Ideal Commonwealths*, ed. by Henry Morley (London: George Routledge and Sons, 1899), pp.51-167 (pp.63, 97, 99-100), and Thomas More, *Utopia*, ed. by George M. Logan and Robert M. Adams (Cambridge: Cambridge University Press, 1988; repr. 1995), pp.18, 51, 53.

34. [Xenophon], *Xenophons treatise of householde*, trans. by 'Gentian Heruet' (London, 1532), ff.11v-12r; [Aristotle], *Aristotles politiques, or discourses of gouernment. Translated out of Greeke into French*, trans. by 'I. D.' (London, 1598), pp.50, 54, 56, 92, 95, 145-7, 191-3, 339, 343, 347, 356, 362, 363, 382-3, 392.

35. Keith Wrightson, "Sorts of People' in Tudor and Stuart England', in *The Middling Sort of People*, pp.28-51, (p.43). This is obviously a speculative point, although the Stationers, for example, do seem to have been Aristotelian in their separation (in the *Remonstrance*) of the cultural and the economic, echoing Aristotle's belief that the marketplace should be sited outwith (in the suburbs?) the cultural and political heart of the city (*Politics*, 1331a-b).

36. Xenophon, *Economics*, IV. 2-4, quoted in Meyer, p.11.

37. Plato, *Republic*, 495d-496a, quoted in Meyer, p.14.

38. Aristotle, *Politics*, 1328b-1329a, from *The Politics*, ed. by R. F. Stalley, trans. by Ernest Barker (Oxford: Oxford University Press, 1995), pp.271-2. It should be noted that 'mechanical' does not carry all before it in twentieth-century translations of these passages. For example, the Loeb Classical Library's edition of Xenophon prefers 'illiberal' (implying a contradistinction with the 'liberal arts'); and, more recently, the Oxford University Press edition of Plato talks of 'paltry professions' and 'servile business'. See Xenophon, *Memorabilia and Oeconomicus*, trans. by E. C. Marchant (London: William Heineman, 1923), p.391 and Plato, *Republic*, trans. by Robin Waterfield (Oxford: Oxford University Press, 1994), pp.217-18.

39. Quoted in George Unwin, *Industrial Organization in the Sixteenth and Seventeenth Centuries* (London: Cass & Company, 1957), p.211.

40. The social prejudice was not apparent in the definitions of the word in the dictionaries of the period with lexicographers such as Robert Cawdrey, Henry Cockeram and Thomas Blount equating 'mechanick' with handicrafts, although Blount, writing in the 1650s, seemed more ambivalent, suggesting also 'a man of Occupation' and 'a Tradesman' (based on a search of *The Early Modern English Dictionaries Database*, ed. by Ian Lancashire (University of Toronto, 1996), available on-line at http://www.chass.utoronto.ca:8080/english/emed/emedd.html). An impressionistic review of library catalogues at the Bodleian Library and the British Library, along with various word-lists, seems to suggest that the usage of 'mechanick' was increasing in frequency through the seventeenth century.

41. Christopher Brooks, 'Apprenticeship, Social Mobility and the Middling Sort, 1550-1800', in *The Middling Sort of People*, pp.52-83 (p.79).
42. Francis Bacon, *Novum Organon (1620)*, ed. and trans. by Peter Urbach and John Gibson (Chicago: Open Court, 1994), pp.26, 44, 131.
43. See Unwin, pp.204-10. For a sensitive analysis of this period of artisan protest, see Norah Carlin, 'Liberty and Fraternities in the English Revolution: The Politics of London Artisans' Protest, 1635-1659', *International Review of Social History*, 39 (1994), pp.223-54.
44. *A Brief Discourse Concerning Printing and Printers* (London, 1663) (Wing B4578).
45. Cyprian Blagden, 'The "Company" of Printers', *Studies in Bibliography*, 13 (1960), pp.3-17 (pp.5-6, 9-10).
46. *Discourse*, pp.23-4.
47. *Discourse*, pp.18-23.
48. *Discourse*, p.4. This analogy with the disproportionate growth of the 'Appendix' was perhaps not simply a whimsical comparison. As Professor Ian Maclean noted at a recent Oxford University seminar, in order to evade imperial book privileges in this period, Continental publishers would produce 'new' editions of classical texts with ever fatter scholarly apparatus ('The trade in learned books 1570-1630', paper presented at the *Seminar on the History of the Book*, All Souls College, Oxford, 24 January 1997).
49. *Discourse*, pp.7, 13. Note the echo of the *Remonstrance*'s contrast of the poor state of the English book trade with the continental situation.
50. *Discourse*, pp.15-17.
51. *Discourse*, p.6. It is not entirely clear who they mean here, although no doubt men like William Caxton and Richard Grafton (neither of them a Stationer) were the most likely candidates.
52. *Discourse*, p.15. See Blagden, 'Company', *passim*.
53. Richard Atkyns, *The Original and Growth of Printing* (London, 1664) (Wing A4135); [Richard Atkyns], *The Original and Growth of Printing* ([London?], 1660) (Wing A4134).
54. It was over the disputed heritage of the law patent that Atkyns had come into direct legal conflict with the Company. See *DNB*, s.v. 'Richard Atkyns'; *A Dictionary of the Booksellers and Printers who were at work in England, Scotland and Ireland from 1641 to 1667*, ed. by Henry R. Plomer (London: The Bibliographical Society, 1907), s.v. 'Richard Atkyns'.
55. *Original*, p.2.
56. *Original*, sig. B2r-v, p.7. Atkyns was referring to 21 Jac. 1, c.3 §X, which exempted these manufactures from anti-monopoly legislation. 'Salt-Peter' is potassium nitrate, a constituent of gunpowder.
57. *Original*, pp.2-6. In fact, Atkyns implied that the impetus for searching for the Oxford origin of English printing came from his belief that printing could not have been introduced into England as a purely commercial venture by Caxton.
58. *Discourse*, p.1. It is, of course, entirely possible that the printers had Atkyns's broadside of 1660 in mind when they wrote this.
59. *Original*, pp.11-13.
60. *Original*, pp.7-8. Both Atkyns and the *Discourse* drew attention to this etymology of 'mechanick' that emphasized both a manual and a mental dexterity – although Atkyns preferred to characterize the mental agility as lowly cunning rather than the *Discourse*'s rather more enlightened 'ingenuity'.
61. *Original*, p.10.

62. *Original*, p.19. I have reproduced the original black letter as italic.
63. Joseph Moxon, *Mechanick Exercises, or, The Doctrine of Handy-Works. Applied to the Art of Printing* (London, 1683-4) (Wing M3014); reprinted in Joseph Moxon, *Mechanick Exercises on the Whole Art of Printing*, ed. by Herbert Davis and Harry Carter, 2nd edn (London: Oxford University Press, 1962). All references to *Exercises* hereafter will be to the Davis and Carter edition, unless otherwise noted.
64. Joseph Moxon, *Mechanick Exercises, or, The Doctrine of Handy-Works* (London, 1677-80) (Wing M3013); Benno Forman's introduction (p.xxvi) to Joseph Moxon, *Joseph Moxon's Mechanick Exercises or the Doctrine of Handy-Works: applied to the arts of smithing, joinery, carpentry [&] bricklaying* (New York: Praeger Publishers, 1970), a facsimile reprint of the 1703 edition.
65. Neither Davis nor Carter seem to have acknowledged this rather subversive edge to Moxon's manual; Forman, on the other hand, was keen to champion the revolutionary nature of such an act. See *Exercises* (1970), pp.xi-xiv.
66. *Mechanick Exercises* was not entered in the Stationers' Company Register; Moxon never entered any book he published. See *A Transcript of the Registers of the Company of Stationers from 1640-1708 A.D.*, ed. by G. E. B. Eyre, 3 vols (London, 1913-14; repr. Gloucester, Mass.: Peter Smith, 1967) and William Proctor Williams, *Index to the Stationers' Register 1640-1708* (La Jolla, Calif.: L. McGilvery, 1980). Moxon did not utterly eschew a corporately-modelled book trade, but his sole mention of the Company in the *Exercises* deals only with the annual printers' feast, and is confined, echoing the *Discourse*, to the 'appendix'. Moreover, he was well aware that the Company 'Grandees' (as Moxon calls the officers of the Company) might have little in common with their 'mechanick' printer-colleagues: such officials were commonly invited to the printers' feast 'although [they were] perhaps no Printers'. See *Exercises*, pp.329-31.
67. *Exercises*, p.395. Incidentally, there was no such semantic shyness for his son: James Moxon in his *Mechanick Powers* (London, 1699) (Wing M420) began by claiming the 'noble' mechanical arts, to be '[a]mong the chiefest and most useful ARTS, which God. . .hath granted to Mankind' before moving on to explain (somewhat disappointingly) that he meant 'mechanick' in its most simple scientific sense: 'the quantities of moving Forces, and of the times in which the Motion is made' (sig. π2v, p.1).
68. *Exercises*, pp.396-7.
69. *Exercises*, pp.xlv, 395. Note the unfavourable comparison with the continent. Davis and Carter do not mention that this 1677 preface, which was appended to all succeeding editions of 'volume one' of the *Exercises* (the printing volume was never apparently reprinted), was altered in these subsequent editions to include a paragraph in which Moxon explicitly styled himself as a Baconian 'philosopher' seeking out the secrets of the trades. See *Exercises* (1970), 'Preface'.
70. To characterize his intended audience as genteel may be too simplistic; Forman notes that Moxon's distinctive method of selling his *Exercises* in 'monthly' instalments would have placed the volumes within the price-range of the contemporary 'mechanick' (*Exercises* (1970), pp.xi-xii).
71. *Exercises*, pp.3-12, *passim*. It is interesting to note that the printing volume alone featured human figures in its illustrations. I owe this observation to Martin Moonie.
72. For a passionate argument in support of this, offering some American evidence, and in which Moxon is cast as almost the sole reason for England's early start during the industrial revolution, see Forman's introduction to *Exercises* (1970), pp.v-xxvi. Forman notes (p.xv) as part of his evidence for an intended 'mechanick' audience that the

Exercises had no dedication to a noble patron. This was not the case with the printing volume which was dedicated to the surviving partners of the Oxford University Press – perhaps precisely the gentlemen-mechanicks Moxon had in mind (*Exercises*, pp.1-2).
73. D. F. McKenzie, *Bibliography and the Sociology of Texts* (London: The British Library, 1986), p.7.
74. Wrightson (1994), p.50.

George Hawkins (1705-1780): Bookseller and Treasurer of the English Stock of the Stationers' Company

ROBIN MYERS

Introduction

THE PAPERS relating to the trading and domestic life of George Hawkins, Treasurer of the English Stock from 1766, were left at Stationers' Hall when he died there in 1780, at what John Nichols described as (and was, for those days) 'a very advanced age' (75 years). He died, 'intestate a widower without child or parent brother or sister uncle or aunt nephew or niece leaving behind him Sarah Bowden spinster his cousin germane who . . . renounced the right to letters of administration of all and singular the goods, chattels and credits of the deceased'.[1] It was left to the Company to take out letters of administration and clear up his effects when his successor as Treasurer of the English Stock moved into the house. Somehow the collection of Hawkins's miscellaneous papers, vouchers and other financial documents relating to his domestic life and bookselling business got overlooked.

Sidney Hodgson, the Company's first archivist, came across them and arranged them in a rough and ready way, within the outer covers of company reports; Ellic Howe, a *protegé* of Mr Hodgson, used those relating to binding in *A list of London Bookbinders, 1648-1815*,[2] and for some of his entries they are the only source.[3] I don't know of anyone else's looking at them until I came across them when I was invited to index all the unclassified documents in the muniment room in 1975. Ten years later, when I was putting the archive in order for the Chadwyck-Healey microfilm publication, I returned to the Hawkins papers and made a much more detailed calendar of them[4] and put them into acceptable archival order.[5] They include three or four rough ledger or balance sheets – but no ledger – lists and vouchers for advertising, for books bought from other booksellers, for bookbinding, for printing, for paper, for stationery, for purchases at trade sales.[6] There are a few subscription lists – not always identifying the work being subscribed for. The fullest of them is a draft list for Patrick Forbes's edition of *A full view of the public transactions in the reign of Queen Elizabeth*, 2 volumes, octavo, 1740-41; it lists 8 large paper copies, including complimentary copies for the Prince of Wales and the Prince of Orange, and 10 small paper copies for various noblemen and gentlemen. All in all, they give a pretty complete picture of Hawkins's trading and personal life.

There is next to no private correspondence, apart from a couple of ill-written, ill-spelt letters from a Sarah Bowden (probably the cousin germane of the letters of administration).[7] On 13 March 1773, she writes from Windsor:

i recieved your very kind presant of good tea, for whith i return my sencercere thanks but wold have aded much to your kindess, if you wold a sent a Line and Let me know you are In good Health, as to my self i have a bad cold and coff at presasant, i have not bin out this week past but hop when the weather comes arm i shall git better, I beg you will make the most of your Holydays and if shold come near Windsor that i may have the plesure of seein you, but not a put you to Enny Charge as i did before i am Sr with grate Recept your Humble Servant. . .

In September, she hoped he

got home safe, and had know return of your Complaint. . .Sr I cant conclud my scrole without return in thanks for your very kind visset and good intertainment i was in grate hops of havein your compeny to Brakfast as ye Morning was so fine, it was all reddy but makeing the Tea. . .

The vast quantity of personal vouchers tell us a good deal about Hawkins's domestic arrangements – there are invoices from apothecaries, carpenters, farriers, hatters, jewellers, lawyers, locksmiths, a nurse to look after his ailing mother, 'paying a man for washing bottles', tailors, undertakers, upholsterers, bills for firkins of ale, 'canary' wine, candles, carpets, cleaning feather-beds, coals, loaves, lobsters, oysters, tobacco, shaving, refurbishing a wig.

In the intervening years I looked them over from time to time with a proprietory interest, but in the days before the *Eighteenth Century Short Title Catalogue*,[8] the Maslen edition of the scattered Bowyer ledgers and McKenzie, *Stationers' Company Apprentices,* Volume 3, *1701-1800*[9] and without any ledger to provide a guide through the morass of small vouchers, it was too daunting and I turned to other projects. I was conscious that, once I had made them public through the Chadwyck-Healey microfilm, it was only a matter of time before someone else would have the fun of piecing the jigsaw puzzle together and revealing the image of this fairly typical retail and wholesale (or publishing) bookseller of the mid-eighteenth century.

The *ESTC on CD-Rom* has revolutionized imprint studies, making it possible to compile a reasonably complete list of publications as well as tracking down advertisement lists in the backs of books.[10] The indexes in Terry Belanger's thesis on the trade sales – still, and alas likely to remain, unpublished – speeds the search for auction purchases.[11] These two resources allow us to identify what Hawkins published; but the retail trade is another matter altogether. Although we can get a good idea of what books Hawkins sold retail, from whom he bought his stock, what he had bound, the prices and terms by piecing together vouchers and lists in the Hawkins papers – it is time-consuming work, and then we don't know if it tells the whole story.[12]

Background and Parentage

Hawkins's paternal grandfather was a Buckinghamshire gentleman; his father, Richard Hawkins, a Citizen, Armourer and Brazier; his mother, Miriam Peacock, the daughter of a tailor where Richard Hawkins lodged.[13] George, the eldest of three surviving children, was baptized, February 1705. He was apprenticed to Samuel Ballard, bookseller of Little Britain, in 1720 with a premium of £40. His father died a few months later and in March 1725, he turned himself over to Thomas Woodward whose shop was the Half Moon between the Temple Gates over against St Dunstan's Church in Fleet Street, close to the shop which Hawkins occupied from 1739 to 1766. He was freed 5 May 1730, published his first work in 1734, married in 1736, set up in Fleet Street in 1738, was widowed in July 1747, lost his mother in 1756, his sister in 1762 and left off trade in 1766, moving into Stationers' Hall in 1767. These are the bare facts of his life.

George Hawkins, Publisher (1734-77)

That Hawkins's grandfather was a gentleman, that he had property in Worcestershire, and that his father could pay a largish premium argues background prosperity and an *entrée* into the best bookselling circles. But for all the plethora of vouchers and his name on some 136 imprints, which should give an exact sense of Hawkins's style of life and his status in the book trade, it is surprisingly difficult to place him in context, particularly (although unsurprisingly) in his early years.

The death of his father only months after he was bound to Ballard may have affected the family fortunes, with perhaps a mother, sister and younger brother to support. Could this account for his turning over to Woodward, shifting his trading epi-centre from the area north of Stationers' Hall to Fleet Street farther west, arguing a pull towards the legal London and the west end trade of the Strand? That he did not cut himself off entirely from his first place of activity may be argued from his accepting his second apprentice, Thomas Sedden, turned over to him in 1744 by John Oswald, bookseller in Little Britain.

Definite facts about his *modus vivendi* in the years before he set up in 1738, near Temple Bar, are few and far between. That he started in a small way we may surmise but the four years between his coming out of his time in 1730 and beginning to trade on his own account, are almost a blank; he may have worked journeyman for Woodward and he entered works at Stationers' Hall on behalf of Andrew Millar a couple of months before coming out of his time, for Jethro Tull and for Woodward.[14] In this interim period, he launched his publishing career with 500 copies of a pamphlet, *The Loyal Tory*, printed for him by Charles Ackers at a cost of £5.17s.3d in March 1733/4.[15]

His course as a general bookseller and publisher, and his personal life were under weigh before he moved into his first shop in Fleet Street, near Temple Bar in 1738. In 1735, Hawkins published, jointly with Thomas Woodman, the sixteenth-century courtesy book, Gozlicki's *De Optimo Senatore*, 1568, translated as the *Accomplished Senator*; the next year, 1736, the year of his marriage to Anne Wheeler, he started buying shares in copies and books for resale at trade sales.[16]

In 1739, he moved a few doors to the east to larger premises at Milton's Head, between the Temple Gates. He rented another shop 'in the season' according to Nichols, at 12 guineas per annum in Tunbridge Wells. It made sense to move out of London in the summer months when trade virtually came to a halt with the ending of the law term and the removal of the nobility and gentry to the country or to spas such as Tunbridge Wells.[17] The imprint of William Petyt's *Jus Parliamentarium*, 1739, a splendid folio in two parts, published jointly by six booksellers and sold 'at their shops', includes both his addresses.[18] For a few years he shared or leased the premises with Henry Eyre,[19] whose *Brief account of the Holt waters, containing 112 Cures*, Hawkins published in 1743, suggesting the traditional tie-up between the sale of books and retail medicine.[20] By the beginning of 1740 he had published eighteen works and bought quantities of law reports, highly saleable in that location, as well as 24 copies of Chamberlayn's *State of Great Britain*. He remained at Milton's Head for 26 years. From this point his business grew; in 1741, he rented a larger country shop with a house 'upon Tunbridge Wells Walks' at a rent of £15 per annum.

Evidence for his domestic life and trading is given in the invoices of Edmund Dennes the carrier, from 1741 to 1759, for transporting parcels, hampers, baskets, trunks, boxes and bottles to and from Tunbridge Wells. Hawkins was still paying rent (or perhaps subletting) the Tunbridge Wells premises in 1771. Bills, 1749 to 1779, from farriers and for the stabling, purchase and sale of a horse shew that from the early 1740s, although he might not keep a carriage, he was able to live in style; and by the mid '50s he was in a very fair way of business and was bookseller to the Prince of Wales – the custom of that royal bibliophile, the future George III, would have been worth having although it was not an official royal warrant.[21]

In common with booksellers and collectors in every age the books were outgrowing their space and in 1757 he rented a room at £3 p.a. over the vestry or 'quest room' of St Dunstan's Church on the opposite side of Fleet Street. He was still paying the rent in 1770, although he had sold all but one of his copyrights by the time he moved into Stationers' Hall at the beginning of 1767.

His was a general list; his name appears in some 136 imprints and most of the works of which he was sole publisher seem to have been on commission or 'for the author', though rarely so designated.[22] We are left to deduce this from evidence assembled from a variety of sources – the imprints, entry in the Stationers' Registers, the Bowyer and Ackers ledgers and, of course, the Hawkins papers. Unfortunately we have no contracts to provide ultimate proof but we have a few scrappy authors' receipts from which we can deduce a commission – such as two payments made in 1758 for 200 copies of Joseph Harris's anonymous *Essay on Money*, 1757,[23] and a note to Henry Strachey, 20 February, 1739 for ten guineas 'with the like sum for me received by him for the *Index to the Records*'.[24] Then there is a civil if scribbled note (see fig.1), 6 July 1747, from John Upton, Prebendary of Rochester asking Hawkins to pay £20 to 'Dr Collier of Commons & place it to the account of yr humble servt: I should have given you notice of this by letter but had not time; so hope you'll pardon it, nor do I write this as a demand, but a request'.[25] Hawkins entered Upton's *Canto of the Fairy Queen*, 'on the abuse of travelling a canto in imitation of Spenser' to the author in the Stationers' Register, 2 December 1746.

In his first ten years of trading Hawkins published five volumes of poetry 'for the author'. The first and most successful was William Somervile, *The Chace* (1735) which Hawkins took over from Thomas Woodward who entered 'Proposals for a Poem on Hunting on royal

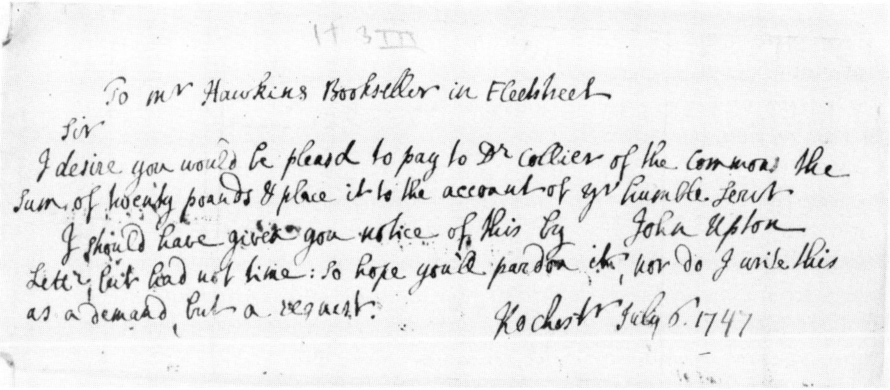

Fig.1. Note to Hawkins from John Upton, author of *A canto of the Fairy Queen*, 1746. Stationers' Company miscellaneous documents, Series I H3 iii.

paper' on 3 February; Bowyer printed '750 copies of quarter-sheet' of *The Chace, a Poem* and on 13 May Hawkins entered it to the author, William Somervile, and deposited the statutory nine copies.[26] In the first year, 1735, it came out in quarto, octavo and duodecimo, 'printed for G. Hawkins and sold by T. Cooper'. Further editions followed in 1743, 1747 and 1757, printed by Bowyer and distributed by the Coopers, first Thomas and after his death in 1743, by his widow, Mary.[27] After 1757, it passed out of his hands. Another, to us surprisingly, successful volume of poetry was *Love Elegies written in the Year 1732*, 'wrote by a gentleman lately dead and justly lamented'.[28] It is unlikely that anyone would have heard of James Hammond if the Earl of Chesterfield had not decided to publish a handsome slim folio, with a preface extolling the poet, of the banal love elegies in 1743, 'printed for G. Hawkins and sold by T. Cooper', with further editions in folio, octavo and duodecimo 1743, 1745 and 1747.[29] Only once did Hawkins publish any faintly memorable poetry – Young's *Night Thoughts*, once on the English syllabus at Oxford but now long forgotten, mainly published by Dodsley night after night, so to say. Nights

7 to 9, *'The Complaint. Or, night-thoughts on life, death and immortality'* were printed by Samuel Richardson for G. Hawkins and sold by M. Cooper.[30] The rest of Hawkins's list was pseudo-classical, neo-romantic verse of no distinction – all with the imprint 'printed for G. Hawkins and sold by T. [or M.] Cooper' 1739 to 1764.[31] Only *The Solitary, an Ode inscrib'd to Ralph Allen Esq, of Bath, price 6d* [1747] may be of passing interest through Allen's friendship with Pope;[32] but who would now look at *A Poem on Chess*, 1764 and reprinted the same year; or *The Fireside, or a Pastoral Soliloquy* by Isaac Hawkins Browne, 1746 with notes by John Upton.

In the 1760s and 1770s Hawkins did a considerable retail trade in literature and literary periodicals, buying single copies from other booksellers of, among others, Beaumont and Fletcher, Shakespeare and Pope from Charles Bathurst in 1763, *The Spectator* and *The Guardian* from Robert Marshall in 1773;[33] and bills from William Cooke, James Darbyshire, George Heath and other bookbinders include volumes of Gray, Thomson, author of *The Seasons*, Young and Newton's edition of Milton's *Paradise Lost* and *Paradise Regained*.[34] He also bought newspapers wholesale from the Langfords, 1757 to 1760, for the country trade,[35]

In the days before medicine was regarded as a profession, medical books were often published as a form of advertising – Henry Eyre's *Holt Waters*, already noted, is a case in point. Hawkins's list includes *An Historical and Critical Treatise on Gout*, 1740 and 1742 by Dr Thomas Thompson, physician to the Prince of Wales; William Forster's *Treatise on the Causes of most Diseases incident to Human Bodies and the Cure of them*, 1746; Thomas Gataker's *Observations on Venereal Complaints*, 1754 and 1755.[36]

Located between the Temple Gates, law books were predictably a staple of his list and he did a brisk retail trade in law reports and cases bought at trade sales and from other booksellers – at the Queen's Head, 17 November 1739, he bought (lot 12) copies of Hobart's, Finch's, Sander's, Levinz's, Lucas's, Fawesty's and Ventris's reports and four copies of Shower's Cases – at Gosling's sale, 5 October 1742 (lot 5), 119 copies of Gilbert's *Cases in Equity*, with a quarter of the copy, and (lot 13) 139 copies of Salkeld's Reports. He bought Ward's and Burn's *Justices, the Laws of Evidence*, multiple sets of the *Statutes at Large* both at trade sales and from various booksellers, one of which he had bound, with the index, by Margaret Folingsby in 1760. Law books figure in Cooke's and other binders' lists, either sewn in boards, or calf, lettered, once grandly with 'red leaves etc'.[37] He bought an 8th share in the *Attorney's Practice in*

King's Bench at Woodward's sale in March 1752[38] but it seems as though he and the others in the imprint had bought stocks from Lintot or were distributing for him rather than publishing in the modern sense.[39] This was also the case with the other four standard legal textbooks printed by Henry Lintot or his daughter Catherine, 1741 to 1759.[40]

There was no shortage of theological commentary, often published at the author's expense; such was Vinchon Desvoeux, *A Philosophical and critical essay on Ecclesiastes*, 1760, printed by Bettenham at a cost of £70.14s.6d.[41] Desvoeux sent Hawkins a 'list of presents', copies that he wanted sent to, among others, a number of English and Irish bishops and academics in the Low Countries. Hawkins also published some eighteen or twenty occasional sermons, quarto or octavo pamphlets, paid for by those, be it the University of Oxford, the Lord Mayor, or 'the Lords spiritual and temporal in Parliament assembled', who commissioned the preacher. In 1740, Hawkins published, jointly with Robert Gosling and printed at the Clarendon Press, Walter Harte's sermon on *The Reasonableness and advantage of national humiliations upon the approach of war*.[42]

Harte, a friend of Pope and Young, and Canon of Windsor, was later to be the star in Hawkins's list with his *History of the Life of Gustavus Adolphus*, lavishly produced for the author and sold by Hawkins, 2 volumes, 4°, 1759, at a cost, to Gents. of £1.16s bound and to the trade £13 per 10 sets with 4 months credit 'signing notes'. Ten leading booksellers, most of them Hawkins's partners at one time or another, bought sets.[43] Chesterfield, with a characteristic sneer, condemned Harte's style as 'full of all isms but anglicisms'.[44]

Hawkins had shares in several large-scale works such as the English edition of Bayle's *General Dictionary, historical and critical*, folio, 1738, late editions of Chamberlayn's *Present State of Great Britain*, with 14 others, 8°, 1743-56, and Philip Miller's *Gardener's Dictionary*, with 16 others, folio, 1756 and 1759, and *The gardeners kalendar*, 8°, 1765.[45]

Hawkins published five classical texts (Epictetus, Dionysius of Halicarnassus, Livy, Sallust, Xenophon) all of them as sole publisher, but he may well have done a larger retail trade in classical texts and commentary. This is suggested by an undated, anonymous, priced list of the 'Latin Classicks cum Notes Variorum, in 4to. . .' The hand is unknown to me; it may be Vaillant's or Nourse's.[46] Likewise the quantity of French books bought, December 1759 to late 1768, from his one time fellow apprentice, the Huguenot bookseller, Paul Vaillant, shews that Hawkins had customers for books in French.[47] The importing of foreign books was a highly specialist business and Hawkins would never have meddled with it.

The Roman History, from the building of Rome to the ruin of the Commonwealth, 11 volumes, 4°, 1738-71 by Nathaniel Hooke is not a riveting work except as an indicator of current taste and as publishing history – a case study of a successful work published for the author.[48] James Bettenham, who printed it until he retired in 1766, entered it to the author, 3 October 1735.[49] Hawkins published the first two volumes but Hooke died in 1763 when Volume III was in the press and the Tonsons, Hawkins and Thomas Longman took over the copyright in equal shares, commissioning Dr Duncan Stuart to complete a four volume edition. Hooke's daughter continued to receive payment on that edition whose print run was the customary 500. After Jacob Tonson died in 1767, his share was divided between a varying number and assortment of leading booksellers who, in 1771, were Cadell, Strahan, John Rivington, Johnston, Baldwin and Robson. *The Roman History* made money, and perhaps reputation, for Hawkins and when he gave up trading he noted, 'January 1767, copys now sold except Rom. History and Court and City Register'. He expected £400 in profit from the 'new edition'.[50] Among his papers are details of his dealings with printer, plate-makers and engravers, advertising, printed subscription notices sent to gentlemen or members of the trade etc. Hawkins drew up a sheet of details of production and other costs for publication of the last volumes in 1771.[51]

Hawkins's business throve throughout the later 1740s and 1750s and he was prosperous enough to be able to give his wife a slap-up funeral with a fine elm coffin 'sett off in the best manner. . .plate of inscription & flower on the top, all gilt with gold, lined and ruffled with crape. . .12 men in mourning processed with 12 large branchlights, with candles of wax. . .' The cost was £19.7s.8d. His mother, who died in 1756, was given a more modest send off costing £6.10s.6d with a mere 'best finished covered coffin' at 4 guineas, 'a superfine shroud pillow' at one guinea and 'use of the best pall' for 10s. Whether or not this is indicative of the relative status of wife and mother, who is to say?

Treasurer of the English Stock

'That marked connection, both consanguineous and professional, between the Church and the book trade in the seventeenth century had turned in the eighteenth into a similar association between lawyers and Stationers in Fleet Street and Chancery Lane.'[52] The Company's role had diminished until only entry in the registers for copyright protection with the submission of free copies for legal deposit and the binding of apprentices had any real impact on the London book trade. Hawkins entered little in the register – his name appears a mere ten times in 33 years, six times on behalf of the author or another bookseller.

The members of the Company continued to eat convivial dinners, draw pensions when they fell on hard times and draw good dividends if they were fortunate and rich enough to own a share in the English Stock.

Hawkins was typical of a reasonably prosperous mid-century bookseller in his association with the Company, as in much else in his personal and trading life. Many of his trading partners and associates (booksellers, printers and binders) sat on the Court but the Company probably had little impact on his daily life. He traded too far west for much contact, both shop and warehouse were almost at the limits of the City and the lawyers of the Inns of Court and the Westminster and country gentry had more direct effect on his trade than Stationers' Hall.

At the same time he was very much a Citizen and Stationer, bound at the Hall, freed and cloathed as a Stationer, binding his apprentices, and freeing one, at the Hall, holding stock shares and being elected to the Court in December 1763 in 'one of the biggest – and broadest based – calls of Assistants. The number first proposed was twelve; this was increased to fifteen and finally to eighteen',[53] thus strengthening the Court's defences against the Yeomanry when Jacob Ilive made a last ditch stand against the inequalities in the Company in 1762.[54]

Hawkins, at number sixteen, was among the last to be called, probably accounted an inoffensive man who would give no trouble and would support the Court's decisions. There is no means of knowing how he, or any Assistant voted (votes) on Court, but he was assiduous in his attendance during his three years as an Assistant.

What induced him to apply for the post of Treasurer or Warehouse keeper (the Court had ruled that the latter was to be the title but continued to use the former by default) is matter of speculation. Hawkins's business was flourishing and he was well able to maintain his lifestyle – on moving to the Treasurer's House on the north side of Stationers' Court he ordered a mahogany dining table, 19 yards of best Wilton carpet, and 10lbs of the best old feathers for his bed (though they only cost 8 guineas)[55] – but he was, by the standards of the day, at 61, an elderly man who, again from the evidence of increasing expenditure on medicines and purges, may have felt he was in failing health. He had no family and a rent- and tax-free house attached to Stationers' Hall, with no domestic worries, with 10s allowance for coals, an annual gratuity and a salary of £60 p.a. in exchange for giving up trade, may have appealed.

Rules for the 'Treasurer or warehouse Keeper' (revised in 1755) had been drawn up by the Court in 1724, after trouble with bookselling Treasurers defrauding the Stock. The incumbent must 'voluntarily cease the trade both as shop and chapman and apply himself solely to the Company's service. . .have leave and liberty only to sell and print any impressions of such copys as shall be his own proper right. . .' And, because they had had a great deal of trouble with Treasurers who got out of hand they specified that 'if of the Assistants not to act as such for he is then to be in the capacity of a servant to the said Court'.[56]

Consequently Hawkins resigned from the Court at the beginning of March 1766, gave up his shop and moved into the Treasurer's house at the beginning of 1767. In the draft balance sheet headed 'State of my affairs, Jan: 1.1767', he noted his debts amounted, in all, to £1200, his credits £1451.4s.9d which with £400 'supposed profit on new edition of Roman Hist.' totalled £1851.4s.9d, shewing that he was good for the £1000 bond demanded of the Treasurer (another precaution dating from 1724).[57] Apart from the last volumes of Hooke's *Roman History*[58] all he published after he ceased trading was, in 1777, with 29 others, *Heraldry in miniature,* a standard duodecimo reference work. He did, however, sell a few books retail.

The Rules specified the hours of attendance 'in the warehouse under the comon dining parlour of this Company now used for the sale of books belonging to the Stock'. These were 'every week from Monday morning to Saturday night throughout the whole year. . .from Lady Day to Michaelmas from 8. . .to 12, 2. . .4 Holy Days always excepted.' They also specified the sort of account books to be used as 'a day book, a posting book, an acquittance book, a book of business relating to the Universities, a book for business relating to Parts Fines and Forfeitures, a book for rents received. . .'

Publishing and selling the Stock's copies took a great deal of the Treasurer's time. He had clerical and porterage assistance (but I don't know how much). There were four Stock Board meetings a year, with the minutes to write up, and he had to deal with compilers, printers, the Stamp Office, booksellers' accounts, collect rents from the Stock's or the Company's tenants in the premises round Stationers' Hall. Almanack Day in November must have been pandemonium – the almanacks were loaded on to the tables in the hall and the booksellers' carriers flooded in to collect their consignments – it may have been somewhat less frenetic during Hawkins's last years after the Company's claim to perpetual copyright was quoshed and Carnan's rival almanacks made such a large dent in the sales. Christmas and Midsummer, when dividends were paid to the Stock partners, were also busy times, involving a good deal of paperwork. Invoices in Hawkins' hand from the late 1760s to January 1780 itemize 'Working the warehouse 5s', '100 reams to the Stamp Office 2s',[59] '4 times to the Stamp Office 2s', 'carrying Tate 24 in the Warehouse',[60] 'Going to the Printers & Workmen 4s'.[61]

The Treasurer had also unscheduled calls on his time and patience. On 12 October 1771, the unhappy James Mackenzie wrote from Gravesend to protest against his eviction for non-payment:

I am sory that you have Don so by Me. . .Dear Sr you know that I made aplycation to you for sum speady Relief by your condescending to take them Nots in wich it was Utmost in my Power to offor you in wich I was in hopes you woud ben so kind as to take it in consideration to save me from Ruin and my Wife and Famaly it would have don had you taken the Nots and have given me time But now a lass I am undun for ever by you forsing me from Home to leave my Business and Famely and Wife in the most melancoly situation by the death of a child in wich was buried last weak. . .

John Wallis, bookseller who was declared bankrupt, 2 January 1778, was, on 12 February, more literately, '. . .ashamed to have troubled you so much with my Note for £22 but the difficulty of getting in monies due to me plead my excuse. . .I will make a point of paying it this week' [presumably he did not] with many thanks for your Indulgence. . .'[62]

Not mentioned in the rules were errands such as that of Thomas Wright, compiler of Season's, Partridge's and Old Moore's (Vox Stellarum) almanacks who wrote shakily (though he lived until 1797) on 10 November 1779 (see fig.2):

I have sent you a parcel by the Peterborough Wagon. . .viz a Lump of Butter and 2 cheeses and my Wife and Daughter sends their complements and desires you to buy and send 'em 16 yards of Chinee or dark cotton for 2 gowns and 2£ of green tea and I will return the money they say goods are bought cheaper in London than in the country or at least they think so. I did fully design to come to London this summer but I've had a Rheumatick disorder in both my Hands. . .that I could do no journey. . .I am just recovered to my former state of Health and gotten into my study again from which I have been absent some months. I see by the Paper that the Almanacks are published the 16th Instant therefore if you please to send mine by the Peterborough Wagon. . .

His wife adds a postcript explaining that 'chinee is hard to get in the Country. . .'

In addition the Treasurer had been given the job of entering copies in the Register, formerly done by the Clerk. An item in Hawkins's invoice,

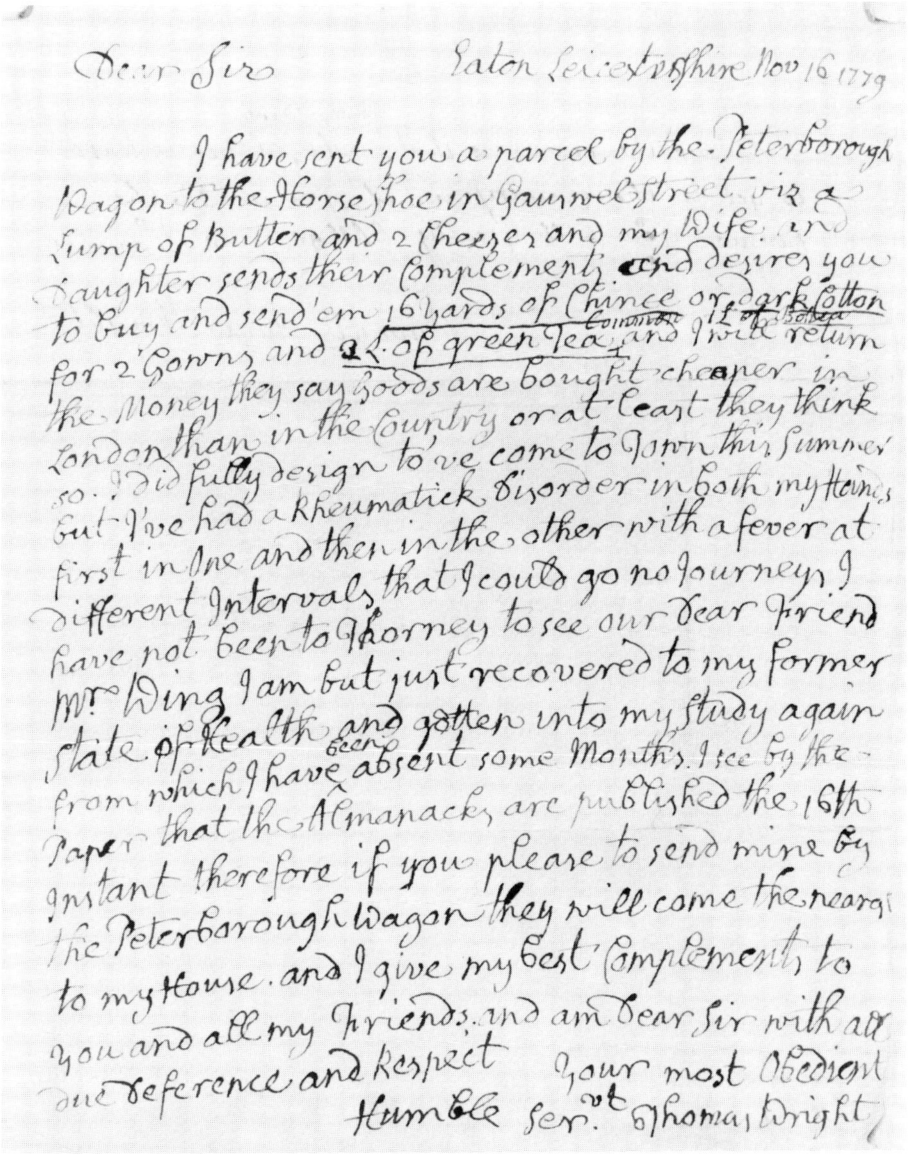

Dear Sir   Eaton Leicestershire Nov 16 1779

I have sent you a parcel by the Peterborough Wagon to the Horse Shoe in Gaunwel Street, viz a Lump of Butter and 2 Cheeses and my Wife and Daughter sends their Complements and desires you to buy and send 'em 16 yards of Chince or dark Cotton for 2 Gowns and 2 L of green Tea and I will return the Money they say Goods are bought cheaper in London than in the Country or at least they think so. I did fully design to've come to Town this Summer but I've had a Rheumatick Disorder in both my Heines first in One and then in the other with a fever at different Intervals, that I could go no Journeys. I have not been to Thorney to see our Dear Friend Mr Wing I am but just recovered to my former state of Health and gotten into my Study again from which I have been absent some Months. I see by the Paper that the Almanacks are published the 16th instant therefore if you please to send mine by the Peterborough Wagon they will come the nearest to my House. and I give my best Complements to you and all my Friends and am Dear Sir with all due Reference and Respect Your most Obedient Humble Servt Thomas Wright

Fig. 2. Letter from Thomas Wright, almanack maker, to Hawkins as Treasurer of the English Stock, 16 November 1779. Stationers' Hall, Series I H2 ii.

15 April 1769, is for 'Makeing up Register Books 3s'. The job does not look, on the face of it, like a soft option. In an age when there was no retirement a man soldiered on until relieved of his post by death; but the wind was sometimes tempered to the shorn lamb and the Company would give an ageing Treasurer an assistant who often succeeded him when he died. In 1779, when Hawkins was probably beginning to fail, John Wilkie was appointed his assistant and made Treasurer after Hawkins died at the hall in April 1780.

With no will and no family, the subsequent clearing up must have been quite a task – hence the papers left at the hall, hence my paper today.

References

1. Probate grant.
2. Ellic Howe, *A list of London bookbinders, 1648-1815*, London, The Bibliographical Society, 1950.
3. For the bookbinders used by Hawkins, both for stock and for retail sale, see Appendix II.
4. With the help of first, Alison Shell, then Alison Emblow, and finally Anna Greening.
5. Robin Myers, *The Stationers' Company Archive: An Account of the Records, 1554-1984*, (Winchester: St Paul's Bibliographies, 1990), Series I, Box H (Hawkins) pp.131-43, also Box M, relating to the English Stock.
6. These are rough memos, more detail is found in the Ward and Longman sets of trade sale catalogues in the Bodleian and British Libraries, though each of the three sources has something not found in the others. For details of the booksellers from whom Hawkins bought stock, see Appendix I.
7. The signature is clearly 'Bowden', the letters of administration and Court Book minutes are as clearly 'Borden' but it is more than probable that this is one and the same person.
8. The project was set up in 1976 but it was several years before it was generally available.
9. Published, 1978; D. F. McKenzie, *Stationers' Company Apprentices, 1603-1700*, 2 vols, 1961 & 1974, were not relevant to Hawkins. D. F. McKenzie and J .C. Ross, *A Ledger of Charles Acker*, 1968, identified 2 works printed for Hawkins.
10. Giles Mandelbrote has pointed out that only separate bound-in sheets of advertisements are noted by ESTC.
11. Terry Belanger, *Booksellers' sales of copyright: aspects of the London book trade: 1718-1768* Columbia University, New York, 1970.
12. See Appendix I, II and III, retailers, bookbinders and printers used by Hawkins.
13. 'He is a brasier and lodgeth at Mr Peacocke, a taylor in South Hampton Court in ould Southampton Buildings against Grays Inn.' Rough marriages Guildhall Library 6548, 20 September 1703.
14. Young's *Tragedy of Sophonisba*, entered for Millar, 1 March 1729/30. Millar was not admitted to the Livery (by redemption) until 1738; to Jethro Tull, *The Horse Hoing* . . . 1 June 1730; to Thomas Woodward, Francis Atterbury's Sermons, 18 March 1734.
15. For details, see Appendix III, printers used by Hawkins.

16. Hawkins bought copyrights or shares in copyrights, as well as stock for resale at some 15 sales between 18 May 1736 and 8 January 1765.
17. I am indebted to Arnold Hunt for pointing this out during discussion following this paper.
18. William Petyt (1636-1707) published three works on parliament in his lifetime; they were the basis for the posthumous *Jus Parliamentarium: or, the ancient poer. . .of the most high court of Parliament. . .*William Petyt, Late of the Inner Temple, and Keeper of the Records in the Tower of London. Nourse. . .M. Green. . .Caesar Ward, Richard Chandler. . .George Hawkins. . .and Thomas Waller, 1739.
19. It must have been considerably larger for Henry Eyres paid £1 personal tax while Hawkins paid 10s, where in the first shop he had paid only 5s. I am grateful to James Raven and Antonia Forster for tracking down this information for me.
20. I am indebted to Michael Harris for reminding me of this.
21. George III's father, Frederick, Prince of Wales, died in 1751. Hawkins is called Bookseller to the Prince of Wales in Chamberlayn's *Present State of Great Britain*, 1755 and 1756 editions and in Nichols, *Literary Anecdotes of the Eighteenth Century*.
22. The list of the works he published, either as sole or part owner of the copyright, identified through imprint search of the ESTC, is much too long to include in this paper.
23. Joseph Harris, *An Essay upon Money and Coins*, 2 parts, London, printed and sold by G. Hawkins, 1757. 8°.
24. Henry Strachey (1671-43), *Index to the Records, with directions to the several places where they are to be found. And short explanations of the different kinds of rolls, writs etc. to which is added, a list of Latin sir-names, and names of places. . .*London, printed for G. Hawkins, 1739. 8°. ESTC attributes the *Index to the Records* to Strachey but this voucher proves his authorship.
25. 'Commons', presumably Dr Collier of Doctors' Commons and Upton is asking Hawkins to settle a lawyer's bill.
26. J. D. Fleeman, 'William Somervile's "The Chace", 1735, PBSA 55, 1964, pp.1-7 and D. F. Foxon, *English Verse 1701-1750*, 2 vols, Cambridge, 1975, S562 I 742. For details of works printed by Bowyer for Hawkins, see Appendix III.
27. Thomas Cooper died in 1743, Mary in 1761.
28. Introduction by the Earl of Chesterfield.
29. *Foxon*, H22, H23, H24, H25.
30. Foxon Y50, Y52, Y54, Y61, Y62.
31. If you except Samuel Butler's *Hudibras*, Zachary Grey's edition with the Hogarth cuts, published 12mo in 1761 and 8° in 1764. Hawkins bought 183 out of 3000, 'the purchaser of this lot has a right to the last impression on paying paper and print'.
32. Foxon S551.
33. For list of booksellers from whom Hawkins bought for retail sale, see Appendix I.
34. See Appendix II.
35. But there is no evidence in the Hawkins papers that he owned a newspaper; for details of his purchase of newspapers for resale, see Appendix I.
36. Published by Hawkins with the Dodsleys, sold by M. Cooper.
37. See Appendix II.
38. There were various editions of *the Clerk's Instructor*, first published as *The Clerk's English Tutor*, 1733; ESTC gives Hawkins's name, with eight others, in the 2nd edition of 1741.

39. For a discussion of the eighteenth-century meaning of 'published' see D. F. Foxon, review of McKenzie & Ross, *Ackers Ledger*, *The Library*, V. xxv, 1, 1970, pp.65-73.
40. As the holder of Sayer's patent Lintot, or after his death his daughter Catherine, appears as the printer of all the important law books to appear between 1743 and 1759, such as Sir George Cooke, *Practical register of commons pleas*, 1743; Job Mill, *Practice of conveyancing*, 1745 and 1746; John Lilly, *Select Pleadings*, 4th edition, 1758; Robert Richardson, *Attorney's practice in court of commons pleas*, 1746 and 4th edition, 1759. See Appendix III.
41. See Appendix III.
42. Wednesday 9 January 1740, printed at the Theatre for R. Gosling and G. Hawkins, London, 8°. See Appendix III.
43. For printers and engravers used for the *Gustavus Adolphus*, see Appendix III.
44. See attached table of publishing history.
45. ESTC gives only the 1756 edition of Chamberlayn as Hawkins's, but the title-pages of the set in the Society of Antiquaries includes his name, 1743-56. *The gardeners dictionary* was published for the author and the second issue entered to eight booksellers, Hawkins having 1/32nd share, 30 March 1759.
46. The bookseller has written 'they may all be got in sheets & consequently uniformly bound. . .if the Gentleman who has desired to know the above prices, let him send back this List that we may regulate the prices by it. . .'
47. See Appendix I for details of books bought from Vaillant.
48. Nathaniel Hooke (1678?-1763) the younger, was the nephew of Nathaniel Hooke the elder, an Irish Jacobite and prolific writer; Hawkins published two other of the younger Hooke's works, the scandalous and successful *Account ('written with the assistance of Nathaniel Hooke') of the Dowager Duchess of Marlborough. . .in a letter to herself from my Lord*, 5 editions, printed by Bettenham, 8°, 1742; and *Observations*, 2 editions, 4°, 1758.
49. For details of printers and engravers used for *Hooke*, see Appendix III.
50. It was such a popular and lucrative work that the Scottish bookseller Dow smuggled in a 3-volume octavo Irish pirated edition in 1775 (see below, p.161).
51. There was an 11 volume edition in 1810, but it is not part of the Hawkins story.
52. Cyprian Blagden, *The Stationers' Company, a History 1403-1959*, 1960, p.249.
53. Blagden p.233.
54. Ilive led a rebellion of the Freemen or Yeomanry in an attempt to get a fairer deal for them. He incited the Freemen to withold their Quarterage dues, but was outmanœuvred when the Court sued defaulters in the Court of Requests. See Blagden pp.232-3.
55. The carpet, bought in March 1767 @ £5.17s, the feathers in April @ £1.5s, the dining table in June @ £1.11s.6d.
56. The rules had been drawn up on the election of Thomas Simpson, who was an Assistant at the time.
57. His debts included £200 'on a bond' to Sarah Bowden, £300 to the jeweller, Peter le Dru, £300 to Tonson, £200 to Child's Bank, £100 to Wakelin, the lawyer. Credits included £300 stock in his St Dunstan's warehouse, £500 for the copy of the Roman History and £400 profit expected on the new edition, £160 for his Livery share.
58. Vol.10, 1767, vol.11, 1771.
59. To get paper for almanack printing stamped.
60. This is Tate & Brady, *The Singing Psalms*, a steady seller.
61. *The Singing Psalms*. An invoice in Hawkins's hand, May and June 1771, for 'delivery

of brevier Psalms etc' notes, 'These have been taken away by Mr Catherall under his arm.' (Series I Box M 12).
62. John Wallis, book, map and printseller of Ludgate Street, from 1777 to 1805, bankrupt 1778, his son Edward succeeded him, 1818-47.

Appendix I

Booksellers and newspaper sellers who supplied George Hawkins wholesale (a selection)

Bookseller or Pamphlet Seller	Title	Cost	Dates of purchase & payment	Binding	Notes
Charles Bathurst	1 Com. prayer 24mo 1 do best Cutts 1 Beaumont & Fletcher 10v 7 Popes Works 9v 8vo Shakespear 9v 18mo Greys Hudibras 2v 1 Canon of Criticism 1 Raleigh's History in 1v fol 6 Port Royal Greek Grammar 2v Bibles, prayer bks, & c.40 other works	£30.8s.6d	Mar 50- July 63 £85.8s.5d	Turkey morocco quires quires calf calf quires	
Charles Bathurst	1 Arnold on Wisdom 1 Biographia Britannica 3v 1 Common Prayer 8vo 1 Votes	£9.8s.10d	Jan-Apr 57 pd 17 May		
Charles Bathurst	Blackstone 4v	£3.10s	Feb 1770	boards	
Charles Bathurst	Statutes umpteen vols	£108.11s.4d	Aug 63- Aug 64	sewed or quires	bought in dribs & drabs month by month

Charles Bathurst	14 Statutes 14v 4 Blackstone Mills Conveyancing etc	£41.5s.6d	1764-5	boards, sewed boards	Statutes bought at various times, various vols, Blackstone also bought in dribs & drabs
Sam. Bladon	5 Modern History 3v fol 5 Modern History 8v 8vo	£24	Dec 58 Jan 59 pd 12 Feb 59		
Sam Bladon	2 Modern History v9 fol	£2.4s	July 61		
Sam Bladon	3 Modern History v12 fol 2 do v13 2 do v14	£7.14s	Oct-Dec 62 pd May 64		
Sam Bladon	3 Parliamentary History 24v	£13.10s	pd Jan 63		rec'd for Miller & Tonson 'by a note ... 13 Dec last at 6 months'
Caringon Bowles	1 English Atlas	£2.7s.6d	Dec 63		
Peter Brett	Newspapers for 8 weeks	£1.0s.6d	Dec 62-Feb 63 pd		8 weeks @ 2s.6d per week

Appendix I

Bookseller or Pamphlet Seller	Title	Cost	Dates of purchase & payment	Binding	Notes
John Brindley	25 Iliade amaro di . . . 25 Swifts free thoughts 12 ? on Voltaire 12 Army proceedings General Claystom of Horsemanship 6 Theatre of the Warr 18 Garrats' Designs 2 sets of Ovid 5v Halfpennys Town Houses Architecture delineated etc	£18.6s.1d	Aug 36-Nov 50 pd Feb 1759	 quires	'rec of Mr Hawkins . . . for Mrs Brindley <signed> Jas Robson'
D. Browne	Woods Institutes Bradys History of England 3v Banburys Reports	£3.4s.6d	bt & pd Feb 56		
Dan Browne	2 set Statutes at Large 6v	£20.11s.6d	May 1758	quires	
Thos Caslon	1 Bible large 4t single 1 do	£1.8s	Nov 62	calf quires	
Thos Caslon	1 Bible larg 4to Cam single leaf 1 Newtons Tables 12 Oxford Testaments 12 Wealds Spelling 24 Bibles non.p. sets of psalms 1 sheet almanac	£6.1s.4d hlf	65-Jan 66 pd March 66	calf calf	

Thos Caslon	1 Spectator 8v			calf lettered
	1 Holwells Indostan 2 pts	£3.5s	pd Jan 67	calf lettered
	1 Van Sittart 3v			calf lettered
	1 Churchills Works 2v			
Thomas Caslon	2 Common Prayer	£1.17s	1768	calf
	1 Life of Wicklife 8vo			calf lettered
	1 Sharpes Introduction 8vo			calf lettered
	1 Souths Grammar 12mo			calf lettered
	1 Harmers Letter of Philadelphia			
	1 New Duty of Man 8vo			calf lettered
	1 Complete Distiller			calf lettered
	1 Camb Euclide 8vo			calf lettered
Arthur Collins	Sidney Collections of State Papers	£3.3s	pd Sept 46	
Thomas Davies	Rapin & continuat'n with cuts 5v	£5.15s	Feb 69	got Davies per Char Barker
Thos Davies	3 Machiavels Works	12s	July 62	for Davies per M. Hingeston
Lockyer Davis	Marryn's Abridgement of the Phil Tans. v8 & 9	£2.4s	Aug 62	signed C. Reymers 'for L. Davis & self'
Andrew Dury	Roque's Map of London	£1.16s	Aug 58	
George Freer	1 Johnsons Shakespear 3v	£58.15s.5d	Jan-Apr 66	calf lettered
	4v Biographia Britan fol			boards
	1 Johnsons Shakespear 8v			lettered
	1 Debates Lords & Commons 22v			
	1 Dict. Geographique 10v royal			lettered
	1 Encyclopedie 21v fol			

Appendix I

Bookseller or Pamphlet Seller	Title	Cost	Dates of purchase & payment	Binding	Notes
Benj. Dod	Bibles various 14 Watsons Clergy 5 Harte's Gustavus	£13.4s less £6.10s	Nov 54-58 pd		Harte sold to Dod thus total pd £26.11s
Hitch & Hawes	1 Humes Essays 4to 1 Hillery on Africa ? 1 Potton Contusions	17s.6d	Apr 60	quires quires calf	quite a complicated transaction not worth itemizing
Sam Hooper	Baskerville Bible	£.13s	Oct 63		
John Knapton	3 Poslthwayt's Dicty 2v 4to 1 Johnsons do 2v fol 1 Tillotsons do 2v fol	£17.18s.8d	Feb, Mar 57	quires quires quires	
Thomas Langford	6 dozen + 2 London Evening 6 dozen + 2 General Evening 3 dozen + 1 Evening do 7 dozen + 5 Chronicles 2 dozen + 1 Gazettes single	£2.12s.1d	Sept-Dec 57 pd		Probably bought to send with orders for books from country customers
Thomas Langford	149 London Evening Posts 76 Generals 56 Chronicles	£2.0s.4d	June-Aug ? 58 pd		

Thomas Langford	139 London Evening Posts 74 General 65 Chronicles	£2.1s.5d	Sept-Dec 58 pd	
Tho Langford	220 approx London Evenings 8 Gazettes	total torn off	date ditto	itemized in 11 lots of Evenings, singles of Gazettes
Mary Langford	98 Chronicles 150 London Evenings 101 General Evening Posts	Mar-June 59	£2.11s.5d pd	
Thomas Langford	129 General Evenings 129 London Chronicles 76 London Evenings	£3.6s.6d	Sept-Dec 60	including 12s.7d 'left unpaid of laster quarters bill'
Mary Langford	84 General Evening 72 London Evening 82 Chronicles	£1.18s.1d pd		other similar bills for 59-61
William Lewis	500 A Scheme in Philosophy large 4to plate @ £2.6s per 100	£12.6s	May 60 pd	
Thomas Longman	1 Locke Works 3v 4to 1 Robertsons Scotland 2v 8vo 1 Dalrymples feudal law 1 Gordons Tacitus 5v 1 Sterns Works 15v 1 Bartletts farriery	£5.1s.4d	Aug 1773	quires do do do do do

Appendix I

Bookseller or Pamphlet Seller	Title	Cost	Dates of purchase & payment	Binding	Notes
Thomas Longman	1 Elements of Criticism 2v 1 Don Quixote (Jarvis) 4v 1 Dalrymple on feudal system 1 Dr Price on the National Debt 1 Millar Dictionary 4to	£2.0s.3d	Apr 1774	quires quires quires	
Robert Marshall	1 Spectator 8v 1 Guardian 1v 1 Popes Works 6v 1 Dyches Dictionary 1 Goldsmiths England 4v	£3.1s.7d	March 73	calf lettered do do do do	'reced at the same time the above contents in full for the use of Mrs B. Law'
Andrew Millar	3 Birch's Royal Society 2v 6 Burns Justice fol 1 Humes Essays 4to 2 Hooke	£8.18s less £3.16s for Hooke = £5.2s	June 56	boards	
Andrew Millar	12 Burns 8vo	£4.13s	Nov 56-Feb 57 pd Feb 58		

Andrew Millar	6 Humes Essays Ormonds Life 3v Maitlands Scotland 2v Demosthenes 6 Sullys Memoirs 5v Palmyra 6 Burns Justice fol	£25.10s	Apr-Nov 59 pd Oct	qu Let'd boards Lettered sewed qu hf board qu	'cash & note for Burn'
Andrew Millar	11 Robertsons Scotland 2v 1 Johnsons Dictionary 2v fol	£12.8s.6d	Sept-June 56 pd Apr 57	quires	
John Nourse	1 Chambers Architecture	£2.2s	Aug 59	boards	
William Owen	Dictionary of arts	£1.5s.4½d	Apr-June 56		
William Owen	Warner on prayer Female Conduct Law of Evidence Chapman on venereal disease Russell on Sea Water Wallis's Dictionary Biographia Dict 6v Salmons Grammar 6 Wards Justices Bacon 3v etc	£13	Oct 58-Jan 66 pd Jan 67	calf lettered calf calf calf boards calf boards calf quires quires	
Elizabeth Reeve	Millers Jests 2 Attorneys Pocket Book	13s.1d	Mar-Dec 47 pd Aug 59		
John Rivington	40 titles various	£37.19s.1d	57-8		too many to list

Appendix I

Bookseller or Pamphlet Seller	Title	Cost	Dates of purchase & payment	Binding	Notes
John Rivington	1 Newtons Prophecies 3v 8vo 1 Johnsons Dictionary 2v 8vo 1 Wards Oratory 2v 8vo 1 Delany's Life of David 2v 8vo 1 On Language Saved 1 Revelations examined 4to 1 Abstinence 1 Clarke's Pyles Paraphrase 4to	£3.4s.7d	64-65	quires quires board quires quires board	
John Rivington	45 works most single copies	£37.19s.1d	pd Sept 64	quires boards	
John Rivington	1 Postlethwayts Dictionary fol	£6.12s	Nov 63-Dec 65 pd Aug 72	boards qu board	'accounts sorted Sept 7 1764 . . . and another Oct 16 1765 . . . balance of £72.3s.1d
William Sandby	12 Parl History 5v 6 Lisles Husbandry 4to 1 Lisle 25 Dialogues of the Dead	£11.11s.6d	Mar 58	sewed quires gilt Lr'd quires	
Edward Sayer	1 D. Lisles Atlas	£5	Mar 59	hf board	

Robert Sayer	1 English atlas fol	£2.12s.6d	July 63 pd Aug 63	bound	'received … for Mr Robt Sayer <signed> J. Bennett'
P. Smith	46 Pamphlets on interest	16s.6d	Jan 1750		
Richard Thurston	'Books of Cotton & King Esq'	£4	27 May 62		
Paul Vaillant	1 Tableau de Penitence 12mo 1 Theologies du Coeur 2v 12mo 1 Guion sur le nouveau Testament 8v 12mo 1 Oevres de Bourignon 20v 12mo & 8vo	£3.7s	Feb 60	quires	
Paul Vaillant	1 Memoires de Monegon 9v 12mo 1 Regles pour former un avoret 12mo 1 Fables de la Fontaine 2v 12mo 1 Barbeyrac Morale des Pans 4to 1 Grotius Droit de la Guerre 2v 4to 1 Liturgie 8vo 1 Essay sur le Commerce 12mo 1 Memoires de Torg 12mo 1 Histoires des ? 13v 4to 1 Paraises (?) Fables 4 sheets fo 1 Bossuet Histoire des Navigation 4v 12mo	£6.16s	Sept 54-Feb 60 pd Dec 62	quires quires	

Appendix I

Bookseller or Pamphlet Seller	Title	Cost	Dates of purchase & payment	Binding	Notes
Paul Vaillant	1 Opera Machiavelli 2v 4 1 Boyer 4 1 Sully 8v 4 1 Memoi: de Netz 4vo 1 Culture des terres tom 5 1 Recueil de voyages 12v 1 Elements of Agriculture 1 Figures del encyclopedie tom 2 3 1 Dictionai de Michelet 3v fol 1 art de parler Francois 2v 1 encyclopedie tom 8 & 17 fol 1 figures	£29.17s.7d	63-64 pd Feb 68		sewed quires
Paul Vaillant	1 Principles de la Vie Chretienne 12mo 1 Schurman Operas 1 Oeconomie Divine par Poiret 7v 12mo 1 Preservatif contre le Fanatisms 1 Pratique de la Vraye Theologie 2v 1 Poiret Cogetationes 4to	£1.18s	Dec 59 pd		
J. Whiston & B. White	Alex Trallianus Gr. R. Stephanie Aretaeus Gr. Lat. Xenophon Leunelavii Trans of Xenophons Grecian History by Newman	£3.11s.6d	Jan-Apr 57		

J. Whiston & B. White	St Augustinius de Civitate 2v Kennets Hist of England 3v Bradley's Botan. Dict. 2v		Sept-Nov 57 pd Jan 58	'best'
Whiston & White	Aristophanes Justius Life of Erasmus Elzivir Classics 52v 6 Du Hamels Husbandry 1 do	10s.6d £36.15s	 1757 pd Feb 19 57	boards morocco quires boards
Whiston & White	Juvenatus Maittaire Horatius Sandby 2v London Magazine 28v Eginatus de Vita Caroli Magni Darts Canterbury Seneca Variorum 3v Howes Sermons Murdins State Papers Bousset Interests des Princes 4 tom. 4to Wicqueforts Embassade 3 tom 4to Dormat Loix Civiles fol	£16.6s	pd Sept 62	board lettered quires sewed
Whiston & White	Scipio Livy History Surgery 'parcel of books'	£3.9s.6d	64-65 pd Apr 68	
John Wilson	1 Prideaux Connection 4v 1 Lee on Botany sold him 3 Hooke v1 & 2: & 5, v8 2 Harte's Gustavus 2v	£10.17s.2d	boards	
Thomas Wilson	Rushworth's Coll. 8v fol	£4.10s	pd Mar 63	

Appendix I

Bookseller or Pamphlet Seller	Title	Cost	Dates of purchase & payment	Binding	Notes
Edw Woodcock	the books of Richard Ashworth Esq	£100	pd Dec 63		
John Wren	1 Johnson's Dictionary	£300 approx	1961-63		some 20 invoices, single copies of Eng lit, topography etc

Appendix II
A Selection of Bookbinders used by George Hawkins

Binder	Title	Style	Date	Cost	Notes
Gottfried Borneman			May-Dec 63		
John Boys	Gustavus 2v	hf board let'd	May 67	2s.6d	
	Harris' Voyages	lettered		8d	
	Johnson Dict 8vo	hf board let'd		5s	
	3 Simpson Epictetus	covered on ye back calf		4d	
Bayles & Staples	stationery vols		May 73	17s	for SC?
John Boys	Hooke v1 3 Nautical almanac	hf board let'd boards lettered	Mar 75	total £1.7s	16 items, mix of own books & English Stock
John Boys	16 Hooke various vols other own vols	most board lettered	Aug 71	£4.4s.2d	
John Boys	own vols	ditto	n.d.	£2.6s.1d	also a bookseller
Mrs Brindley			Aug 36-Nov 58		
John Colborne	Newton's Milton Voltaire 17v Keplers Travels Moores Fables	morocco borders gilt gilt extra gilt extra	May 58	£3.15s.4d	

Appendix II

Binder	Title	Style	Date	Cost	Notes
John Coles Stationer	Folio vellum book cont 8 large skins	binding in vell & headboards	Sept 42	£1.18s.6d	stationer at the Sun & Mitre Chancery Lane Fleet street
Coles & Evans	Broad quarto demy	1 qr ruled 6 lines bound in Vellum	Jan 1778		dr on Stationers Company
William Cooke	some 2000 volumes	mainly calf gilt lettered, some boards	Jan 57-July 58	£39.19s.8d	another similar sized & many small ones – this is the tip of the iceberg; Hawkins used Cooke 1757-63
William Cooke	many		1759-63		Hawkins' main binder
William Cooke	House of Commons Journals 28 vols & 2nd Vol Index		April 25 1762	£3.15s	printed receipt
Jas Darbyshire			1756-60		not all itemized

Jas Darbyshire	c.100 vols	lettered	Nov 58	13s.11d	also a bookseller
Richard Dymott					
Margaret Folingsby	Statutes Index to Statutes Temple's Works, 8 vols Reports	sewed boards	1760	£18.9s.3d	
M. Folingsby	Statutes	sewed	1763 & 1764		
George Heath	Hooke 4v Blackstone 4v Churchills Poems 2v Greys Hudibras 2v Newton Milton ditto Regained Gil Blas 4v Cottons Virgil Youngs Works 4v Gays Poems 2v Thomsons Works 4v Priors Poems 2v Somerviles Chace	all calf lettered	May 1772	£2.12s.8d	noted in Howe
Anthony Hilker	map of the world	to pasting on cloth fitted up with roles pulleys etc compleat case with do	Jan 1763	18s	
John Hughs		'for binding'	1761-62	£11.17s.8d	

Appendix II

Binder	Title	Style	Date	Cost	Notes
Johnson (Ed ?)	2 Common Prayer 1 Cam Psalms 12 Bibles 12 Testaments 12 Bibles 12 Duty of Man 1 Bible Cam 24 Bibles 1 Common Prayer 1 Goldsmith 6 Bibles 12 Common Prayer	rough calf rules, extra registers & case pf plain plain calf let on side bands let on side extra hotpressed cases plain plain sheep put in vell cover glt calf lettered calf lettered	Oct 60-Apr 65	£15.17s.2d	dr on Benj Dod
James Marks	30 titles	various, including extra, turkey, gilt leaves etc also boards	Jan 68-Nov 61	£6.2s	
James Marks	14 titles	various inc. vellum	Mar 62-May 63		
James Marks	12 titles various	calf lettered	62, 63, 66		3 other bills
James Marks 1 qr rules 6 lines bound in Vellum			Mar-May 58 pd July 58	£4.1s	
John Miller	Carters Epictetus	'bound'	June 78	7s	

Appendix III
A Selection of Printers and Engravers used by George Hawkins

Printer or Engraver	Title	Date	Cost
Charles Ackers	The Loyal Tory, 300 copies	20.3.33	£5.17s
	The Bachelor or Salamanca, 1000 copies (with Bettesworth, Hitch & Davis)	27.12.36	£3.15s.4d of £11.5s. total
	Vol.2 750 copies	24.1.39	£10.7s. total
Anthony Allen, shared with Bettenham & Bowyer	Gustavus Adolphus	1759	
Isaac Basire, engraver	plates for Hudibras	1761	
James Bettenham	Bayle's Dictionary	1738	
	Tasso	1738 until	
	Hooke's Roman History	1766	
	Public Trans. of Q. Elizabeth	1740-1	
	Duchess of Marlborough's Memoirs	1742	
	Livy tr. Freinsheim	1744 & '45	
	Port Royal Greek Grammar v, ii		
	Dionysius		
	Britons & Saxons not Popish	1747	
	Abridgments of new method of learning Greek	1748	
	Life of Pendock Neale	1749	
	Des Voeux, Essay Ecclesiastes	1758	
	Hudibras	1760	
	Poem on chess	1761	
	de la Tour d'Auvergne	1764	
		1740 & '65	

147

Appendix III

Printer or Engraver	Title	Date	Cost
William Bowyer	Somervile, the Chace	1735-57	
	Anderson, Right of Mankind to debate religion	1735	
	A touch of the Times, a ballad	1740	
	Scamnum Ecloga	1740	
	Ballier's Epitaph	1740	
with A. Allen & Bettenham	Boyle, Horace imitated	1742	
	Pococke, Description of the East	1743-5	
	Windham, Glacieres	1744	
	Port Royal Grammar, vol.I	1758	
	Onely, Relief of the Poor	1759	
	Gustavus Adolphus	1759	
James Harrison	Hooke, Roman History, vol.i		
John Hughs	Thompson, on Gout	1745	
Thomas Kitchen, engraver	maps & plates for Gustavus Adolphus	1759	
Henry Lintot	Clerk's instructor on King's Bench	1741	
	Cooke, Practical Register	1743	
	Job, Practice of Conveyancing	1745 & 46	
	Lilly, Select Pleadings	1758	
Catherine Lintot	Attorney's Practice in . . . King's Bench	1759	
Mrs Miller, engraver	Hooke, frontispiece		
James Noyes, copper-plate Printer	Hooke, worked 4,500 cuts, vols.1-3, 5th ed. & 4,000 front., maps & 2 plates	1770-71	
John Purser	Common Sense	1738-39	
Oxford, Clarendon Press	Harte, Reasonableness . . . (sermon)	1740	
	King, Tres Oratiunculae	1743	
	Simpson, Religion & Learning	1761	
	Sharpe, Want of Universality	1766	

Appendix III

Printer or Engraver	Title	Date	Cost
Samuel Richardson	The Complaint, nights 7 to 9	?	
William Richardson & Samuel Clark	Sharpe, Rise & Fall of Jerusalem	1761	
Charles Rivington, printer	Gustavus Adolphus, appendixes	1759	
John Rivington, printer	Miller's Gardener's Dict'y, engraved plates	1759	
Charles Say	Cox, Letter on Inoculation	1757	
William Strahan	Hooke, vol.ii		
Anthony Walker, engraver	Maps & plates for Gustavus Adolphus	1759	
Henry Woodfall	Coventry, Philemon to Hydaspes (ornament evidence)	1744	

Smugglers, Reprinters, and Hot Pursuers:
The Irish-Scottish Book Trade, and Copyright Prosecutions in the Late Eighteenth Century

WARREN MCDOUGALL

THIS PAPER LOOKS AT what was happening on the frontiers of the British book trade, still nominally policed through the Stationers' Company in London. It examines the activities of the people who tried to stop Irish reprints being imported to Scotland, and of those who brought them in, and presents evidence to show there were more of these books circulating in the country than has been thought.[1] The story takes in: a hitherto unrecognized smuggler from Stirling, William Anderson; Charles Elliot of Edinburgh, who bought smuggled books while maintaining a trade with the copyright holders; and the Scots booksellers who were taken to court for selling Irish and Scottish reprints of the same London title. It begins on the streets of Glasgow.

Excise seizures 1781-82
According to Customs records only a hundredweight of books, valued at £12, were imported legally from Ireland in 1781 (see table below). More than that, though, was being smuggled in the cart of the Saltcoats carrier, John Barclay, which trundled up to the Weighhouse in Glasgow on 2 August that year. Barclay had evidently made this run without mishap before, but today the wagon was stopped and searched by three Excise officers, Patrick Corbett, Robert Semple and Alexander Brisbane.

The Excise found three large bales addressed to William Anderson, bookseller in Stirling. When examined later these were seen to contain Dublin editions of London titles: Edward Gibbon's *Decline and fall of the Roman Empire*, printed for William Hallhead, 1781, 20 copies each of the first two volumes, 70 copies each of the remaining four; 50 copies of Johnson's *Dictionary*, the 3rd edition, printed by W. G. Jones for Thomas Ewing, 1768. Stitched in marble paper were: 30 copies each of the second and third volumes of Johnson's *Lives of the poets*, the title page missing; two copies of John Richard's *A tour from London to Petersburgh*, printed for W. Wilson, 1781; two copies of William Hayley's *An essay on history in three epistles to Edward Gibbon*, printed for C. Jackson, 1781; two copies of Hayley's *An essay on painting*, printed by Patrick Byrne, 1781.

Corbett and the others reported the books had been run in a vessel from Dublin to Saltcoats, and added: 'Mr Anderson has been in practice of bringing large quantities of books from Ireland without payment of dutys which can be proven if wanted & always lodged in the possession of Mr. [Daniel] Dow Schoolmaster in Saltcoats.' News of the seizure spread quickly. Anderson came from Stirling and offered Corbett £25 sterling for the return of the books; this was refused, and a few days later a Hugh Colquhoun tried the same bribe with Corbett and Semple, again unsuccessfully.[2]

William Creech of Edinburgh, who was associated in copyright ventures with William Strahan and Thomas Cadell, members of the Stationers' Company, wrote to them suggesting they prosecute Anderson; he would liaise with R. E. Philips, the Secretary to the Board of Customs Commissioners in Scotland, as well as James Walker, a Writer to the Signet, who acted as agent in piracy prosecutions. A few days earlier, Strahan had been complaining to Creech about the damaging effects of piracy on his copyright profits: 'for this plain reason, that the Irish immediately reprint upon us in a cheap size and not only run away with the whole American Trade, but even import them, with Impunity, into all the Western Coast of Britain. Nor are we able, as you well know, to prevent this' (4 October 1781).[3] Strahan agreed with Creech's proposals: 'Anderson of Stirling, I have been told long ago, is a very large Importer of Irish Editions of new books, by which he has got a great deal of Money, and is therefore the most proper Person of any to make an example of; and I hope we shall be able so to do; that he may be obliged to refund some of his ill-got gains' (18 October 1781). The action was swift: on 27 October, a messenger-at-arms served Anderson with a summons – on behalf of the pursuers, Strahan and Cadell, and James Dodsley – for pirating Johnson's *Dictionary*.[4]

Meanwhile, Philips, the Customs Secretary, ordered that the Excise men question the Saltcoats carrier again. Corbett and Brisbane stopped John Barclay in Glasgow on 16 October, but he 'refused to give up the name of his employer, pretending he did not know who he was'. They had a look inside the wagon, and found two more bundles of smuggled books, one for Dunlop & Wilson of Glasgow, the other for Anderson of Stirling. Examination in the Customs warehouse showed Dunlop & Wilson were getting nine copies of Johnson's *Lives of the poets*, Dublin, for Whitestone, Williams, Colles, and others, 1781, volumes 3 and 4. The books for Anderson were eight copies of William Blackstone, *Reports of cases determined in the several courts of Westminster Hall*, Dublin, for Whitestone, Chamberlaine, Colles, and others, 1781, two volumes.

John Girvin, acting land surveyor at Glasgow, knew the Commissioners were interested in this case, and he did some leg work. He visited Dunlop and Wilson, but Wilson 'disclaimed all knowledge' of the books. (Strahan and Cadell would add them to their prosecution list.) Girvin examined the Blackstone. 'Having never heard of the publication,' Girvin said, 'I called two booksellers to view it & they said they do not think it is, as yet, published in London.' Girvin asked his superiors to send a copy to the Commissioners: 'I hope the Preface of the book will sufficiently apologise for this singularity, & shew their Honours what a worthy family suffers by so fraudulent importations, over and above the injury to the Revenue and trade of this kingdom.'[5]

During a meeting chaired by Adam Smith, whose own work had been reprinted in Dublin, the Customs Commissioners heard that the bales stopped on 2 August had been brought in from Dublin to Saltcoats on the brig *Polly*, Magnes Garrett master, and Garrett had passed them on to Robert Barclay, son of the Saltcoats carrier. The Board decided that 'the several Papers on this subject be put into the Hands of the Gentleman who is employed for the London Booksellers, for his Information, and that the Solicitor shall give any assistance he can in this Business.'[6] Dow and Anderson had been linked, and now Garrett, who was a shipmaster in Saltcoats.

Smuggled books continued to be seized by the Excise. The carts of the Irvine carrriers John Watt and James Stevenson were stopped in Glasgow on 2 January 1782 by Brisbane and Angus McDonald. Cards sewn onto the bales were addressed to Morison and Son, Perth, care of Mr Templeman, bookseller in Irvine. All the books seized were Dublin-printed: four copies each of Robertson's *History of Scotland*, 2 volumes, *History of Charles V*, 3 volumes, and *History of America*, 2 volumes; 10 copies of Johnson's *Dictionary*, 25 of Paton's *Navigation* and four of *History of Modern Europe*. Strahan and Cadell took out a summons against the Morisons, too.

The first Excise seizure may have arisen by chance, in a search for unpaid duties, the second because of a quest for information, but the Morisons' came after Secretary Philips had sent 10 guineas to be shared by the officers. The fourth, again in Glasgow, was made in the hope of getting more money. In March 1782, Semple stopped 19 bundles of books, weighing three hundredweight, belonging to the Glasgow bookseller John

Liddell. Semple said he 'suspected the bundles to contain books of a kind with those he & others were lately rewarded for', although he had no evidence such as place of importation. The Customs officers in Glasgow did not support the seizure and were sympathetic to Liddell, telling the Board he 'bears a very fair character in this City, keeps a Circulating Library, and at certain periods goes through the country auctioneering'. The books were described as mainly novels, plays, history and divinity. However, Girvin, the land surveyor, spotted a set of Hume's *History* and six sets of Moore's *Travels through France*, both Dublin-printed, in sheets; the Board, possibly with Creech assisting the Secretary, noted that others on the list were also prohibited – Enfield's *Sermons* and Farquhar's *Sermons* – and ordered that all four titles be detained, with the remainder going back to Liddell.[7] Liddell became the fourth bookseller caught in similar circumstances to be prosecuted by Strahan and Cadell.

The officers involved wanted more money for their troubles. The reward system motivated the Customs and Excise ranks – after seized goods were condemned, the officer making the seizure was entitled to at least a third of the proceeds after various expenses were met. But what worked for rum or tobacco, did not apply to books. The penalties provided by the Copyright Act of 8 Anne were forfeiture of a penny a sheet, and damasking, and those of 1739 Importation Act were damasking, a fine of £5, a fine of double the value of every book, one half of which was to go to the Crown, the other half to whoever sued for it – and it was invariably the literary proprietor who sued. When the Customs condemned seizures, books for damasking had no value. In 1783, Semple, Corbett, Girvin and McDonald complained that the unbound books they had seized amounted to to 16,263 sheets, but that apart from the ten guineas Secretary Philips had paid out for the first seizure, they had received nothing.[8] The Board did not reply to this. The men had to wait until 1785, when two boatmen at Greenock found a large quantity of Blair's *Sermons* and Johnson's *Dictionary* being smuggled from Dublin, before they and the other officers shared £10 sent by Creech.[9] It was probably Creech who provided the reward for the first seizure of 1781. When he was asked to comment on a long list of smuggled titles in 1786, Creech said, 'If any of the books were my property, I would think it my duty to reward the officers.'[10] I have not seen evidence in the Customs letterbooks that many other booksellers did this; nor is there any sign that the Stationers' Company rewarded the men.[11]

Stationers' Hall

Stationers' Hall was crucial to the operation of the Scots book trade in the second half of the eighteenth century. Registration, in accordance with the Act of 8 Anne, was the central reference point for Scots protecting their own literary property, taking the right to reprint lapsed or non-entered titles, or trying to deny piracy at the Court of Session. Their belief in the Hall was founded in the copyright prosecutions brought by London booksellers in Edinburgh in the 1740s. The Scots defenders argued there that the Act meant ownership of literary property was limited, not perpetual, and that a title had to be entered in the Stationers' Register to be protected for 14 years, or 28 years if the author were still alive. The Court of Session agreed to this, along with the stipulation that an action by a copyright owner had to begin within three months of an alleged piracy. The court also ruled that pursuers were not entitled to damages as well as the penalties of the Act (an issue that continued to be raised as the London booksellers sued for large damages in the 1770s and 1780s). Because of the Court of Session ruling, so favourable to the Scots, and the stand-off at the House of Lords Appeal of 1751, the Scots were reprinting for 25 years before the case of Becket v. Donaldson settled the issue for Britain in 1774.[12]

When Gavin Hamilton of Edinburgh published volume one of David Hume's *History of Great Britain* in 1754, he made certain of entry by going to Stationers' Hall himself to sign the Register. A perusal of the Register shows Scots took it seriously, none more so than Charles Elliot, who invested heavily in copyrights, mainly of medical works, and who placed 43 entries in the Register, starting with Robert Simson's *Elements of Conic Sections* in 1775.[13] Elliot was in the go-it-alone tradition of Hamilton. The pre-eminent publishers of the leading Scots authors from the late 1760s, however, were John Balfour and William Creech in Edinburgh, and William Strahan and Thomas Cadell in London.[14] Their determination to protect their expensive copyright in the work of William Robertson, David Hume, Hugh Blair and others, put some pressure on the smuggling trade and on illegal reprinters in Edinburgh. In this they would be joined by a number of other heavyweight booksellers from London.

Much of the Scottish trade was in reprinting. The London literary proprietors saw the reprinters, not as people producing cheap books to the benefit of their country, but as pests taking the bread out of their mouths. Edward Dilly told Creech the Edinburgh booksellers who petitioned the House of Lords in 1774 'consist chiefly of low pirates'.[15] Strahan lumped reprinters and pirates together, and in 1778 a disaster at the Apollo Press of Edinburgh, which produced cheap copies of English poetry for John Bell's 109-volume London edition, quite cheered him up. 'I perceive that Martin's Printing house is burnt down,' he said to Creech, 'and I heartily wish it may have the Effect you suppose, in checking the Progress of Piracy, which has already nearly the ruined the Trade altogether.'[16] He lamented in the same year: 'The Importations from Ireland, I am afraid it is not in our Power to prevent. That and the laying open Literary Property in Britain, are two incurable Evils, which are likely to render Bookselling one of the most unprofitable and precarious, and of course the most disreputable, of all Trades.'[17]

Nevertheless, the Londoners chose not to attack the principle of limited copyright in the Court of Session, but instead concentrated on curtailing illegal reprinting of a copyrighted work, and importation from Ireland. The Act of 8 Anne protected through registration of copyright. The 1739 Act prohibited importation of a work for sale if it had been published in Britain during the previous 20 years: so, while reprinting was legal in Ireland, the editions became illegal when entering Britain.

London copyright holders took action in the Court of Session against particular imported titles being sold in Scotland. They also sought twice to prevent books coming in at the western ports, asking the Scottish Customs Commissioners to head off Irish editions of Blackstone's *Commentaries* and William Robertson's *History of America*. The Board circulated ports with its first warning on 12 January 1768: 'We have been informed that there has lately been printed in Ireland a pirated edition in Octavo of a book printed and published in England, entitled "Commentaries on the Laws of England" in Quarto, and of which the property still remains in the author Mr. Blackstone; we direct you to take notice that all such books as are brought into Great Britain, are forefeited by the Acts of 8 Anne cap 19 & 12 Geo cap 36 – and you are to give the strongest injunctions to all officers in your precinct, to use their utmost endeavours for seizing the same, or any other pirated edition printed abroad.'[18]

Edward Burrow, the collector at Port Glasgow, sprang into action: only eight days later he wrote to show that he had personally seized books brought from Dublin on the *Loving Ann*, David Dunlop master. The books had been entered as Irish, and therefore admissable on payment of duty if no questions had been asked, but Burrow's inspection showed they were 'only reprinted there'. There were 32 titles, most in multiple copies, and a number were described as 'tore', which I take to mean lacking title pages. They included Shakespeare's *Works* and Dryden's *Works* with false

London imprints; *The history of the Chevalier des Grieux*; *Amelia*, Dublin; Swift's *Works*, tore; *The adventures of a* guinea, London; *The cobler of Preston*, Dublin; *Flora; an opera*, Cork; Churchill's *Works*, London; *Clarissa*, Dublin; *The Sermons of Mr. Yorick*, tore; *The builder's jewel*, London; *The History of the Canary Islands*, tore; Robertson's *History of Scotland*, tore; *The history of Miss Delia Stanhope*, Dublin; *The Female Quixote*, Dublin; *The history of Lady Julia Mandeville*, Dublin. *The history of Miss Jenny Salisbury*, Dublin; Gay's *Fables*, London; *The Vicar of Wakefield*, Cork; *The history of Sir Charles Grandison*, London; *The history of Sir George Ellison*, Dublin; *The North Britain*, London. Burrow's final entry was: 'A pirated edition in octavo on the Commentaries on the Laws of England by Wm Blackstone Q[ui]res'.[19] The leaving of this to the end suggests a flourish by Burrow; on the other hand, the list shows what would have been imported if he had not searched.

The importation of Blackstone continued. The Board renewed its circular on 25 October 1769, and in 1772 wrote to the western ports: 'The Board has been informed that notwithstanding the directions contained in their letters . . . Commentaries on the Laws of England, still continues to be imported from Ireland, they therefore direct you again to admonish all the officers in your District to be particularly careful in the execution of their duty so that further complaints can be avoided.'[20]

In 1777 the Board circulated an order to the nine western Ports: 'Mr John Balfour, in behalf of himself and William Strachan & Thomas Caddell of London, purchasers of the History of America written by Doctor Robertson, having represented to the Board that they are apprehensive that a pirated edition of the said book will soon be smuggled from Ireland contrary to law, and desiring that the strictest search may be made on board all ships coming from Ireland, not only for the above edition, but for all such books that come within the said predicament. The Commissioners enjoin you and all the officers within the precinct of your port, to use your utmost endeavours to prevent the importation of any prohibited books, and to seize all such as shall be brought in, wherever they shall be found. R. E. P[hilips]'[21] Port Glasgow and Greenock did not pick up any Robertson this time. However, this order appears to have had an effect on the amount of Irish-printed books being imported openly.

Imports and Exports

Scottish-Irish trade in unbound books going through Scottish Customs 1755-1780[22]

Customs estimated these books at £8-£16 a hundredweight (112 lbs), taking the value at a median £12.

	Duty paid imported from Ireland cwt.lbs	total £.s.d	Duty free exported from Scotland cwt.lbs	total £.s.d
1755	0.0		2.0	£24.
1756	0.0		0.0	
1757	0.0		0.0	
1758	0.0		0.0	
1759	0.0		36.0	£432.
1760	0.0		32.0	£384.
1761	0.0		8.0	£96.
1762	7.56	£90.	20.84	£249.
1763	*Irvine 4.0	Irvine £48.	Irvine 22.56	Irvine £270.
1764	12.70	£151.10	48.30	£579.4.3
1765	4.7	£48.15	9.0	£108.
1766	1.90	£21.12.10	8.0	£96.
1767	21.93	£261.19.3	16.56	£198.
1768	10.90	£129.12.10	17.29	£207.2.1
1769	Irvine 18.39	Irvine £219.	Irvine 27.53	Irvine £327.
1770	17.32	£207.8.6	35.64	£426.17.2
1771	9.61	£114.14.4	44.56	£534.
1772	9.0	£108.	27.56	£330.
1773	7.28	£87.	25.20	£302.2.10
1774	25.84	£309.	17.0	£204.
1775	3.0	£36.	15.0	£180.
1776	6.56	£78.	8.56	£102.
1777	11.0	£132.	3.0	£36.
1778	0.0		6.0	£72
1779	0.0		18.44	£200.14.3
1780	1.0	£12	0.56	£6.4.3
1781	1.0	£12.	1.56	£18.

	Duty paid imported from Ireland	total £.s.d	Duty free exported from Scotland	total £.s.d
	cwt.lbs		cwt.lbs	
1782	0.0		2.66	£31.1.5
1783	2.56	£30.	14.108	£179.11.5
1784	0.0		26.76	£320.2.10
1785	1.80	£20.7.1	4.60	£54.8.7
1786	0.0		9.28	£112.1.5
1787	0.91	£9.4.3	7.32	£87.8.7
1788	1.28	£15.	3.90	£46.14.3
1790	0.0		0.0	

* National figures not available for 1763 and 1769: calculated for Irvine only.[23]
Over the period, Scotland exported to Ireland 69 hundredweight of bound books, valued at £10–£12 a hundredweight, or a median of £11. Some of these were taken by individuals for their own use.[24]

Books exported from Scotland were classified as 'British' and therefore duty free. Books from Ireland were of 'foreign composure, not French', and the duty for unbound was 7s.7d, and a fraction of a penny, per hundredweight. This imposition might have been reason in itself for avoidance of Customs by some importers. The Irish imports listed above were those that were given a certificate at the Irish port, were reported by the captain, and entered in Scotland upon payment of duty: it was intended that they come through Customs. They do not include books that were smuggled in or books that were seized from ships. The official Irish imports exceed Scottish exports in 1767, 1774 and 1777. What were these books? Surely they included reprinted English titles – reprinting was the staple of the Irish trade.[25] The seizure made by the Port Glasgow Collector in 1768, and those described below, show the kind of titles. The sudden drop of regular entries in 1778 parallels the Customs Commissioners' increased attention in the Irish reprints.

Anderson and Dow at Irvine

Irvine was the main port for the legal Scottish-Irish book trade, accounting for the bulk of the exports and imports in the period. The Irvine Collector's Quarterly Account books give the ship and captain, destination, weight of the books, duty on imports, the name of the shipper outwards, and say who was entering the books imported. Sometimes the book exports from Irvine surpassed the official national total, as in 1761, when the *Nugent*, with James Boyd or John Orr as master, made four trips to Belfast with 17 hundredweight of unbound books, and the *Thomas & Ann*, Thomas Fulton master, took two hundredweight to Dublin.[26] The difference between this and the national figure of eight hundredweight might be explained by the Customs discounting large amounts of books returned to western Scottish ports from Ireland 'for want of sale'. In this year at Irvine, for example, four hundredweight of British books were returned from Dublin for Robert Bell.

The leading shippers of books through Irvine by legitimate means, and therefore the main shippers in Scotland, were William Anderson and Daniel Dow. Anderson appeared 4 April 1767, bringing in three hundredweight 86 pounds of books from Dublin in the *Peggy & Jean*, Andrew Steel, master, for which he paid £1.8s.8d duty. Magnes Garrett, in the *Mayflower*, took books in both directions for Anderson: to Dublin with nearly four hundredweight of books in April 1768, back in June with 10 hundredweight, the duty being £3.16s.[27] From 1769 to 1771, Anderson brought in 17 book shipments from Dublin, 43 hundredweight 32 pounds; at the same time he sent 73 hundredweight to Dublin in 13 vessels. Anderson was at Irvine to enter the books until March 1769; his imprint as a bookseller in Stirling appears in 1770. Dow first began to ship and receive books for Anderson in August 1769 and continued to do so in his name until early 1771.[28] From then on Dow took over, and the Irish books he received accounted for a large part of the Scottish imports. In 1774, he took 20 hundredweight in six shipments from Dublin, while James Schaw received five hundredweight. Dow and Captain Magnes Garrett of Saltcoats owned the *Craufurd* and this ship was often used.[29]

On 3 October 1775 Dow paid £1.2s.9¾d duty at Irvine on three hundredweight of Irish books, which Garrett had brought from Dublin on the *Craufurd*.[30] He was smuggling books by the following year. In August, 1776, Garrett's ship, coming from Dublin, was boarded by officers from a Scottish Customs cutter based at the Old Kirk, or Inverkip, at the mouth of the Clyde. Alexander Thomson, the commander, said when he searched the vessel he found six parcels of unbound books of Irish printing. Since the books had no clearance from Customs at Dublin, Thomson seized them. The books were addressed to Daniel Dow, bookseller in Saltcoats, and consisted of 14 sets of Smith's *Wealth of nations*. 3 vols, 8vo; 21 sets of Gibbon's *Decline and fall of the Roman Empire*, 2 vols, 8vo; one Churchill's *Sermons*, 12mo; a set of Hooke's *Roman History*, 3 vols, 8vo; 28 Direction Books for St George's Channel.[31]

Seizures at Port Irvine

Some of the Irvine Collectors' Letterbooks have survived for this period, and these show a number of book seizures.[32] Common reasons for stopping books from Ireland at Irvine were the lack of the required certification and/or an attempt to avoid duty, after which the legality of the books would be queried. Sometimes, though, illicit reprinting was the primary reason. When suspicious books were held, a list of the titles was sent to the Board in Edinburgh, and instructions awaited.

In September 1762, in the *Assistance* from Belfast, the land surveyor stopped four small bundles containing unbound folio Bibles with Apocrypha, and some odd volumes of Hume's *History* in sheets, because they had no address; the master, John Young, said he did not report them because they were going to America. The Board let Robert Urie retrieve the books as long as he exported them.[33] In 1764, 25 copies of Lady Mary Wortley Montagu's *Letters* were seized along with other prohibited titles. They comprised three hundredweight 56 pounds of unbound books, which James Alexander, master of the *Warrington* from Belfast, entered and paid the duty for Alexander Kincaid of Edinburgh and James Knox, bookseller in Glasgow. The accompanying letter of James Hay of Belfast somehow caused the Comptroller to go to the shore and have the land surveyor open the packages. The books were forfeited, and the duty repaid.[34]

In 1765 a hundredweight of books was seized; when they were condemned, the Board's solicitor sent instructions on how to make them waste paper, which suggests the procedure was new to the Port.[35] When the *Prosperity* arrived from Belfast in October 1766 John Thom the Master 'through inadvertancy' forgot to report four bundles of unbound books along with his other cargo, so they were taken to the warehouse, where they were seen to be 10 Bibles and 57 quires of *Poor Robin's Almanack* for 1767. James Meuros, bookseller in Kilmarnock, said he had not commissioned them, and to save the Irish owners putting him to trouble and expense, he asked that they be returned to Belfast. Meuros changed his mind and asked for delivery, but the books were condemned.[36] Robert

Urie petitioned in 1767 for the return of seized books but the Controller was told to damask them and make them into waste paper.[37]

The Customs kept a 'List of seizures of customable & exciseable goods to be condemned', which gave the reason for the seizure and the recoverable worth of the goods. Condemned books were damasked and had no value. In 1766, the *Jean & Betty* of Irvine was seized, along with 'a parcel of unbound books, rum, brandy, sope, salt'; the reason for seizing the books was non-payment of duty. Unbound Bibles were condemned in 1767 for non-payment of duties at Irvine. In 1775 a parcel of books was seized 'having been first published here'.[38]

Drunk in Charge of an Irish Piracy

On 15 September 1773, acting on information from Patrick Corbett of the Excise, four Customs men went to the River Clyde in Glasgow and boarded a gabert, a boat used for loading and unloading other vessels. The first parcel they found contained 36 Bibles in sheets. John Cummine, the land carrriage surveyor in charge of the raid, gave the parcel to James Wallace, a land carriage waiter, and carried on rummaging. Instead of taking the Bibles to the Customs warehouse, Wallace stopped off at a public house in the Broomielaw, and there the Glasgow printer Joseph Galbraith, who had ordered the books from Ireland, and the gabert owner, Archibald Campbell, formed a plan. They got Wallace drunk, and Galbraith pressed six shillings into his hand and told him to go and bribe someone for the parcel of Bibles; the other books they knew would be seized. Wallace laid the books down in the pub, and set off for the gabert.

Meanwhile, the Customs officers had found 27 more Bibles, 100 *Apocrypha*, 25 'sermon books', 15 primers and 180 history books, all unbound. Corbett, standing by, was first to be offered the money by Wallace. Corbett turned him down, and advised the others to do the same, saying it was a snare laid for them to get them in trouble with their superiors. Unsuccessful, Wallace returned to the public house, but the Bibles were gone.

The Bibles Cummine had were probably the same kind as the stolen ones, and he learned from Alexander Kincaid, the King's Printer, that they had a fraudulent design to evade Customs. Cummine reported: 'The Bibles in question were printed in the name of Mr Watkins, predecessor to the present King's printer in Edinbro, and were Page for Page with his, as we are informed by Mr Kincaid, but that we apprehend was by way of deception & makes Galbreath's case the worse as it shews he must have ordered them from Ireland under the Imprimatur purely to deceive the officers.'

On 20 September Cummine sent Galbraith a stern official letter: 'First you are to be represented to the Board for offering Bribes to one of the Customs' Officers & likewise deluding the Officer with false persuations, that by so doing you & companions got him intoxicated with drink, when you & some of your companions deforsed him of the Bibles, for which you shall be brought in at the utmost Rigour of the Law for so doing. And in the second place you are to be represented to the King's Printer for causing any prints to be printed in Ireland in Mr Kincaid's name . . . to defraud the King from the Revenue of Excise of both paper & prints, for which the penalty follows, £500 sterling. To this you'll please give your answer now . . . returning the same Bibles with bearer.'

Galbraith coolly sent back a bill by the bearer, saying that if the Customs did not return his 36 Bibles in two months, they were to pay him £3.13s sterling. The Customs wanted to prosecute, and even interviewed the public house owner to try to get evidence. But Wallace had been so drunk – 'or as he calls it stupid & infatuated' – that he could not have testified accurately, and without this there was no proof against Galbraith.[39]

Books stopped at Port Glasgow and Greenock

The Customs could not stop smugglers using the Clyde coast. In 1768 the Port Glasgow Collector, Edward Burrow, wrote to the Board to say he found 'the method of smuggling has now taken a diff[eren]t turn in this river, and that the cutters concerned in that illicit trade, instead of coming up the river so far as the Old Kirk [Inverkip, five miles from Greenock] & there discharging, do land their cargoes in Arran, from whence it is convey'd in open boats to different places up the river, & there secretly hid & deposited till the same can be carried off, & the boats immediately go away.'[40] Senior Customs officers of Port Glasgow and its member port, Greenock, were asked by the Board in November 1785 for their observations on smuggling, and the picture they gave was of a service not coping. They said a considerable quantity of prohibited goods were being smuggled into their area, such as spirits, tea and salt, and in the herring season there were around 400 boats off the coast, which smuggled with impunity; the high duty on commodities, particularly on tobacco, created the illegal trade. Salaries were too low, and younger and fitter men should be employed at the waterside, in place of the decrepit older ones who could not follow instructions.[41] At the Ports, the ships were not always searched thoroughly, either deliberately or through inefficiency.[42] It was in this context that Irish books were smuggled into the west of Scotland.

How many books came through Port Glasgow and Greenock unreported is unknowable. However, the officers there did examine incoming books more closely than their counterparts at Irvine, and this was recognized. The annual import figures of books from Ireland, when compared with the Collectors' quarterly accounts for Irvine, show that Irvine was the port of choice for shippers getting books through Customs. By 1786 the bookseller Charles Elliot considered Greenock too strict for smuggling. In earlier years, though, there was still an attempt at bluff by the bookseller. The Glasgow waterside officers opened a parcel of unbound books from Dublin 12 November 1767. They said these had been entered as Irish, but were different works first published in England and reprinted in Ireland, 'and some said at the bottom to be printed in London, though manifestly of type with those printed in Ireland'. The shipper said officials at Greenock had not objected to similar books, so why should they, and this caused the Collector, Edward Burrow, to make enquiries there.[43]

Earlier in 1767 a parcel of books and pamphlets was seized for non-payment of duties and damasked.[44] Edward Burrow found many titles when he was looking for Blackstone's *Commentaries* in 1768, as previously described. Irish printed books were condemned in 1777 for importation contrary to to the 1739 Act.[45] It was probably on shore in Glasgow that Peter Wright, land carriage waiter, seized six parcels of Irish books in sheets in May 1777: 2 *Receuil Francoise*, 32 Boston's *Memoirs*, 2 Parnell's *Poems*, 4 Sherlock on *Death*, 2 Pope's *Homer* 2 vols, 12 Raynal's *History* 2 vols, 2 *Essays on praise of women*, 23 Ambrose's *War with devils*, 8 Hill's *Arithmetic*, 12 Goldsmith's *Essays*, 18 Young's *Works* 6 vols, 8 Haddington's *Poems*, 9 Delincourt's *Christian consolations*.[46]

Books returned from Ireland 'for want of sale' were stopped frequently at Greenock and Port Glasgow, and the procedure required to claim them reveal a number of Irish-Scottish trade connections. William Duncan of Glasgow claimed for books sent from Belfast to New York and returned to Greenock in 1761.[47] James Magee of Belfast returned books to John and James Robertson of Glasgow, James Meuros of Kilmarnock, and Anderson at Stirling in 1777, and sent back John Brown's *Dictionary of the Holy Bible* to Anderson in 1783.[48] The books for the Robertsons got off the ship without a certificate from Belfast, but were seized on shore by an officer, who thought they were Irish books. William Gilbert of Dublin returned Plans of Edinburgh to Alexander Kincaid, in 1786, and books to Charles Elliot twice in 1787.[49] Alexander Wilson & Sons of Glasgow sent five boxes of type to John Magee of Dublin for printing a newspaper and these were stopped at Dublin because the wrong weight was on the certificate.[50]

Attempts continued to be made to get books in illegally. A Collector's letter to the Board described a seizure made in July 1784:

We humbly acquaint your Honors, that Robert Punton & George Todd, Boatmen at Greenock, from some suspicions arising to them in rummaging the Matty, Daniel Ferguson Master, arrived from Dublin, brought to the Customhouse there, on [1 July], eleven parcels of books bound and unbound, which they alledged were intended to be privately got on shore – and having directed them to be brought up to the warehouse hither and examined we find.

That eight bundles contain 310 copies half bound, and 100 copies stitched in paper covers, of Dr Blairs Sermons, and 9 bundles contain six copies of Dr Johnsons Dictionary of the English Language, the fourth edition, printed at Dublin 1775.

Doctor Blairs Sermons are all marked in the title page, London printed 1784, and belong to one Thomas Stewart, who was formerly a bookseller in Glasgow, and came passenger in said ship, being now settled in Dublin, who came and threat[e]ned the Collector with a Protest, and demanded their delivery; but with which he refused to comply, considering the words "London printed 1784" as only a deception.

The other 3 bundles are addressed to Mr Charles Elliot, Bookseller in Edinburgh.

As this trade of importing Irish books ought no doubt to be checked, we have commended the two officers for this instance of their attention, to prevent these bundles being got on shore, and we humbly pray your Honours directions concerning them.

17th July 1784.
PS The Collector understands Dr Blairs copy's right of the Sermons to be now in Mr Creech and others, to whom he has sent 2 volumes and desired him to lay them before your honors.[51]

It is a vivid sketch: the bundles not intended for regular entry, the bluster of the owner, the false imprint, the large number of the pirated Blair, the officers looking for a reward, the awareness of Creech's interest. Blair's *Sermons* were a prime copyright for Strahan, Cadell and Creech, vol.1 being in its 12th edition, vol.2 in its 9th. The duodecimo brought in from Ireland reprinted both in one volume.[52] Johnson's *Dictionary* was the two-volume quarto published at Dublin by Thomas Ewing; Strahan, Cadell and Dodsley owned the copyright. The Board ordered the books to be sent to Creech in Edinburgh, along with the titles seized by the Excise in 1781-2. Creech reimbursed the Collector 16s.4d for the carriage, and sent a £10 reward for the officers involved – the two boatmen and Brisbane, Corbett and Semple; the Board said it was 'to be distributed in proportion to the value of the books'.[53] Stewart was not the only book smuggler aboard the ship: the three bundles for Charles Elliot, sent by William Gilbert of Dublin, also contained Johnson's *Dictionary* and were due to be taken off secretly, too.

Charles Elliot

Charles Elliot had a shop in Parliament Close from around 1771 until 1790. In these years he built up a large bookselling and publishing business, selling books in Scotland, America, Ireland, Europe, London, and English provincial towns. In London, his main connections were with the George Robinsons and Thomas Cadell. He traded nearly £5,000 worth of books to the Robinsons between 1782 and 1788, nearly £4,000 to Cadell in the same period (Elliot Ledgers). There were other London correspondents, including John Murray;[54] and he opened a shop in London in 1786 in partnership with his brother-in-law, Thomas Kay. He published a great deal, specializing in the work of the Edinburgh medical men. The records of this substantial bookseller have survived.[55]

Elliot's correpondence includes many letters to Irish booksellers and to his friend, William Anderson of Stirling. Elliot paid Anderson to be his supplier of illegal reprints from Ireland. 'I must pay Mr Anderson 10 p[ercen]t or take the risque upon myself,' Elliot told a Dublin bookseller. 'I believe the former is my surest way.'[56] Elliot's attitude to illegal Irish reprints changed over the years. At the beginning of his career he sought them out, and in 1775 he ordered from Anderson, specifying that they had to have false 'London Titles': up to 6 copies of Hume's *History of England*, 8 vols; up to 6 Blackstone's *Commentaries*; 6 Robertson's *History of Scotland*; 6 Davidson's *Virgil*, 2 vols; 6 or 12 *Gulliver's travels*; 1 or 2 Voltaire's *Works*, 24 vols; 1 or 2 Hooke's *Roman History*, 8 vols.[57]

In 1776 a group of leading booksellers in the city formed the Edinburgh Booksellers' Society; Elliot joined, and was present when they agreed that no member would buy books falling within the Queen Anne Copyright Act, unless they were published by the legal proprietor.[58] However, in 1777 he asked Anderson for 6 Hume's *History*, a dozen Davidson's *Virgil*, 1 *Humphrey Clinker*, 2 *Yorick's Sermons*, and told him to send to Ireland for a small format *pharmacopoeia*. Elliot rationalized that his sets of the Hume had been bought before the Society was formed.[59] Later in the year he warned Anderson about an order: 'I hope all the Dublin books have London titles, at least the capital one[s].'[60] Elliot and

Anderson exchanged books rather than pay cash. 'I have no doubt what you say of the exchange being in my favour,' Elliot said in 1781, 'were there not so much Irish and contraband books, being more than two thirds of these . . . I have not the same advantage of sales as in others, as I cannot expose them publickly, and were I not getting them from a Gentleman of your honour I would not touch a book.' Elliot was discussing an exchange valued at £249. He accepted the reckoning, but would not enter it in his books or keep a copy in case Anderson should be caught.[61]

In 1779 Thomas Cadell queried the books marked Dublin in an Elliot sales catalogue, and Elliot replied that any there, were outside the copyright statute and had come from the stock of the late William Auld. 'I do not look upon myself as obliged to give so strick [sic] an account of my transactions but I wish by all means to be clear of the smallest suspicion which I think you have once or twice hinted on this head agt. me. I have sent books to Ireland and generally got very bad accounts of them but never in my life recd. one single book from the Country.'[62] This was not true, although at the time his Irish-printed books had all come from Anderson.

Elliot was in touch with a number of Irish booksellers to whom he wished to sell books. In 1774, John Magee was in Edinburgh with an order from his father, James Magee of Belfast. Elliot sent octavo Bibles back with John, but had to ask Anderson for the 100 copies of Hervey's *Meditations* Magee wanted.[63] In the same year, Elliot began a correspondence with Thomas Ewing of Dublin, sending over 500 proposals for Van Swieten's *Commentaries upon Boerhaave's Aphorisms*, 18 vols 12mo. Elliot said he had heard about Ewing dealing in medical books from students from Dublin.[64] John Hay Junior of Belfast saw Elliot in Edinburgh and ordered Ramsay's *Songs*.[65] Elliot also did business with the Dublin booksellers James Williams, William Hallhead, James Sleater, William Wilson, and John Magee. Luke White was a frequent correspondent from 1782, William Gilbert from 1783.

Anderson visited Ireland in the spring of 1776 and invited Elliot along. Elliot regretted he could not go, but gave Anderson commissions in Dublin – to call on Ewing and ask what he thought about the Van Swieten proposals; to ask Williams what had happened to a medical manuscript sent by Lewis Borthwick of Ireland; to sell the Van Swieten and Rollin's *Ancient History*, 10 vols 12mo; to get papers for Dr Cleghorn from merchants in St Mary's Abbey; to look for a good correspondent.[66]

When Sleater of Dublin offered in 1778 to sell him books, Elliot was ambivalent. 'I am sorry to say that Irish books does not answer here Cleverly. Such books as are not property we have them within ourselves, such as are property it is neither fair nor proper to sell or keep them.' However, he agreed to take 22 titles from Sleater, for £30.19s.6d, including 4 *Annual Register*, 19 vols, and 4 Gray's *Poetical Works*. 'I should be very well pleased to have the Annual Register London Titles, as I frequently export books. It is in this way I get clear of Irish copies.' He urged Sleater to take some of his multi-volume publications. 'You have no risque in receiving my books but I have a great one in getting over yours.'[67]

The willingness to oblige an Irish bookseller he hoped would take his books arose again in an introductory letter to William Wilson in Dublin. An Irish medical student had recommended the name, so Elliot sent his 220-page catalogue and asked Wilson to sell on commission. He said they were not free in Edinburgh to sell reprints of British property, and it would be doubly cruel of him to do so, because he had some copyrights himself. But 'if at any time I can with propriety take or dispose of any of your copies will cheerfully do it. You may perhaps be a stranger to the mode of proceeding here in these cases, they are exceeding troublesome and dangerous.' However, 'I think a man of honour should not altogether be bound by law & Acts of Parl[iamen]t.' Wilson should let Elliot know what he had, since he exported a great deal.[68]

Elliot was pleased when Gilbert took 50 copies of Cullen's *First lines of the practice of physic* in 1784; he said Thomas Cadell was taking 1,250, but he recognized the field was wider in London. Elliot preferred Gilbert and tried to support him against White. Hearing White intended to reprint the Cullen, he had some words with him by letter, then said to Gilbert: 'I can easily see he's a queer fellow. Do not be browbeat by any of your neighbours. I am convinced if you were buying 100s I could supply you in many common books as you print in Dublin – if you will stand by me I shall stand by you.' He even offered to print an edition for Gilbert that would be the same price as White's, on the condition that it was not reimported to Britain to compete with his own.[69]

Luke White was told several times by Elliot not to send copyrighted books without an order. Smuggling problems began for the Edinburgh man when White ignored his directions. In the spring of 1783 Elliot ran out of copies of a medical school text, William Cullen's *Materia Medica*. The current edition was owned by William Creech, but was, apparently, out of print, so Elliot asked White to send Irish reprints of the Cullen as well as works in French. This White did, and added on speculation a number of Dublin reprints of English copyright. Learning about these, Elliot told White to warn Gordon & Millar, booksellers and agents at Greenock, so that they could enter the bale with Customs and pay duty; he was sure there would be no problem getting it in if this were done. White did not write to the agents, and the captain did not report the bale, which had the wrong initials on it – EE instead of CE. Customs officers took the mysterious unclaimed package and left it in the warehouse. Elliot petitioned the Commissioners, saying he did not know what White had sent, and no fraud was intended. The Board sent for a list of title pages, then ordered the port to detain Cullen's *Lectures on the Materia Medica*, 2nd edition, Dublin, for Whitestone, 1783; John Jortin's *Sermons on different subjects*, 3rd edition, Dublin, for Whitestone, Sleater, Williams, Wilson and others, 1783; Thomas Pennant, *The journey from London to Chester*, Dublin, for Luke White, 1783; Robert Wood, *An essay on the original genius and writings of Homer*, Dublin, for William Hallhead, 1776; *Elements of general history translated from the French of the Abbe Millot*, Dublin, for Price, Potts, Cross, Jenkin and others, 1779.[70]

Elliot still needed the *Materia Medica* for the students. He told Gilbert to send him 40 or 50 copies care of Daniel Dow at Saltcoats, and to follow Dow's directions; Gilbert was, however, 'to clear them out properly at the [Dublin] Custom house'.[71] Elliot told Dow: 'you may say to [Gilbert] how he should direct – it is not books properly prohibited – but I wish to avoid trouble'.[72] Dow evidently got them through successfully. Elliot was not prepared to give up on the 23 copies sent by White, and he got them a year later. Dr Cullen even wrote to the Commissioners, saying he would not have any copies for sale in Britain for some time, and he had no objection to Elliot getting them from Ireland. The Board consented, as long as the duty was paid, and a moderate sum was given to the officer who stopped them.[73]

In 1784 on speculation, Gilbert shipped six copies of Johnson's *Dictionary*, 4th edition, Dublin, 1775; he at first said he would send them by Elliot's preferred routes, by either Dow at Saltcoats, or Alexander Forsythe, bookseller in Ayr, and Elliot thought 'all was safe'.[74] But Gilbert changed his mind and sent them to Greenock. Elliot told Gordon & Millar that Gilbert 'has taken out a Clearance but in case of detection I wish you could get them on shore privately, the Duty is a mere trifle, but the last things I had coming were kept 12 mo[nths] before I got them.'[75] They were still on the ship when they were seized along with the 410 copies of Blair's *Sermons* and the Johnson's *Dictionaries* being smuggled by Thomas Stewart. Elliot told Gilbert he was wrong to send the Johnson by

Greenock, and he would probably never get them back. He gave it a try, anyway, and petitioned the Commissioners that Gilbert thought the copyright on Johnson had expired in Britain, and he hoped they would send the books back to Dublin. He concluded: 'I am happy to find the Officers at the Port of Greenock are so attentive, by w[hic]h the smuggling of Property books into this Country will be chequed, & I hope altogether prevented, few being so much interested in the protection of Literary Property in this country as, Gentlemen, Charles Elliot.'[76] It did not work.

In 1786 a consignment of books from White was once more seized at Greenock. Elliot reminded White he had ordered only French titles, and said he was sorry White had sent British copyrighted books. He said Greenock confiscated such books without reserve; Saltcoats or Ayr were the places to use, with a proper agent. Elliot said he did not want to run the risk of ordering English titles, and he might well have been worried about his reputation. 'It is, do you know, a kind of affront to have such detected.'[77] The books had not been examined yet, so Elliot told the Customs Board he was expecting only French ones, gave a list of titles, and said, 'Cause some of the officers that can read so as to distinguish French from English to inspect the said two bales or bundles'.[78] The sarcasm was picked up along the line. John Schaw, the land surveyor at Greenock, to whom Elliot had sold books over the years, said he had read what they were 'as well as we can' and drew up a list of English books not mentioned by Elliot. Schaw said none of them had title pages, but he believed them to be Dublin printed and some private property.[79] The list was passed to William Creech for his opinion. He said, 'Your gentlemen at Greenock and Port Glasgow not only read and write well, but distinguish very properly the books importable from the others.' Creech scanned the title-less volumes and, after identifying them, commented on the forging of title-pages in Scotland:

1.   Law dictionary 5 vols. This probably Cunningham's Law Dictionary, and if so it is property. I never heard an original work of this kind being composed and printed in Ireland.
2.   Voyage to the Cape of good Hope. This is Sparrman, a late London publication in two vols quarto, the property of Mr. Geo. Robinson.
3.   Cook's Voyages, the property of Mr Caddell and Mr Geo. Nicol, London.
4.   Essays on the Intellectual Powers of Man. This is Dr Reid's work, a late publication & the property of Mr. John Bell, Edinburgh; English Dictionary – if Johnson's, not importable. No books printed or reprinted in Britain within 20 years being importable from Ireland.
5.   Plays for a Private Theatre. This I know nothing of. If Haley's, it is property.

6. Raynall's History of the East & West Indies. This J. O. Justamond's translation is the property of Mr. Caddell, London.
7. Moral & Political Philosophy. This is a late publication by Mr Paley of Carlisle and is the property of Mr Faulder, London.
[bundle] no.2
1. Horatii Opera – not property.
2. History of Ireland, by the Editors of the Modern History – this is a parce [part] publication from the Modern History & belongs to the proprietors of that work.
3. Adelaide and Theodore, or Letters on Education. This translation is the property of Mr Caddell, London. If not an original translation of Ireland, not importable into Britain.

The other articles in No.2 being Latin and French books are not property & are importable on payment of the dutys.

What Mr Schaw observes points out is a fraud frequently practised. Books printed in Dublin which are British Property are often without title pages to disguise them, and title pages are afterwards printed in Scotland, bearing that the books is printed by the real proprietor in London or Edinburgh. If any of the books seized were my property, I would think it my duty to reward the officers.

W. Creech
Edinburgh 9 March 1786

In consequence of the report I made yesterday respecting the books that were property and not importable into Britain, I beg leave to inform you that having the authority from Mr Caddell & Mr Strahan of London, I shall take charge of these articles and be answerable as upon former occasions.[80]

Elliot did not sound perturbed by the seizure. 'The Custom house people are exceedingly troublesome,' he told White. 'I have not yet got any of the Books. I dare say I will get the French but the English I will never see. They have been so alarmed of late by importations that nothing can escape by Greenock.'[81] He was right about the books: the Board ordered that those that were property to be delivered up to the owners or their agents, and those printed in Britain within the last 20 years be forfeited; the Latin and French books were not property and could be admitted to entry. The Board also told the port that literary proprietors could prosecute for penalties, and also that the importers of illegal books, meaning Elliot, could be prosecuted by any person.[82] Elliot received the French titles a few months later, complaining mildly that he got them cheaper from Lyons. His main concern was to show that if White took 300 or 500 copies of any book not reprinted in Dublin, Elliot could supply them cheaper than Dublin printing. 'If it was not the danger we run I could sell many Books from Dublin but I am determined never to run the risk.'[83] When White subsequently said he was sending reprints worth £66 Irish – they were to go via Chester – Elliot declined them.[84]

Pursuers and Defenders

London copyright holders, members of the Stationers' Company, often pursued cases in the Court of Session to stop particular titles imported from Ireland being sold, and to halt the reprinting and sale of piracies in Scotland. A Writer to the Signet acted as agent, or attorney, during the procedures at the Court Session; James Walker was the agent in a number of cases. A summons was drawn up with the charges and the redress sought, and the booksellers and printers were served by a court messenger-at-arms and ordered to appear. The case was usually heard by a single judge sitting in the Outer House, but could go to the Inner House in front of a panel of judges. If the judge agreed with the pursuers, he gave a Decree, or judgment, against the defenders. Getting a Decree was the primary objective for the pursuer: it sustained his copyright, served as a warning, and the procedure leading to it caused the pirate to spend time and money. In cases concentrating on one or two main offenders, various other booksellers and printers might be summonsed but would never appear, and possibly were not expected to. A Decree in Absence was given against them and a point made; it could be taken up if they continued to sell a named piracy. A primary source for the copyright cases is the unextracted processes in the cases, at the Scottish Record Office. The unextracted processes always contain the summons but vary in the amount of other papers remaining in the bundle.

There was a consistency in the stances of defenders and pursuers in the piracy cases. The defenders required their accusers to show power of attorney to the Scots lawyer, the entry in the Stationers' Register, and the copyright agreement with the author or owner of the literary property; the pursuers also had to prove their case was brought within three months of an offence. The pursuers cited the terms of the 1710 Copyright Act and the 1739 Importation Act and asked for the penalties – damasking and a penny a sheet under 8 Anne; forfeiture, a fine of £5, and double the value of every book for the importations. The pursuers usually put a size to the editions in the complaints, but these were guesses, or a ploy – as when they said in several cases that the defender had been involved with a number of editions of 10,000 copies each. Clearly the pursuers were concerned about the amount of illegal books, Irish and Scots, being printed and sold. Their problem was in learning the actual number of copies, and most times they were in the dark. The Court of Session would not grant their requests to sequestrate the contents of book-trade premises, and the Scots bookseller would resist giving information. On some occasions, though, the pursuers achieved their goal – they were able to have the Edinburgh printers interrogated about piracies of Lord Chesterfield's *Letters* and Sterne's *Works* and *Sentimental journey*, for example, and they knew the numbers and titles taken in the Excise seizures of 1781-2. The Pursuers often asked for enormous damages – £1,000 or £2,000 – but the Court of Session's position was that there were no damages in common law available when the pursuers were also asking for penalties, and I have not seen evidence that the defenders had to pay such sums. The pursuers asked for their expenses in bringing the process, and this they would get if they were awarded the Decree.

The London copyright booksellers were on the look-out for piracies. In 1772 one of the Dillys wrote to Kincaid & Creech: 'Gentlemen . . . if you can possibly hear of any bookseller in Edinr that has taken from the Irish booksellers Entick Dict. Spelling, Langhornes' Plutarch, or any other of our London property please to inform me directly and I will give orders to the Attorney to Prosecute immediately. Shall be glad to hear how he goes on with [William] Anderson for selling Nugents Dict – Mr Cadell will be glad to be informed of anything belonging to him is offered by the Irish Booksellers.'[85] Charles and Edward Dilly currently had separate actions against Anderson of Stirling and William Gordon of Edinburgh for importing and selling 'many copies' of Thomas Nugent's *A new pocket dictionary of the French and English languages*, Dublin, printed for James Williams, 1770, in contravention of the 1739 Act.[86]

Early in 1773 William Johnston, of Ludgate Street, London, pursued the piracy of two titles. For Henry Brooke's *The fool of quality*, his advocate showed entry at Stationers' Hall of four volumes in 1769, and the fifth in 1770. He said that between 1769 and 1772, one or more editions of 3,000 copies had been printed or sold in four and in five volumes duodecimo by John Reid, printer in Edinburgh, William Darling, Robert Clark, Alexander McCaslan, John Wood and James McCleish, booksellers in Edinburgh, and by William Anderson. The printer John Robertson was dropped from the summons.[87] The second piracy was Tobias Smollett's *The expedition of Humphry Clinker*, which Johnson and Benjamin Collins of Salisbury said had been printed and sold in an edition of 3,000 copies, in 1771-2, by the Edinburgh printer Robert Mundell, the Edinburgh booksellers William Darling, Charles Elliot, Robert Clark, John Wood, James Dickson, Alexander McCaslan, and by William Anderson.[88]

In December 1774 *Letters written by the Right Honourable Philip Dormer Stanhope, Earl of Chesterfield, to his son* . . . Edinburgh, printed for C. Macfarquhar, and sold by the booksellers, 1775, 4 vols 12mo, was finished printing and copies were reaching Edinburgh shops. When he heard about this, and that an Irish edition was also being sold in Edinburgh, James Dodsley, who had paid around £1,500 for the copyright, had the agent James Walker take out an interdict to stop the sale of both. The injunction was against a large section of the Edinburgh trade, including Creech and John Balfour.[89] The real targets were the publishers of the edition – Macfarquhar, Elliot, and George Douglas, paper merchant. There were two cases. The first, during which Dodsley had to take out a security of £500, ended in July 1775 with the interdict against selling the Irish and Edinburgh editions being made permanent during the remaining term of Dodsley's copyright. The defence that the Edinburgh edition was legitimate – it was different from Dodsley's because of new material, and Dodsley did not get permission from Lord Chesterfield directly – was rejected by the court. Dodsley then tried to get damages and penalties. Macfarquhar, Elliot and Douglas were the only defenders represented. Summonses for selling the Irish and Scottish editions were taken out against, in Edinburgh, William Millar, William Gordon, John Bell, William Gray, James Brown, James McCleish, William Darling, James Dickson, John Wood, and Gavin Alston, and in Glasgow, James Knox, John Smith, Peter Tait, and Dunlop & Wilson; a Decree in Absence was given against them when they did not appear. Big numbers were put in the charge: that in the last four months of 1774 they had all participated in three pirated editions of 10,000 copies and had imported another edition of 10,000.

The pursuer made an issue of the secret preparation of Chesterfield's *Letters*. Macfarquhar said his name on the imprint showed he did not think of it as piracy. If he had, 'he could have concealed his name from public view, and ushered this Scotch edition into the world, "London printed", as spurious editions and literary encroachments usually are.'[90] As the case went against him, Macfarquhar offered to make a deal: give Dodsley £100 for the right to sell the Edinburgh edition; or sell all the copies to Dodsley, or a bookseller on his behalf; or give Dodsley 500 copies.[91] To Dodsley, this conjured up a vision of an infinite Scottish piracy: 'Numberless copies of the book, in the same form, paper and type, and, perhaps, even dignified on the title page with the name of *Colin Macfarquhar* as printer, might come to be distributed, and all under the pretence of being part of this very impression, without his having it in his power to detect the fraud.'[92]

Dodsley wanted the copies confiscated because he feared the edition might be exported to America. Macfarquhar said through his lawyer, however, that he could not hand in the books because he had now exported them all to Ireland. Called up before the judges, Macfarquhar confessed he had been lying. Of the 1,500 copies printed, 1,000 had been sent to England, 300 had been sold locally, and his partner Douglas had 200. Half the English copies had already been sold there. The court put him on a surety of £200 to get the unsold copies back from England within five weeks, and ordered that they be damasked along with the remainder of the edition. In all, 700 copies were damasked. The case did not end until 1777 because Macfarquhar and Douglas intended to appeal to the House of Lords; but they were advised against this.

Thomas Becket raised an action in Edinburgh in 1773 against Martin & Wotherspoon and others there, and John Barrie and others in Glasgow, for printing and selling a Scottish edition of Laurence Sterne's *Works* and for selling an Irish edition.[93] He left the process hanging and said he thought he had succeeded in stopping the sale, but in June 1775 David Willison printed another edition of the *Works* and of *A sentimental journey*, and there were imported Irish copies of Sterne being sold. Becket was joined by Cadell and Strahan in the new prosecution.[94] The pursuers needed to know the size of the impression and applied for a sequestration order to seize copies in a dozen premises – because 'the defenders obstinately refuse to give any information' – but the court would not grant this.[95] Instead, they gained an interdict, apparently for a month, to stop sales of the Irish and Scottish Sterne, then were granted a Decree in Absence against Charles Elliot, William Gordon, John Bell, William Gray, James Brown, James McCleish, William Darling, James Dickson, John Wood and Lachlan Forsyth. None of these booksellers took part in the case: the defender was Willison, and he offered the pursuers his printing profit, £30. This was rejected by Strahan, who wrote to Creech: 'I am entirely of your opinion with regard to the Pirate of Sterne; both because £30 is no adequate Compensation for the offence; by which he must have made at least four times the Money, but chiefly to prevent, by some striking Examples, the Continuance of that pernicious Traffic. I have therefore written to Mr Walker (of whom I am glad you have so good an opinion) to prosecute the offender to the utmost, without listening to any Terms of Accommodation whatever.'[96]

Willison eventually admitted that he had printed 1,000 copies of *The works of Laurence Sterne* for the paper-maker Robert Douglas, with 15 extra, and that he printed 500 copies of *A sentimental journey*. He produced an entry for Douglas from his printing ledger: '1775 June 10. To Sterne's Works, 7 vols, 80 2/3 shts Small Pica Bible Crown 12mo 1000 cop @ £1.5.4 p sht. allowing 1/10d more than proportion for odd 2/3 sht. £102.5s.4 8/12d.'[97] The pursuers had him undertake a 'judicial examination', to answer under oath questions put by a lawyer for the court, but in the three hours there he gave little away and did not say what booksellers received copies.[98] Becket, Cadell and Strahan had produced certificates from Stationers' Hall for only volumes 3 to 7 of the *Sermons* and for *A sentimental Journey* and they restricted their claim to penalties to these. The court ruled in 1778 that Willison should pay them a penny a sheet, £112.19s.11½d sterling, and that they had the right to damask all the copies if these should ever be discovered within the term of their copyright. They were also given expenses.[99] None of this stopped the sale of illegal Sterne reprints in Edinburgh: during the case, Elliot asked Anderson (1777) for two sets of *Yorick's Sermons*. Perhaps this was from the missing Edinburgh edition, or simply Anderson's usual Irish suppliers.

Early in 1781, to stop the piracy of *A father's legacy to his daughters by the late Dr. Gregory*, Strahan, Cadell and Creech prosecuted the Edinburgh booksellers John Bell, James Dickson, Alexander Brown and Patrick Anderson.[100] Now, Creech would help organize the prosecutions over the Excise seizures, but he wanted to keep quiet about his involvement. After Anderson's summons had been served, Strahan wrote to Creech: 'I am glad this Prosecution of Anderson is carrying on vigorously. Your Name, to be sure, has no business to be mentioned in this Matter, and shall not by any body here. Tis a Pity we cannot get at Dunlop and Wilson, who certainly were not ignorant of the Contents of the Parcels. I wish we may be able to put a Check to this illicit Trade, which tears up our Property by the very Roots.'[101]

Strahan and Cadell did prosecute Dunlop and Wilson, but the Glasgow booksellers were cleared.[102] Liddell of Glasgow was charged by Strahan and Cadell with pirating David Hume's *History* and Dr John Moore's *A view of society and manners in Italy* and *A view of society and manners in France, Switzerland and Germany*. The pursuers used a blanket statement for this and the following Anderson and Morison summonses: that the defender had printed or sold three illegal editions of 10,000 copies each, and had also imported an edition of 10,000 copies, part of which had been seized. These are remarkably high quantities to expect of a bookseller moving his books around Glasgow in a wagon. Liddell did not come to court, and with no defence presented, the judge gave a Decree against him in Absence.[103] Anderson was charged by Strahan, Cadell and James Dodsley with pirating Johnson's *Dictionary*. He defended the case, and began by querying whether the 1739 Act was still in force, making the prosecution show it had been renewed.[104] The pursuers said Anderson had been selling and importing books illegally for a number of years, and that he had commissioned the copies of Johnson from Ireland; they said Anderson's attempts to get the seized books back proved they were his property.[105] The remaining papers in the case are lost – they were borrowed by legal clerks subsequently and not returned to the bundle; an inventory shows, though, that Anderson was fighting his corner.[106] A Decree was given against him on 18 December 1782.[107]

Robert Morison and Son of Perth were contrite. They were charged in two court actions that ran together – by Strahan and Cadell with importing William Robertson's *The History of Scotland, The History of Charles V,* and *The History of America,* and by Strahan, Cadell and Dodsley with importing Johnson's *Dictionary*.[108] According to the formula in the summonses, the Morisons were involved with 40,000 illegal books each time. The proceedings brought this and the two £1,000 claims for damages down to earth. James Boswell, lawyer for the Morisons, said they had ordered the books in November, 1781, on the application of a bookseller in Ireland: 'this they did ignorantly and in the belief that since the Irish bill[109] there was neither evil nor danger in importing them, in which idea they were encouraged not only by the bookseller in Ireland, but by the open manner in which Irish books are bought and sold in this Country, and they accordingly imported them not by any means in a secret way but openly and avowedly, the consequences of which they were immediately seized and the present action brought.' Since they had no intention of encroaching on the pursuers' property, 'from the moment they understood their mistake, in place of defending it or entering into any litigation upon the subject, as they understand many of the booksellers in this Country were to do, to acknowledge the fact at once.' Boswell said the Morisons had never done anything of this kind before, and never would again.[110] Six copies of each of the Robertson and 12 copies of the Johnson had been confiscated altogether. The pursuers said that since the Morisons had 'fairly and candidly acknowledged their fault', they would restrict their penalties to the value of the Robertson copies, £2.15s, and to that of the Johnson, £7.13s. The judge modified this to a total of £6, including expenses.[111]

When Anderson and the Edinburgh printer John Robertson published an edition of Fanny Burney's *Cecilia*, the court ruled that the Act of

8 Anne provided penalties, not damages, but because the book was a deliberate fraud, Anderson had to pay a sum to Thomas Payne and Thomas Cadell. Payne and Cadell bought the copyright to the book but neglected to enter it at Stationers' Hall. Anderson and Robertson reprinted an almost exact replica, copying print, paper and title page, and were sued for damages in 1787. They were prohibited from selling copies with the same title page, and had to pay the expenses. Anderson was ordered to pay damages of £10.[112] At the same time, Andrew Strahan, Cadell, and Daniel Prince of Oxford prosecuted Anderson and Robertson for publishing an edition of William Blackstone's *Commentaries on the laws of England*. Anderson learned he was required by the court to do what a Scots defender tried to avoid – say how many copies he sold. In the Minute of his evidence, we catch an ironic voice from Stirling: 'Mr Anderson answered that hitherto he has taken no share in the management of the present process, having left it entirely to the other Defender Mr Robertson to conduct in any manner he thought proper. How far Mr Anderson was well advised in reposing this unbounded confidence in the other Defender Mr Robertson it is needless at present to enquire.' Anderson said he had sold 299 copies of the *Commentaries* to persons with whom he kept accounts, and 50 or 60 were exchanged with booksellers but not entered in his records.[113]

Summary and conclusion

The Morisons of Perth referred to 'the open manner in which Irish books are bought and sold in this Country'. Irish reprints came to Scotland in various ways. There were significant imports into Irvine for some years up to the mid-1770s, brought in by William Anderson and Daniel Dow. Open importation almost stopped at the time of the searches ordered by the Customs Commissioners, but books arrived covertly. Some Irish-printed books came on vessels into port but were never meant to see Customs. The officers at the ports studied made a number of seizures, and the scale of these is a pointer to the number getting through by various means. The gabert searched on the Clyde in 1773 would have unloaded the books from another vessel. Books were run from Dublin to avoid Customs altogether: Magnes Garrett took them off his brig at Saltcoats in 1781 and avoided detection at the shore; five years earlier the smuggled books he was carrying had been stopped at sea. Distribution inland was by carrier's wagon. The Excise seizures on Glasgow streets over a few months in 1781-2 stopped books going to Stirling, Glasgow and Perth, and a bookseller from conveying his stock; this has the air of normal business being interrupted. The preference of book runners for Irvine and Saltcoats over Port Glasgow/Greenock is shown in the activities of Dow and Anderson, the official imports and the Irvine Collectors accounts up to 1777, and in the arrangements made by Charles Elliot.

William Anderson was a major figure in the traffic in Irish reprints and Scottish piracies. Charles Elliot paid him a commission to bring in books for Ireland; in 1782 two-thirds of Elliot's exchange with him was 'Irish and contraband books'. A leading Edinburgh bookseller with his own copyrights, Elliot traded with eminent London booksellers, yet took Irish reprints for export and advised Irish booksellers how to get illegal reprints through. Customs records and Elliot's corrrepondence give evidence of a Scottish-Irish book trade.

The Scottish book trade in the second half of the century relied on registration at Stationers' Hall for their own copyrights, as a guide to what they could reprint, and as a line of defence in the prosecutions brought against them. Registration was also central to the London booksellers pursuing Scots under the 1710 Copyright Act and the 1739 Importation Act. When London booksellers brought charges in it was often over two versions of the same title, the Irish and Scottish, being sold in Scotland at the same time. The Court of Session processes provide detail of a number of editions and of the interplay in the book trade. The Londoners had some successes in court, and a bookseller like Elliot could not openly sell illicit books in Edinburgh, yet Anderson continued.

Often the reprints were exported from Ireland to Scotland with false London titles, and Charles Elliot wanted at least the capital ones to be in that state. The Bibles left in a Broomielaw public house in 1773 were designed in Ireland, on order from the Glasgow printer, to look like those by a King's Printer of the 1750s. Many books came in without a title page – William Creech said it was 'a fraud frequently practised'. This disguised the book during importation, and in Scotland, a fake title page would be printed to imitate that of the London or Edinburgh publisher.

References

1. Mary Pollard, *Dublin's trade in books 1550-1800*, (Oxford, 1989), pp.74-109, found, in a preliminary investigation, few seizures by Customs and little sign of an influx of Irish reprints into Britain.
2. All described in Glasgow City Archives: CE60/1/13, Customs letterbook, Port Glasgow and Greenock, Collector to Board, 26 Sept. 1781.

3. SRO: RH4/26A/3, Dalguise Muniments, Creech Correspondence, Strahan to Creech; cited with permission of Anderson Strathern, W. S., Edinburgh. I am grateful to Richard Sher for pointing out the relevance of these letters to this study.
4. SRO: CS229/S6/17, unextracted process, Strahan and Cadell against Anderson.
5. GCA: CE60/1/13, Port Glasgow and Greenock, Collector to Board, 23 Oct. 1781, with Girvin's letter of 19 Oct.
6. SRO: CE17/1, Customs Board Minute book, pp.218-219, 14 Nov. 1781.
7. GCA: CE60/1/14, Port Glasgow and Greenock, Collector to Board, 16 March 1782, including the titles of Liddell's books, with Girvin's letter of 15 March; CE60/2/321, Board to Collector, 9 April 1782.
8. GCA: CE60/1/15, Port Glasgow and Greenock, Collector to Board, 3 May 1783.
9. GCA: CE60/2/323, Port Glasgow and Greenock, Board to Collector, 8 March 1785.
10. GCA: CE60/2/275, Port Glasgow and Greenock, Board to Collector, Creech's opinion, 9 March 1786.
11. Pollard, pp.76-7 on the Stationers' Company promising rewards to officers after the 1739 Importation Act; the money was to come from penalties and forfeitures.
12. Warren McDougall, 'Copyright litigation in the Court of Session 1738-1749, and the rise of the Scottish book Trade', *Edinburgh Bibliographical Society Transactions*, vol.V part 5 (1988), pp.2-31; John Feather, *Publishing, Piracy and Politics: an historical study of copyright in Britain* (London, 1994), pp.64-96.
13. *Records of the Worshipful Company of Stationers 1554-1920*, ed. Robin Myers (Chadwyck-Healey, 1985), part one reel 7, p.25.
14. See Richard B. Sher, '*Charles V* and the book trade: an episode in Enlightenment print culture', in *William Robertson and the Expansion of Europe*, ed. Stewart J. Brown (Cambridge, 1997), pp.164-95, and Sher's continuing work on the publishing of the Scottish Enlightenment.
15. Dalguise Muniments, Dilly to Creech, 30 April 1774.
16. Dalguise Muniments, Strahan to Creech, 28 Aug. 1778.
17. Dalguise Muniments, Strahan to Creech, 19 Nov. 1778.
18. SRO: CE14/3 Scottish Customs, General Orders Scotland, 1753-85.
19. SRO: Port Glasgow and Greenock, Board to Collector, 20 Jan. 1768, with Burrow's personal return of seizure 6 June 1768.
20. Scottish Customs, General Orders Scotland, 1753-85, 5 March 1772.
21. Scottish Customs, General Orders Scotland, 1753-85, 17 June 1777; punctuation supplied.
22. SRO: Customs, imports and exports, RH2/4/10-25 (photostat of PRO Customs 14); RH20/1-13; Scottish-Irish trade 1774-83 in RH20/24-26.
23. From the Custom Collector's Quarterly Accounts for Irvine. SRO: E504/18/5 and E504/18/7.
24. e.g. James McAdam took 3 cwt of student's books on the *Nancy* for Belfast, James Alexander master, 29 April 1790: Collector's Quarterly Accounts, Irvine, E504/18/12.
25. Pollard, p.66 and throughout for Irish reprints.
26. E504/18/5, Collector's Accounts, Irvine, 1760-5.
27. E504/18/6, pp.235, 253.
28. E504/18/7.
29. Their ownership is referred to in E504/18/12, 4 Aug. and 21 Sept. 1789.
30. E504/18/8.
31. SRO: E504/28/26, Port Glasgow, p.16, 20 Aug. 1776.

32. Glasgow City Archives. Extant for the period under discussion are Collector to Board, CE71/1/1, 1757-60; CE71/1/2, 1765-7; CE71/13, 1772-6; and three letterbooks from Board to Collector.
33. CE71/1/2, 17 and 31 July 1765.
34. CE71/1/2, 13 Sept. 1765, 18 June 1766; CE71/2/55, Board to Collector, 6 Nov. 1765.
35. CE71/1/2, 8 Nov. 1765, 8 July 1766.
36. CE71/1/2, 25 Oct. 1766; CE71/2/55, Board to Collector, 27 Oct. 1766.
37. CE71/2/55, Board to Collector 15 Sept. 1767.
38. SRO: E369/45, Candlemas term 1766, 1767, Lammas term 1775.
39. GCA: CE60/1/7, Port Glasgow Collector to Board, p.159, 2 Oct. 1773; p.188-9, 13 Nov. 1773; p.203, 30 Dec. 1773. CE60/2/269, Board to Collector, p.166 and p.210, 30 and 31 Dec. 1773.
40. GCA: CE60/1/5, 13 Oct. 1768.
41. GCA: CE60/1/18, Port Glasgow, Collector to Board, pp.58-61.
42. An officer at Broomielaw was dismissed for letting a cargo pass (CE60/2/273, 18 Nov. 1782); John Schaw of Greenock was fined for failing to see a cargo he passed did not exist, the captain subsequently sinking the ship for insurance (CE60/2/323 25 Nov. 1784); the rheumaticky tide surveyor at Glasgow did not go on board ships to supervise his tidesmen's searches, and was taken to task when his men missed an illegal shipment of rum (CE60/1/19 4 Oct. 1786).
43. GCA: CE60/2/359, Port Glasgow, Surveyor's copy of letters, p.14.
44. SRO: Exchequer, E369/45, 'List of seizures of customable & exciseable goods to be condemned in Whitsuntide term 1768.'
45. SRO: Exchequer, E369/47, 'List of seizures . . . condemned in Candlemas term 1777.'
46. GCA: CE60/1/9, Port Glasgow Collector to Board, p.295.
47. GCA: CE60/1/3, p.22.
48. GCA: 60/1/10, 3 and 19 Sept. 1777 and CE60/2/70 28 May, 15 Sept. 1777; CE60/1/15, p.137, 2 May 1783.
49. GCA: for Kincaid, CE60/2/275, 18 Sept. 1786, and CE60/2/324 18-26 Sept. 1786; for Elliot, CE60/2/235, 11 May 1787 and CE60/1/19, 10 May 1787.
50. GCA: CE60/2/322, 18 June 1783.
51. GCA: CE60/1/16, Port Glasgow Collector to Board, p.156.
52. *Eighteenth-Century Short Title Catalogue* t104656.
53. GCA: CE60/1/16, Port Glasgow Collector to Board, pp.317-18, 28 Dec. 1784; pp.324-45, 11-13 Jan. 1785; CE60/1/17, p.336, 10 Sept. 1785; CE60/2/323, Board to Collector, 20 Dec. 1784, 6 Jan. and 8 March 1785.
54. William Zachs describes the extensive dealings with Murray in his forthcoming book, *The first John Murray and the late 18th-Century book trade*. I am grateful to Dr Zachs for comments on this paper.
55. Elliot's papers are in the John Murray Archives, London. They probably reached the firm by way of Elliot's daughter, Ann, who married the second John Murray, and were rediscovered recently by William Zachs. I am grateful to Mrs Virginia Murray, the Archivist, for enabling me to work on them. I am currently indexing Elliot's eight outletter books and four ledgers, with the support of a grant from The Bibliographical Society in association with the Antiquarian Booksellers' Association.
56. Elliot to James Sleater, Dublin, 8 June 1778.
57. Elliot to Anderson, Stirling, 14 July 1775.

58. NLS: Ms.Dep.301 no.1. For the Society, see Richard B. Sher's forthcoming paper, 'Corporatism and consensus in the late Eighteenth-Century book trade: the Edinburgh Booksellers' Society in comparative perspective'.
59. Elliot to Anderson, Stirling, 3 April 1777.
60. Elliot to Anderson, Stirling, 29 Oct. 1777.
61. Elliot to Anderson, Stirling, 2 June 1781.
62. Elliot to Cadell, London, 27 Dec. 1779.
63. Elliot to Anderson, 7 May 1774, to James Magee, Belfast, 11 June 1774.
64. Elliot to Ewing, Dublin, 12 May 1775.
65. Elliot to Hay junior, Belfast, 5 Dec. 1775.
66. Elliot to Anderson, Stirling, 4 May 1776.
67. Elliot to Sleater, Dublin, 8 June 1778.
68. Elliot to Wilson, Dublin, 19 June 1778.
69. Elliot to Gilbert, Dublin, February, 20 May and 17 June 1784; to White, Dublin, 7 June 1784.
70. Elliot to White, Dublin, 17 Dec. 1782, 12 April, 9 June and 9 July 1783. GCA: CE60/1/15, Port Glasgow Collector to Board, p.122, 18 April 1783, pp.137-9, 2 May 1783; CE60/2/273, Board to Collector, 16 April 1783; CE60/2/322, Board to Collector, 27 May 1783.
71. Elliot to Gilbert, Dublin, 28 Oct. and 19 Nov. 1783.
72. Elliot to Dow, Saltcoats, 28 Oct. 1783.
73. GCA: CE60/2/322, Board to Collector, 3 May 1784.
74. Elliot to Gilbert, Dublin, 23 June and 8 July 1784.
75. Elliot to Gordon & Millar, 21 June 1784.
76. GCA: CE60/2/322, Collector to Board, 21 July 1784.
77. Elliot to White, 7 March 1786; Elliot to James Millar & Co, Greenock, 8 March 1786.
78. GCA: C60/2/324, Board to Collector, 23 Feb. 1786.
79. GCA: 60/1/18, Collector to Board, 3 March 1786.
80. GCA: CE60/2/275 and CE60/2/324, 8 March 1786; punctuation supplied.
81. Elliot to White, Dublin, 25 March 1786.
82. GCA: CE60/2/324, 15 March 1786.
83. Elliot to White, Dublin, 22 June 1786.
84. Elliot to White, Dublin, 17 Aug. 1787.
85. Dalguise Muniments, Edward and Charles Dilly to Creech, 2 March 1772.
86. SRO: unextracted processes, CS237/D3/12, Dilly v. Gordon; CS237/D3/15, Dilly v. Anderson.
87. Unextracted process, CS229/J/55, Johnston v. Robertson and others.
88. Unextracted process, Johnston and Collins v. Mundell and others.
89. The booksellers John Balfour, William Creech, William Miller, Charles Elliot, William Gordon, John Bell, William Gray, James Brown, James McCleish, William Darling, James Dickson, William Drummond and John Wood; and the printers Robert Fleming, John Robertson, Colin Macfarqhuar. Gavin Alston, Murray & Cochran, and Martin & Wotherspoon. Signet Library: Session Papers 347 (1771-6), No.2, 'Bill of Suspension for James Dodsley', 21 Dec. 1774.
90. SL: April 25 1775, Answers for Colin Macfarquhar, printer in Edinburgh, and others, to the Petition of James Dodsley, bookseller in London, and his attorney, p.2.

91. SL: Dec. 14 1775, Answers for Colin Macfarquhar, printer in Edinburgh, and others; to the Petition of James Dodsley bookseller in London, and James Walker Writer to the Signet, his Attorney, pp.6-7.
92. SL Dec. 18 1775, Replies for James Dodsley bookseller in London, and James Walker Writer to the Signet, his Attorney; to the Answers for Colin Macfarquhar printer in Edinburgh, and others, p.4.
93. SRO: CS16/1/156, General Minute book, 24 July 1773.
94. SRO: CS229/B/3/20, 25 Nov 1775; all the MSS papers in the case are in this bundle, including a receipt and assignments from Sterne.
95. CS229/B/3/20, Petition Messrs Thomas Becket & others 1776; 1 Dec. 1775, Lord Kennet, Minutes in the Process Becket and others against Willison etc.
96. Dalguise Muniments, Strahan to Creech, 2 Feb. 1776.
97. CS229/B/3/20, Excerpts from D. Willison's Books.
98. CS229/B/3/20, Declaration of David Willison [2 Dec.] 1777.
99. CS229/B/3/20, 25 June 1778, Lord Kennet, Minutes in the process Messrs Becket and Company and their attorney against David Willieson.
100. SRO: CS229/S6/3, January 1781; they were summonsed 29 Nov. 1780. John Bell defended the charge; the others had a Decreet in Absence given against them.
101. Dalguise Muniments, Strahan to Creech, 20 Nov. 1781.
102. SRO: *General Minute Book of the Court of Session, commencing 15th January 1782*, vol.1, Edinburgh, 1782, p.304, 1 Aug. 1783.
103. SRO: unextracted process, CS229/S6/32, Strahan against Liddell, 20 June 1782; *General Minute Book of the Court of Session*, vol.1, p.189, 18 June 1782.
104. SRO: unextracted process, CS229/S6/17, Strahan and Cadell against Anderson.
105. CS229/S6/17, 1 March 1782, Condescendence for Messrs Strahan, Cadell and Dodsley.
106. SRO: CS51/21, Receipt and transmission book, 7 Dec. 1784, shows that taken away were an amendment to the charge, two condescendences for the pursuers, answers for Anderson, a representation for Anderson, answers for the pursuers, and a note by Lord Braxfield.
107. *General Minute Book of the Court of Session*, vol.1.
108. SRO: 28 June 1782, unextracted processes, CS229/S6/33 for the Robertson, and CS229/S6/27 for the Johnson. The papers cited below are in both bundles.
109. Ending restriction on Irish trade to the colonies: Pollard, pp.143-4.
110. 1782, Representation for Robert Morison & Son; punctuation supplied.
111. June 1783, Answers for Messrs. Strahan, Cadell and Dodsley; 3 July 1783, Lord Ankerville's note in Representation for Robert Morison & Son.
112. William Maxwell Morison, *The Decisions of the Court of Session*, Edinburgh 1811, Literary Property, 17 July 1787.
113. SRO, unextracted process, CS228/S7/27, Strahan against Anderson & Robertson, 'Minute for William Anderson 1787'.

Wales and the Stationers' Company

PHILIP HENRY JONES

AT A COURT MEETING held on 30 September 1589 it was ordered that Richard Tottell and two others should be 'discharged & Removed from their adsistanceships' in the Company in order to expedite the execution of its business. Tottell was continually absent because he had moved to 'the furthest parts of the Realme',[1] Wiston in Pembrokeshire. The episode epitomizes the attitude of the Stationers' Company towards Wales and things Welsh: Wales lay, both literally and figuratively, at the very periphery of its interest. The few occasions when the Company was compelled to pay attention to Welsh books were when disputes arose over Welsh translations of English books. Thus Dean Nowell's *Least Catechism* in English was part of the privilege of John Day but Richard Jones had had 'the same copie in the welche tonge to him orderly licenced' by the Wardens. A face-saving compromise was signed by Day's son and Jones on 18 June 1578 whereby Jones agreed to print the catechism in the name of John Day and as his assign, but the Welsh copy was to 'properlie belonge' to Jones just as if he had printed the work in his own name.[2] Eiluned Rees has discussed in some detail similar problems which arose in 1630 over a clash of rights to the Welsh Psalms, the patent for the Bible being held by Robert Barker, but the Psalms belonging to the Stationers' Company by virtue of the royal grant of 1603.[3]

The subject of this paper, however, is not the Stationers' Company and Wales but Wales and the Stationers' Company. Although the Stationers' Company could normally afford to ignore Wales, until the end of the seventeenth century virtually all Welsh authors and Welshmen who wished to pursue a career in the book trade had to look to London and thus had to become involved with the Company. If one takes a Wales-centred rather than a London-centred view, two main questions emerge, firstly the contribution the Company's registers make to our knowledge of early Welsh-language books, and secondly, the nature of its Welsh apprentices and their varying fortunes.

In assessing the Company's contribution to the Welsh bibliographical record an appropriate starting point might be to ask how many Welsh-language titles would we remain ignorant of, had the Stationers' archives failed to survive the Fire of London? In other words, how many items from the first 120 years or so of Welsh-language printing are known today only through register entries? Several categories of works would leave no trace. The earliest Welsh-language printed books, beginning with Sir John Prise's *Yny llyvyr hwnn* (*In this book*) of 1546 and its immediate successors, a series of works which owed their appearance to the humanist and fervent Protestant, William Salesbury, had appeared before the Stationers' Company received its charter. Even after 1557, works printed under royal patent would not have been entered. There is, for example, no entry for the greatest Welsh publishing achievement, Bishop Morgan's 1588 Bible, which was covered by Christopher Barker's patent. Welsh books produced outside London would not have been entered. Joseph Barnes commenced the sequence of Oxford-printed Welsh books in 1595 when he printed *Perl mewn adfyd*, a translation of Coverdale's *A Spyrytuall and moost Precious Pearl*, and the Oxford press may have been responsible for as many as three other Welsh-language titles by about 1600.[4] Although no copy has survived of the first edition of 1653 of *Gwaedd Ynghymru* (*An outcry in Wales*) by Morgan Llwyd, convincing evidence exists that it was the first Welsh book to be printed in Dublin.[5]

During the sixteenth century religious and humanist works by Welsh recusants were printed abroad, initially in Milan (1567) and perhaps Paris, and also on clandestine presses in Wales itself. The best-documented of the latter was the press in Rhiwledin cave (near present-day Llandudno) where, in all probability, Roger Thackwell and others printed the first part of *Y Drych Cristianogawl* (*The Christian Mirror*) in 1587, but Professor Geraint Gruffydd has suggested that at various times up to about 1600 there may have been as many as four other secret presses in Wales and the borders.[6] These were responsible for printing the extant *Ynglynion*, sacred verses by Gruffydd Robert, and the *Carolau*, religious poems by Richard White, a copy of which was seen by the pioneering Welsh bibliographer Moses Williams in the early eighteenth century but no longer survives.

Even those Welsh-language books printed in London might not be entered: because they were not worth pirating, entry would simply have been a waste of money. Welsh books were not a commercial venture and virtually all of those published up to the later seventeenth century had to be subsidized. Robert Crowley, for instance, assisted Salesbury's publications of 1550-1, and the London-Welsh stationer, Humphrey Toy, financed Salesbury's New Testament and Welsh Book of Common Prayer of 1567. From the later seventeenth century onwards, religious charities such as the Welsh Trust and the SPCK became important sources of support. A notable seventeenth-century example of a work gaining sufficient popularity to require the protection provided by entry is the collection of popular devotional and improving verse by Rhys Prichard, *Canwyll y Cymru* (*The Welshmen's Candle*):[7] as sales built up and successive editions were required the value of the copy was recognized and the fourth edition was entered in 1672.

Despite these omissions, the Company's registers make a valuable contribution to the historical bibliography of Wales. They record seven otherwise unknown pre-1600 items in Welsh, as well as William Morgan's sermon preached at the funeral of Sir Ieuan Lloyd of Bodidris[8] and Hugh Griffith's '*Epytaphe*' to the same worthy.[9] Between 1600 and 1666 a further six Welsh-language works are known only from register entries. The wording of certain entries (for instance 'a book to be printed in Welshe intituled *A godly meditation of the soule*')[10] suggests that some of these books may have been entered but not printed. Other works may have been published in very small editions, if indeed they appeared at all. Yet other entries, such as the 'cathechesme in Welshe' entered by Richard Jones in 1566-7,[11] and the 'Prymer in Welshe' entered by Thomas Chard in 1599,[12] are for the kind of popular work which was 'thumbed out of existence'[13] and had a poor chance of survival even in English.

To turn from output to personnel: what role did the Company play in the early development of the Welsh book trade? Although estimates of the population of Wales vary, it would appear that it rose from about 250,000 in the 1530s to perhaps some 400,000 by the 1640s.[14] This substantial increase sustained an outflow of emigrants from all ranks of Welsh society to England, a process which had begun in the Middle Ages but gained new impetus from 1485 onwards as the accession of Henry VII opened new avenues to advancement. Welsh emigrants were widely dispersed throughout England,[15] but London was the great magnet and it has been suggested that the Welsh may have comprised about one per cent of the capital's population in the mid-sixteenth century.[16] Some, such as students at the Inns of Court, were temporary residents, but others settled in London permanently. A few, such as the Myddelton brothers, Thomas (1550-1631) and Hugh (1560-1631), younger sons of a prominent Denbighshire landed family, became leading figures in the commercial life of London and were involved in extensive ventures on a national scale.[17] The involvement of Welshmen in the London book trade should be viewed against this background.

Richard Jones, made a Brother in August 1564,[18] proudly proclaimed his Welsh origins through his famous 'Heb Ddieu heb ddim' device which was eventually acquired by Jaggard.[19] Attempts to identify other Welsh members of the Company up to 1562 have relied upon the rather unsatisfactory method of selecting what appear to be distinctively 'Welsh' names.[20] Owen Ap Roger (freed in 1555 and subsequently a troublesome member of the Company) is probably a safe identification,[21] but apparently clear-cut examples of Welsh names prove on closer inspection to be second- or even third-generation immigrants – John Appryce (bound in 1564) was the son of John Ap Price, a deceased yeoman of London,[22] and Giles Appryse (bound in 1565) the son of Rowland Appryse of Hereford.[23] On the other hand, the bearers of such apparently non-Welsh names as Rutte, Hobby, Wall, Crewe, and Egerton all came directly from Wales.

C. Y. Ferdinand's exemplary study of the demography of the Stationers' Company understandably, given the relatively small number of Welsh apprentices, treats Wales as a single unit.[24] However, as has been pointed out, there are significant variations in recruitment between different parts of Wales.[25] In an attempt to illustrate these and highlight other differences I have examined the first-generation Welsh apprentices listed in Arber and in Professor D. F. McKenzie's three lists of Stationers' Company apprentices.[26] For such an analysis, four broad periods suggest themselves: up to 1600, 1601-40 (the latter date is of even greater significance for Wales than for England, as no more than three apprentices from predominantly Royalist Wales were entered during the 1640s), 1641-1700, and 1701-1800.

Of the 205 first-generation Welsh apprentices recorded up to the end of 1800, at least 98 (48%) survived disease and the multifarious temptations of life in the capital and were freed.[27] Setting aside the period up to 1600, where the loss of the records for 1571-6 complicates matters, there are slight variations in the percentage of apprentices gaining their freedom, well over half (56%) of those apprenticed between 1641 and 1700 (37 of 66) doing so, as opposed to rather less than half (45%) of those apprenticed between 1601 and 1640 (25 of 55), and 48% of those apprenticed between 1701 and 1800 (23 of 48). Taking the period as a whole, in most instances the father's occupation did not significantly affect his son's prospects of gaining his freedom. Thus 44.6% of gentlemen's sons were freed and 45.6% of yeomen's sons. The sons of husbandmen and labourers fared rather worse, 38.8% (7 of 18) being freed. The two most striking exceptions are that none of the four sons of esquires were freed, and that 60% (12 of 20) of the sons of clerks gained their freedom. Perhaps surprisingly, only five apprentices are recorded as having run away from their masters. Two of them, Robert Rutte, a gentleman's son from Denbigh bound to Walter Dight in 1596,[28] and Evan Edwardes from Montgomeryshire who was bound to John Smethwick in 1597,[29] vanish without further trace. Two others returned and were forgiven; Henry Hughes, who must have fled shortly after being bound to William Parry on 24 March 1586, was readmitted on 4 October,[30] and Mathew Evans, who ran away at some point from the printer Thomas Ratcliffe to whom he had been bound in 1669, was freed by Ratcliffe in 1678.[31] A fifth runaway, John Bush, a gentleman's son from Carew in Pembrokeshire who was apprenticed to John Kingston in 1630,[32] appears to fall into a different category. Bush was reported as having 'gone beyond sea' by January 1626,[33] a form of words which raises the possibility that he was a Catholic *émigré*.

The county which supplied the greatest number of recruits was Denbighshire (41), followed by Montgomeryshire (31), Flintshire (23), and Monmouth (20). Denbighshire's contribution – a fifth of the total – was, however, concentrated in the pre-1700 period. Only two Denbighshire apprentices were entered for the whole of the eighteenth century, as opposed to ten from Montgomeryshire. Radnorshire, which had provided no more than seven apprentices up to 1700, supplied nine between 1701 and 1800, a figure which may indicate its growing anglicization and consequent isolation from Welsh Wales and its expanding Welsh-language book trade. As Professor McKenzie has pointed out, the remoter Welsh counties were poorly represented.[34] His description of these areas as 'desolate' is certainly true of Cardiganshire and Merioneth; despite substantial population growth the latter did not send an apprentice to London between 1594 and 1683. Relatively prosperous counties such as Pembrokeshire and Glamorgan are also poorly represented, the former with ten and the latter only nine for the whole of the period to 1800. The most probable explanation is that enterprising young men (and a few women) from South Wales tended to take advantage of the area's strong trading links by sea with Bristol: almost an eighth of the 1,426 apprentices bound in Bristol between 1532 and 1542 came from Wales.[35] The absence of any apprentices from Anglesey after 1638 may similarly be attributed to that county's tendency to regard Dublin (and subsequently Liverpool) rather than London as its economic capital. The very diverse pattern of recruitment suggests that Wales should not be treated as a unified whole. The border counties, particularly Denbighshire, Montgomery, and Flintshire, had experienced considerable in-migration from England in the later middle ages and again from the mid-sixteenth century to the

Restoration and were areas of considerable cultural cross-fertilization, the immigrants learning Welsh and immersing themselves in Welsh culture while exposing the Welsh to new cultural influences and giving them some knowledge of the English language. The 'remoteness' of west Wales owed as much to differences in language and culture as to its geography.

Up to 1600, the sons of yeomen (17) constituted the largest group of entrants (47%), followed by the sons of husbandmen (6). Between 1601 and 1640 yeomen's sons remained the largest group (20 or 36%), but gentlemen's sons (18 or 32%) now came a close second. Gentlemen's sons came to the fore between 1641 and 1700, numbering 29 (44%) if two sons of esquires are also included, well ahead of the 17 sons of yeomen (26%). The pattern changed between 1701 and 1801, as the sons of farmers (10) narrowly outnumbered those of gentlemen and esquires (9). Social categories are notoriously difficult to define; in particular it is debatable whether being a 'gentleman' in Wales (where greater emphasis might be placed on lineage than on wealth) was equivalent to being a gentleman in England. The surnames of the gentlemen's sons apprenticed – Nanney, Hanmer, Puleston – are those of families well known to students of Welsh history and may represent younger sons or cadet branches.

Although the sons of craftsmen and tradesmen constituted about a third of all English-born apprentices between 1601 and 1640, comparatively few Welsh-born apprentices fell into this category: only 5 of 35 (14%) up to 1600, 5 of 55 (9%) between 1601 and 1640, and the same percentage (6 of 66) between 1641 and 1700. This marked contrast with England requires further exploration, as does the fact that so few sons of Welsh clerks were apprenticed: only one to 1600, 7 of 55 (13%) between 1601 and 1640, and 5 of 66 (7.5%) between 1641 and 1700. The percentage of apprentices whose fathers were dead at the time of binding declined sharply during the first three periods: 12 of 36 (33%) up to 1600, 10 of 55 (18%) between 1601 and 1640, and 9 of 66 (13.6%) between 1641 and 1700, but then increased markedly during the eighteenth century to 41.5% (20 of 48). An interesting development in the eighteenth century is that London-Welsh charities bound a few apprentices to London stationers, though these were all the children of Welsh parents already resident in London.[36]

As in England, local and family links were important factors in recruitment throughout the period. The importance of religious affiliations is generally more difficult to trace, but it is worth noting that both of the apprentices bound to Andrew and Tace Sowle came from areas of Wales where Quakerism was strong in the later seventeenth century. Joseph Ellis from Y Bala was bound to Andrew Sowle on 13 April 1694 but apparently never freed.[37] His father, Cadwallader Ellis, schoolmaster at Y Bala, may well have been the Cadwalader Ellis of that town who sold the Dublin-printed *Testament y dauddeg Padriarch* (Testament of the twelve Patriarchs) in 1700.[38] Phillip Gwillim, from Casgob in Radnorshire, was apprenticed to Tace Sowle in April 1696 and freed in 1703.[39] In 1711 he printed *Traethawd ymarferol am gyflawn-awdurdod Duw*,[40] a Welsh translation of *A Practical discourse of God's Sovereignty* by Eliseus Cole. Gwillim prospered sufficiently to be cloathed in 1717 and served as Renter Warden in 1727.

The lack of information about the occupations of many masters and the fact that many of them pursued two or more trades means that the following figures concerning the trades to which apprentices were bound can be no more than a rough, minimal approximation. Of the Welsh apprentices bound before 1601, at least 61% (22 of 36) were apprenticed to masters active in the book trade, twenty of them to booksellers (some of whom were also printers and/or bookbinders) and two to printers. One was apprenticed to a 'stationer' and the remaining thirteen to masters whose trade is not recorded. The proportion of those bound to masters active in the book trade between 1601 and 1640 was 56% (31 of 55), twenty to booksellers, nine to printers and two to bookbinders. Two were bound to stationers, two to followers of other trades, and twenty to masters whose occupation is unknown. Between 1641 and 1700, 73% (48 of 66) were bound to members of the book trade. Although 27 were bound to booksellers and one to a bookbinder, the most striking feature is the increase (to twenty) in the number bound to printers. Two masters were simply described as 'stationers', five followed other trades, and eleven cannot be allocated. Finally, between 1701 and 1800, at least 58% of entrants (28 of 48) were bound to masters engaged in some branch of the book trade. Within this group, printing predominated, seventeen apprentices being bound to printers, nine to booksellers and three to bookbinders. In addition, five apprentices were bound to 'stationers', three to printsellers, and one to a copper-plate printer.

Few first-generation Welsh apprentices rose to occupy major office in the Company. Indeed, no more than fifteen (or possibly sixteen) were cloathed.[41] The printer John Salisbury, bound in 1677 to Thomas Cockerill 1 and freed in 1684,[42] has gained a dubious immortality through being described by Dunton as 'a desperate, Hypergorgonick Welshman', a 'Silly, Empty, Morose, Fellow' who 'wou'd hector the Best Man of the trade'.[43] Dunton further notes that Salisbury went to law with the Stationers' Company 'to keep himself from the Livery', presumably in an attempt to avoid the fine of £40 for refusal without reasonable excuse.[44] The two first-generation Welsh entrants who advanced furthest towards high office in the company were Phillip Gwillim (already noted as Renter Warden in 1727) and Rice Williams, son of an Anglesey gentleman, who was bound to the bookseller Anthony Gilman in June 1603, freed in June 1610, cloathed 4 July 1625, and fined for Renter Warden on 22 March 1637.[45]

The commercial success enjoyed by first-generation Welsh stationers varied. Augustine Mathewes, the son of a cordwainer of Betws Cedewain in Montgomeryshire, became one of the most productive printers of his day.[46] Apprenticed in March 1608 to the printer William Hall, he was freed by him in May 1615 and made his first book entry on 27 September 1619.[47] During 1619 he was in partnership with John White (succeeding to the White printing material)[48] and from 1624 to 1626 he had John Norton 2 as partner, a relationship which ended acrimoniously.[49] On 5 July 1623, following an order specifying the number of presses allowed to each printer, Mathewes, who was restricted to one, was ordered to 'take downe' one of his presses and bring it into the hall, before his petition to be a master printer was further considered.[50] He was sufficiently prosperous to be cloathed on 6 May 1630 and in the following year was granted a £50 loan from John Norton's bequest which was duly repaid.[51] On 24 October 1633 Thomas Jones assigned all his copyrights to him.[52] As a large-scale printer – Index 1 to *STC* requires slightly more than a column to list his titles, and in 1636 he possessed three presses – Mathewes succumbed to the temptation of using apprentices and other cheap sources of labour. On 25 September 1620 he was warned at a full Court 'to avoyd ffrances Gastonie a forreno[r] which he keepeth disorderly',[53] on 21 November 1622[54] and 18 August 1624[55] he was ordered to put away apprentices he was 'keeping disorderly', and on 2 April 1627 to 'put away' within eight days three boys he was keeping 'disorderlye in his house' or suffer a penalty of 40 shillings for every eight days he kept all or any of them.[56] Local ties almost certainly lay behind the recruitment of his two Welsh apprentices. John Edwards, bound for 7 years from 29 September 1624,[57] and Thomas Watkins, bound on 6 May 1629 for 8 years,[58] were both from Newtown, a few miles from Mathewes's birthplace. Both apprenticeships ran into difficulties: the entry for Edwards was deleted by order of the Court on 16 May 1629 and he was eventually freed by Henry Skelton on 5 March 1632. Watkins was never freed: according to a 1636 list of 'men brought up to printing against order', Watkins had 'marryed in his Apprentice-hood' and was now working 'abroad for wages, his Apprenticeshipp not being yet expired'.[59]

Mathewes's cavalier attitude to rules and regulations is equally apparent from the series of disputes in which he became involved. He was one of four to incur a fine of £4 each on 4 June 1621 for printing *Withers Motto* (*STC* 25926.5) 'w^(th)out lycense or enterance'.[60] He was in no hurry to pay the fine, and on 26 March 1625 part of it was remitted for 'some services done to the Company', in discovering an illegal press.[61] In 1629 he was in trouble with the Court of High Commission for printing part of Prynne's *The Church of England's old antithesis to new Arminianism* for Michael Sparke,[62] on 9 February 1631 he was fined five shillings for printing without entrance Sir Henry Wotton's *A meditation upon . . . Genesis*,[63] and on 19 January 1632 it was ordered that three reams of bills of lading taken from Mathewes (who had quite improperly printed them) should be handed over to Nicholas Bourne.[64] In 1637, after being 'taken reprinting of *ye holy table*',[65] he was omitted from the list of twenty authorized master printers, his place being taken by Marmaduke Parsons who, it has been argued, had been financing Mathewes's printing activities.[66] Although his name vanishes from the imprints of books after 1638, Mathewes continued to work as a journeyman printer to 1653. Despite his Welsh origins, he was essentially an English printer, and can be associated with only a single Welsh title (albeit one of considerable interest), the earliest printed ballad in the language, *Byd y bigail* (*The shepherd's world*) which he printed for Henry Gosson.[67]

A major tragedy from the standpoint of Welsh-language publishing was the frustration of Thomas Salisbury's ambitious plans to print several Puritan and humanist works in Welsh, the subject of Professor Geraint Gruffydd's 1990 Sir John Williams Lecture.[68] Although Salisbury's name suggests that he belonged to one of the many branches of this important North Wales family, when he was bound to the bookseller and bookbinder Oliver Wilkes on 9 October 1581 his father, Pierce Salberye of Clocaenog, was described as a husbandman. Salisbury was freed on 17 October 1588 and set himself up as a bookbinder and bookseller. In 1593 he first ventured into publishing, having Henry Salesbury's *Grammatica Britannica* printed at the Eliot's Court Press. This was not entered in the Company's registers, nor was his second publication, a Welsh translation of Becon's *Sick Man's Salve* published (if indeed it did appear) with the assistance of a loan of £10 from the London-Welsh merchant Thomas Myddelton. By the end of the 1590s Salisbury was ready to undertake a substantial programme of publishing Welsh books with the assistance of prosperous London Welshmen, most notably Myddelton, who advanced a further £30 in 1602 to pay for the printing of the psalms in Welsh. In

October 1600 Salisbury bound his only Welsh apprentice, Robert Jones, son of a Caernarfon yeoman, possibly to assist in producing these proposed Welsh books. The plague of 1603 totally disrupted Salisbury's plans, and led to financial disaster. Salisbury is listed as receiving relief from the Company when its Poor Book commences in 1608 and lived in poverty and obscurity until his death, probably in early 1623.

The career of Luke Meredith, the son of a Rhuthun gentleman, shows that apprentices of Welsh origin could hope to attain considerable wealth. Bound to Jonathan Edwyn in May 1677, he was freed by the aged and prosperous bookseller Richard Royston in May 1684.[69] Royston thought well enough of Meredith to bequeath him £10 on his death in the autumn of 1686, but a far greater prize fell into his hands when he married Elizabeth, Royston's granddaughter, in the spring of 1687. As well as a bequest of £250, she inherited Royston's very lucrative copies which were to play an important role in the development of the conger.[70] Neither Meredith nor his wife enjoyed their good fortune for long, Elizabeth being dead by 1696 and Luke Meredith dying in the summer of 1700.

Lewis Thomas, the son of a Carmarthenshire gentleman, was bound to the printer Henry Hills 1 in November 1683 and freed by his executors at the beginning of 1690.[71] Thomas was involved in printing and correcting part of 'ye last Edition of the Welsh Bible',[72] and was appointed in 1693 to manage the Oxford Bible Press.[73] He remained in charge until Charles Combes took over sometime before 1720.[74] Because of his knowledge of Welsh, Thomas participated in the production of the SPCK's Welsh Bible of 1717-18,[75] but his relationship with Moses Williams, who exercised overall supervision, was not without its difficulties. Williams later noted:

Mr Lewis Thomas, who was the Contriver of printing the Singing Psalms &c. in that small Character at Oxon, printed off the first Sheet thereof without or rather contrary to my Directions, & that is the Reason Pryse's Letter is left out, & the Index of the Psalms & that of the Hymns put asunder in that preposterous manner.[76]

While not averse to spending convivial evenings with Hearne,[77] Thomas became closely involved in the work of the SPCK, being made a Corresponding Member of the Society in 1714.[78] During the 1720s, following his move to London, he assisted the SPCK's Welsh publishing activities in a number of ways. In 1724 he read and revised John Vaughan's translation of Bishop Gibson's *Family Devotions*[79] and in 1725 he prepared estimates of the cost of producing a new edition of *Canwyll y Cymru* and advised the Society how many copies should be printed.[80] Thomas maintained links with his home town (in 1724 he requested the SPCK to supply books and papers in order to help revive Llangadog school)[81] and, possibly because of these connections, was requested in 1727 to advise the SPCK on 'the most proper Distribution' in Wales of Thomas Richards's translation of *A Pastoral Letter from a Minister to his Parishioners*.[82]

Several years ago, D. V. Glass suggested that it might be worth investigating 'whether there were . . . sizeable streams of trained individuals moving away from London and contributing to the development of trade and industry in other parts of the country.'[83] As far as Wales is concerned, this did not occur. Just as Paul Morgan could find only one example of a Warwickshire youth apprenticed to the Company between 1563 and 1700 who returned to his native county,[84] there were very few instances of Welsh apprentices moving from London to set up business in Welsh border towns (Wales itself would have been a hopeless proposition at that time). One who can be identified is Peter Bodfel from Ceidio near Caernarfon, apprenticed to the radical bookseller Thomas Brewster on 4 February 1656 and freed by him on 6 March 1663.[85] Bodfel's knowledge of Welsh would have been of considerable assistance to Brewster in printing the two 1659 editions of *Canwyll y Cymru*, even though the work's south Wales dialect might well have presented him with a considerable challenge. Bodfel was a witness when Brewster and others were tried in February 1664 for issuing seditious pamphlets. He may well have been coerced into giving evidence, since the following note in the hand of Moses Williams which survives in a copy of the 1664 Welsh Book of Common Prayer,[86] printed by Simon Dover (another defendant in the 1664 trial) for Bodfel and Edward Foulkes, gives a clear indication of Bodfel's true sympathies:

Memorandum that Peter Bodvel the Undertaker of this Book was a Presbyterian Bookseller at Chester & often bragg'd of comparing the King to an Owl the Royal Family to Cranes & the Clergy & their Followers to Apes, by the Capitals in the Morning & Evening service at the Beginning of those Prayers.[87]

By 1666 Bodfel had moved from London to Chester and was admitted to that city's Stationers' Company in 1670.[88] There he sold the only other Welsh title with which he can be associated, the 1672 Welsh New Testament and Psalms, 2,000 copies of which were printed in London by E. Tyler and R. Holt, and were sold there by Samuel Gellibrand, in Chester by Bodfel, and in Wrexham by John Hughes.[89]

London was an unsatisfactory centre for printing books for the Welsh market. As well as the problems of distributing the books, authors found it expensive and inconvenient to stay there for months – as William Salesbury and William Morgan had been compelled to do – in order to correct proofs of matter set by compositors who, more often than not, had no knowledge of the Welsh language. The idea that it would be advantageous to set up a press nearer Wales was not a new one. As early as January 1549, John Oswen, who had just moved from Ipswich to Worcester, received a privilege to print service books and books of instruction for 'the godly edifying and ease of our louying subjects within our Principalitie of Wales and marches of the same'.[90] Despite his privilege and the advantageous location of his press, none of the twenty books he printed were in the Welsh language. One of the arguments used in the University of Oxford's 1584 petition for permission to set up a press was that it would be well placed to supply both the Welsh and the 'Hibernian barbarians' with books.[91] At the beginning of May 1629, the lexicographer Dr John Davies of Mallwyd (who was seeking a printer for his great Latin-Welsh *Dictionarium Duplex*) told Owen Wynne of Gwedir that he had been informed that 'Mr Jones of Whitecrosse-Street, was desirous to remove his presse to the Marches of Wales, and intended so to do'.[92] This would appear to be the bookseller and printer identified in *STC* as William Jones 3, the operator of a clandestine Puritan press between 1604 and 1608. Whatever Jones's intentions may have been (possibly the hope of avoiding close scrutiny of his output), nothing came of his plan and it was not until 1695-6 that the first legal press was set up in the Welsh border.

The key figure in this development, Thomas Jones (1648-1713), was not a member of the Stationers' Company.[93] Born near Corwen in north Wales, he moved to London about 1666 apparently to work as a tailor. By the mid-1670s he had turned his hand to bookselling and published his first work, *The Character of a Quack-Doctor*, in 1676.[94] Welsh books followed, such as a reprint in 1683 of the Welsh primer, *Llyfr Plygain*, in 1684 the violently anti-Catholic *Y Gwîr er Gwaethed yw* (*The truth however dire it be*), doggerel verse inspired by the Popish Plot, and in 1688 the first cheap Welsh dictionary, *Y Gymraeg yn ei Disgleirdeb* (*The Welsh Language in its Lustre*). On 1 January 1679 Jones was granted by Letters Patent 'the Sole Liberty and Lisence of Writing, Printing, and Publishing an almanac in the British Language' which was confirmed by the Stationers' Company at the beginning of March.[95] In view of its customary anxiety to preserve its monopoly, the Company's readiness to allow Jones to publish Welsh almanacs demonstrates its lack of interest in Welsh publications. Jones proceeded to publish an unbroken sequence of almanacs for the years 1680 to 1712. When the Licensing Act lapsed in 1695, Jones moved to Shrewsbury where he set up for the first time as a printer. His Welsh almanacs had encountered rivals before 1695, and from 1698 onwards the almanacs produced by John Jones of Caeau presented a serious challenge. Thomas Jones (something of a paranoiac at the best of times) could do no more than lavish his very considerable powers of invective on the interlopers since the Stationers' Company ignored these obscure local squabbles. Shrewsbury printers soon found that they could pirate London-published Welsh books with impunity, even the Book of Common Prayer, though for the latter a fictitious imprint was sometimes judged to be prudent.[96]

By pioneering the publication of cheap, popular works in Welsh and by creating a network of local distributors for his publications, Thomas Jones paved the way for the inception of legitimate printing in Wales itself in 1718. Even so, the publishing activities of the SPCK in the early decades of the eighteenth century and those of the London–Welsh societies from mid-century onwards meant that Welsh books were still produced in the capital. The chequered career of the printer William Roberts forms a link between the SPCK and the Welsh societies. Born in Llandygái near Caernarfon,[97] Roberts was bound to Anne Downing in December 1708 and was freed by Joseph Downing in December 1721.[98] By 1726 he was at Bartholomew Close, where he bound his first (and only) apprentice,[99] and sold a reissue of the 1717 Welsh translation of Bishop Beveridge's *Private thoughts upon religion*.[100] In the same year he printed Moses Williams's *Repertorium poeticum*, an index to Welsh poetry.[101] When the SPCK decided to reprint a Welsh translation of the Book of Homilies, Roberts (now at Lambeth Hill) agreed to undertake the work for eight shillings a copy in quires or ten shillings and sixpence in calf should the Welsh bishops oblige each parish in Wales to purchase a copy.[102] The SPCK agreed terms with Roberts and he began work. In June 1730 Roberts suffered what he termed a 'misfortune' and by the end of the year had removed to Hamburg as a result of this financial reverse. He continued work on the Homilies,[103] promising in October 1731 that the book would be ready by May 1732.[104] Despite his sending ten sheets of 'exemplars' to the SPCK from Hamburg in May 1733,[105] the edition never appeared. A decade later, in 1743, 'Mr. William Roberts, the Hamburgher' visited William Morris in Anglesey while on his way from Ireland[106] (had he, perhaps, now moved to Dublin?). By 1757 Roberts was once again printing in London, and in 1759 was listed as a member of the Cymmrodorion Society. He printed the Society's *Cofrestr* (*Register*) for that year and for 1762, claiming on his imprint to be the Society's printer.[107] During the early 1760s Roberts entered upon what proved to be a fatal association with the itinerant bookseller Huw Jones of Llangwm.[108] In 1763 he printed for him *Diddanwch Teuluaidd,* a 300-page anthology of Welsh verse.[109] Jones successfully sold the book in Wales but deliberately avoided reimbursing Roberts for its printing so that the destitute printer had to spend the last few months of his life in the workhouse.[110]

As Welsh-language publishing was increasingly undertaken in Border towns and in Wales itself, the Company had little part to play other than its vestigial role in maintaining copyright registers. Certain Welsh books of the first half of the nineteenth century bear the legend 'Entered at Stationers' Hall' to warn off would-be pirates. Someone, sometime, will have to examine the microfilmed entry-books and the post-1842 records at the Public Record Office in order to establish whether these works really were entered, and what contribution the Company's records could make to filling the gap between 1821 and 1909 in the Welsh bibliographical record.

References

I must thank my colleague, Rheinallt Llwyd, and my wife, Mary, for their comments on an earlier version of this paper. Those who are familiar with the field will appreciate the extent of my indebtedness to the researches of Eiluned Rees, in particular to her *Libri Walliae*. All references to *STC* are to the second edition.

1. W. W. Greg and E. Boswell (eds) *Records of the Court of the Stationers' Company, 1576 to 1602* (London, 1930), p.33.
2. Cyprian Blagden, *The Stationers' Company: a History, 1403-1959* (London, 1960), p.55; Greg and Boswell, *Records*, p.7; Geraint Gruffydd, 'Catecism y Deon Nowell yn Gymraeg', *Journal of the Welsh Bibliographical Society* (cited as *JWBS*), 7 (1950-3), pp.114-15; 203-7.
3. Eiluned Rees, 'Welsh publishing before 1717', in *Essays in Honour of Victor Scholderer*, ed. D. F. Rhodes (Mainz, 1970), pp.327-8.
4. R. Geraint Gruffydd, 'The first printed books, 1546-1604', in *A Nation and its Books: Essays on the History of the Book in* Wales, ed. Philip Henry Jones and Eiluned Rees (Aberystwyth, 1997) (in the press).
5. Eiluned Rees, *Libri Walliae: a Catalogue of Welsh Books and Books printed in Wales 1546-1820*, 2 vols (Aberystwyth, 1987) (cited as *LW*), 3408. The fullest discussion is W. Ll. Davies, 'A argraffwyd llyfr Cymraeg yn Iwerddon cyn 1700?', *JWBS*, 5 (1937-42), pp.114-19.
6. Gruffydd, 'The first printed books'.
7. Eiluned Rees, 'A bibliographical note on early editions of *Canwyll y Cymry*', *JWBS*, 10 (1966-71), pp.36-41.
8. Edward Arber, *A Transcript of the Registers of the Company of Stationers of London 1554-1640 AD*, 5 vols (London, 1875-94), II, 484.
9. Arber, II, 466.
10. Arber, III, 84.
11. *LW*, 1868.

12. *LW*, 3433.
13. Franklin B. Williams, Jr., 'Lost Books of Tudor England', *The Library*, 5th series, 33 (1978), p.6.
14. Glanmor Williams, *Recovery, Reorientation and Reformation: Wales c.1415-1642* (Oxford, 1987), pp.90-3, 406-9.
15. Glanmor Williams, 'The Welsh in Tudor England', in his *Religion, Language, and Nationality in Wales* (Cardiff, 1979), pp.171-99.
16. Emrys Jones, 'The Welsh in London in the seventeenth and eighteenth centuries', *Welsh History Review*, 10 (1980-1), p.463.
17. The career of Thomas Myddelton is examined in A. H. Dodd, 'Mr. Myddelton, the Merchant of Tower Street', in *Elizabethan Government and Society: Essays presented to Sir John Neale*, ed. S. T. Bindoff, J. Hurstfield and C. H. Williams (London, 1961), pp.249-81.
18. Arber, I, 278. Why Jones was made a Brother rather than a Freeman is rather puzzling. Peter Blayney has suggested to me in conversation that it might be because he was already a freeman of some other city.
19. Ronald B. McKerrow, *Printers' & Publisher's Devices in England & Scotland 1485-1640* (London, 1913), no.283, discussed p.110; Harry Farr, 'A Welsh Stationer of the sixteenth century', in *Report of the Proceedings of the Thirteenth Conference of Library Authorities in Wales . . . 1946* (Aberystwyth, 1947), pp.12-20.
20. This was the method used by Bob Owen in his unpublished National Eisteddfod essay, 'Ymfudiadau o Gymru i Lundain a Hanes Bywyd Cymreig yn Llundain hyd at 1815', University College of North Wales Bangor, MSS 7343-5.
21. Harry Farr, 'Owen ap Roger or Owen Rogers', *JWBS*, 8 (1954-7), pp.58-63.
22. Arber, I, 251.
23. Arber, I, 286.
24. C. Y. Ferdinand, 'Towards a demography of the Stationers' Company 1601-1700', *Journal of the Printing Historical Society*, 21 (1992), pp.51-69.
25. D. F. McKenzie, 'Apprenticeship in the Stationers' Company, 1555-1640', *The Library*, 5th series, 13 (1958), pp.292-9.
26. D. F. McKenzie, *Stationers' Company Apprentices 1605-1640* (Charlottesville, VA, 1961); *Stationers' Company Apprentices 1641-1700* (Oxford, 1974); *Stationers' Company Apprentices 1701-1800* (Oxford, 1978), hereafter referred to as McKenzie 1-3. I have included as Welsh apprentices Thomas Phillippes (Arber, I, 352), Humphrey Powell (Arber, II, 692), Richard Beaumont (McKenzie 1, 742) and William Roberts (McKenzie 3, 2554/2565). More tentatively, I have classed Peter Bodfel's father as a gentleman.
27. To the 96 recorded as freed, I have added Edward Powell (bound in 1566) and Thomas Daves (bound in 1569), both of whom must have been freed during the 1571-6 gap in the records, since they later had apprentices bound to them.
28. Arber, II, 212.
29. Arber, II, 222.
30. Arber, II, 139.
31. McKenzie 2, 3684.
32. McKenzie 1, 1768.
33. Greg, *Companion*, p.330.
34. McKenzie, 'Apprenticeship', p.299.
35. Williams, *Recovery*, pp.464-5.
36. McKenzie 3 lists five such bindings between 1755 and 1770.

37. McKenzie 2, 4242.
38. *LW*, 4758. This was probably the second Welsh book to be printed in Dublin.
39. McKenzie 2, 4248.
40. *LW*, 1292.
41. The John Jones cloathed in February 1697 may be the John Jones from Wrexham apprenticed to Thomas Ratcliffe in 1671 and freed by him in 1678 (McKenzie 2, 3687) but there are other plausible candidates.
42. McKenzie 2, 882.
43. John Dunton, *The Life and Errors of John Dunton* (London, 1705), p.287.
44. Blagden, *Stationers' Company*, p.159.
45. William A. Jackson (ed.), *Records of the Court of the Stationers' Company 1602 to 1640* (London, 1957), pp.293, 485.
46. McKenzie 1, 236.
47. Arber, III, 306.
48. Arber, III, 700, 703.
49. Jackson, *Records*, pp.196-7.
50. Jackson, *Records*, pp.158-9.
51. Jackson, *Records*, p.224; W. Craig Ferguson, *The Loan Book of the Stationers' Company with a List of Transactions 1592-1692* (London, 1989), p.26.
52. Jackson, *Records*, pp.242; Arber, IV, 307.
53. Jackson, *Records*, p.131.
54. Jackson, *Records*, p.151.
55. Jackson, *Records*, p.169.
56. Jackson, *Records*, p.194.
57. McKenzie 1, 367.
58. McKenzie 1, 370.
59. W.W. Greg, *A Companion to Arber* (Oxford, 1967), p.332.
60. Jackson, *Records*, p.135.
61. Jackson, *Records*, pp.175, 472.
62. *STC* 20457; Greg, *Companion*, pp.243-7, 249-50.
63. *STC* 24905; Jackson, *Records*, p.224.
64. Jackson, *Records*, pp.212-13.
65. Arber, IV, 528. The work in question was a reprint of Peter Heylin, *A coale from the altar*, *STC* 13271.
66. William R. Parker, 'Contributions toward a Milton Bibliography', *The Library*, 4th series, 16 (1935-6), pp. 428-31.
67. J. H. Davies, 'An early printed Welsh ballad', *JWBS*, 2 (1916-23), pp.243-6. Precisely when the undated ballad was printed remains uncertain. *LW* suggests c.1620, but *STC* gives c.1632.
68. R. Geraint Gruffydd, *Thomas Salisbury o Lundain a Chlocaenog: Ysgolhaig-Argraffydd y Dadeni Cymreig* (Aberystwyth, 1991). I have relied heavily on this detailed study for the following account of Salisbury's career.
69. McKenzie 2, 1367, 3974.
70. Norma Hodgson and Cyprian Blagden, *The Notebook of Thomas Bennett and Henry Clements (1686-1719)* (Oxford, 1956), pp.78-9.
71. McKenzie 2, 2134.
72. Mary Clement (ed.), *Correspondence and Minutes of the S.P.C.K. relating to Wales, 1699-1740* (Cardiff, 1952), p.74. In a note Clement suggests that this was the 1690 Oxford-

printed Bible for churches (*LW*, 361-2), but if (as is probably the case) Thomas was still in London, the reference would be to the London-printed Bible of 1689-90 (*LW*, 360).
73. Harry Carter, *A History of the Oxford University Press. Volume I: To the year 1780* (Oxford, 1975), p.190. The transcript of the articles creating a special stock within the Stationers' Company, 6 October 1693, reproduced in John Johnson and Strickland Gibson, *Print and Privilege at Oxford to the year 1700* (London, 1946), pp.181-7, refers to 'Louis Thomas' (p.186).
74. Carter suggests that Thomas was succeeded 'some time between 1713 and 1720' (*History*, p.194) but SPCK minutes and correspondence indicate that Thomas was still at Oxford at the end of 1717 (Clement, *Correspondence*, p.74).
75. *LW*, 363-4. Although the Bible was printed in London, the metrical psalms were printed at Oxford.
76. NLW, Llanstephan MS 105B, reproduced in *The Bible in Wales* (London, 1906), p.41.
77. Carter, *History*, p.193.
78. Clement, *Correspondence*, p.74.
79. Clement, *Correspondence*, p.290.
80. Clement, *Correspondence*, p.293.
81. Clement, *Correspondence*, p.290.
82. *LW*, 3457. Clement, *Correspondence*, p.298.
83. D. V. Glass, 'Socio-economic status and occupations in the City of London at the end of the seventeenth century', in *Studies in London History presented to Philip Edward Jones*, ed. A. E. J. Hollaender and William Kelloway (London, 1969), p.389.
84. Paul Morgan, *Warwickshire Apprentices in the Stationers' Company of London, 1563-1700* (Stratford-upon-Avon, 1978), p.7.
85. McKenzie 2, 514, where he appears as 'Bodnell'.
86. *LW*, 590.
87. National Library of Wales, MS 13254D (Mysevin 33).
88. Derek Nuttall, *A History of Printing in Chester from 1688 to 1965* (Chester, 1969), p.5.
89. *LW*, 475; *Bible in Wales*, p.11.
90. Reproduced in William K. Sessions, *The first printers at Ipswich in 1547-1548 and Worcester in 1549-1553* (York, 1984), pp.99-100.
91. The original Latin petition is quoted in S. Gibson and D. M. Rogers, 'The Earl of Leicester and printing at Oxford', *Bodleian Library Record*, 2 (1941-9), p. 240-5.
92. The original letter is lost but a transcript was printed in the *Gentleman's Magazine*, 60 (1790), pp.23-4. Wynne had earlier sent Davies the following list of 'the names of all the prynters in London' and their addresses:
Mr Iselip, in Pycorner. Kingstons, in Paternoster-row. Stansby, in Thems-street, by St. Peter's church. Dawson, in Trinity-lane. Lownes, and Mr. Younge, upon Bred-street-hill. Fursit, in Nicholas Chamles. Haveland, in the Ould Baly. Flesher, in Little Britton. Mathews, in Ride-lane. Miler, in Blackfriers, by the water-side. Harper, by Blackfriers church. Coates, in Barbican. Mrs Alde, in Butcher's-hall. Mr Jones, in Whitecrosse-street.
To these, Davies added 'one Mr. Beale, a little with out Aldersgate'.
93. The fullest account of the career of Thomas Jones is Geraint H. Jenkins, *Thomas Jones yr Almanaciwr 1648-1713* (Cardiff, 1980).
94. Jenkins, *Thomas Jones*, p.7.
95. Jenkins, *Thomas Jones*, p.9, quoting entry in Court Book, 1 March 1679.
96. e.g. *LW*, 605.

97. John H. Davies (ed.), *The Letters of Lewis, Richard, William, and John Morris, of Anglesey . . . 1728-1765*, 2 vols (Aberystwyth, 1907-9), II, 55, where Lewis Morris calls him 'a fool, a drunken ignorant fellow'.
98. McKenzie 3, 2554, 2566.
99. McKenzie 3, 6298.
100. *LW*, 348.
101. *LW*, 5351.
102. Clement, *Correspondence*, p.298.
103. Clement, *Correspondence*, pp.159, 233.
104. Clement, *Correspondence*, p.165.
105. Clement, *Correspondence*, p.169.
106. Davies, *Letters*, I, 75.
107. *LW*, 1390, 1391.
108. A detailed account of this stage of Roberts's career can be found in G. J. Williams (ed.), *Llythyrau at Ddafydd Jones o Drefriw* (Aberystwyth, 1943), pp.36-8.
109. *LW*, 2917.
110. Hugh Owen (ed.), *Additional Letters of the Morrises of Anglesey (1735-1786)* (London, 1947-9), pp.662-3.

Index

Abergavenny, Earl of, 1, 4
Abergavenny House, 1, 2, 3
Ackers, Charles, 116, 117, 147
Adams, Thomas, 76
Alexander, James, 161
Alford, Roger, 27, 28
Almanacks, printed, 48, 123, 124, 125, 196
Alston, Gavin, 174
Ames, Joseph, 35, 36, 38
Anderson, Patrick, 176
Anderson, William, 151, 152, 153, 160, 166, 167, 173, 176, 177, 178, 179
Appryse, Giles, 188
Appryse, John, 188
Appryse, Rowland, 188
Apollo Press, Edinburgh, 156
Apothecaries, 96
Arber, Edward, 36, 38, 39, 40, 43, 49, 51, 52, 54, 188
Aristotle, 98
Atkyns, Richard, 102, 103, 104
Auctions, of books, 115
Auld, William, 167

Babbington, John, 79, 80
Bacon, Francis, 50, 99, 104
Balfour, John, 155, 157, 174
Ballard, Samuel, 115
Barclay, John, 151, 152
Barclay, Robert, 153
Barker, Christopher, 18, 19, 22, 25, 26, 47, 49, 50, 186
Barker, Robert, 185
Barnes, Joseph, 186
Barrie, John, 175
Barriffe, William, 67, 68
Bassingbourne, Ives, 79
Bathurst, Charles, 119, 130, 131
Battene, John, 28
Bayle, P., 120
Beale, John, 69, 76
Beale, Thomas, 66
Becket, Thomas, 175, 176
Becon, Thomas, 21
Belanger, Terry, 115
Bell, John, 156, 170, 174, 175, 176
Bell, Robert, 160
Berthelet, Thomas, 14
Bettenham, James, 120, 121, 147, 148
Bible printing, 50, 51, 161, 162, 167, 175, 185, 186
Bibliographical Society (London), 52
Binding materials, 2
Bingham, Captain John, 69-73
Birckman, Arnold, 26, 27
Blackstone, William, 153, 156, 157, 164, 166, 177

Bladon, Samuel, 131
Blagden, Cyprian, 39, 46, 49, 54, 93, 94, 100
Blair, Hugh, 155, 165, 169
Bland, Adam, 28
Blayney, Peter, xiii, 11-34, 41, 44, 46
Bloome, Jacob, 75, 79
Blount, Edward, 76, 77
Board of Customs Commissioners, 152, 154, 156, 157, 161, 163, 169, 170, 178
Bodfel, Peter, 195
Bodley, John, 14, 18
Bookbinders
— see Borneman, Gottfried
— see Boys, John
— see Colborne, John
— see Coles, John
— see Cooke, William
— see Darbyshire, James
— see Folingsby, Margaret
— see Heath, George
— see Hilker, Anthony
— see Johnson, Edward
— see Marks, James
— see Miller, John
Booksellers
— see Alston, Gavin
— see Anderson, William
— see Ballard, Samuel
— see Bathurst, Charles
— see Bell, John
— see Bell, Robert
— see Bladon, Samuel
— see Bodfel, Peter
— see Bowles, Carrington
— see Brett, Peter
— see Brewster, Thomas
— see Brindley, John
— see Brown, James
— see Browne, Daniel
— see Cadell, Thomas
— see Caslon, Thomas
— see Clark, Robert
— see Collins, Arthur
— see Collins, Benjamin
— see Creech, William
— see Darling, William
— see Davies, Thomas
— see Davis, Lockyer
— see Dickson, James
— see Dod, Benjamin
— see Duncan, William
— see Dunlop & Wilson
— see Dury, Andrew
— see Elliot, Charles
— see Ewing, Thomas
— see Eyre, Henry

203

— see Forsythe, Alexander
— see Foulkes, Edward
— see Freer, George
— see Gellibrand, Samuel
— see Gilbert, William
— see Gilman, Anthony
— see Gordon, William
— see Gordon & Millar
— see Gosson, Henry
— see Gray, William
— see Hallhead, William
— see Hamilton, Gavin
— see Hawkins, George
— see Hay, John
— see Hitch and Hawes
— see Hooper, Samuel
— see Hughes, John
— see Jackson, C.
— see Johnston, William
— see Jones, Huw
— see Kay, Thomas
— see Kincaid, Alexander
— see Knapton, John
— see Knox, James
— see Langford, Mary
— see Langford, Thomas
— see Lewis, William
— see Liddell, John
— see Longman, Thomas
— see McCaslan, Alexander
— see McCleish, James
— see Macfarquhar, C.
— see Magee, James
— see Magee, John
— see Marshall, Robert
— see Meuros, James
— see Millar, Andrew
— see Morison and Son
— see Murray, John
— see Nicol, George
— see Nourse, John
— see Oswald, John
— see Payne, Thomas
— see Reeve, Elizabeth
— see Rivington, John
— see Robertson, John and James
— see Royston, Richard
— see Sandby, William
— see Sayer, Edward
— see Sayer, Robert
— see Sleater, James
— see Smith, John
— see Smith, P.
— see Sparke, Michael
— see Stewart, Thomas
— see Strahan, Andrew
— see Strahan, William
— see Tait, Peter
— see Templeman
— see Thurston, Richard
— see Tonson, Jacob
— see Vaillant, Paul

— see Wallis, John
— see Whiston and White
— see White, Luke
— see Wilkes, Oliver
— see Williams, James
— see Williams, Rice
— see Wilson, John
— see Wilson, Thomas
— see Wilson, William
— see Wood, John
— see Woodcock, Edward
— see Woodward, Thomas
— see Wren, John
Borneman, Gottfried, 143
Boswell, James, 177
Boswell, E., 44, 53
Bourchier, Archbishop, 102
Bourne, Nicholas, 193
Bowden, Sarah, 113, 114
Bowles, Carrington, 131
Bowyer, William, 148
Bowyer Ledgers, 114, 117, 118
Boys, John, 143
Brett, Peter, 131
Brewster, Edward, 52
Brewster, Thomas, 195
Brindley, John, 132
Brisbane, Alexander, 151, 152, 166
Brooks, Christopher, 99
Brown, Alexander, 176
Brown, James, 174, 175
Browne, Daniel, 132
Browne, Isaac Hawkins, 119
Brudenell, Thomas, 69
Buck, John, 50
Buck, Thomas, 50
Burghley, Lord see Cecil, William
Burrow, Edward, 156, 157, 163, 164
Bush, John, 189
Butter, Nathaniel, 49
Bynneman, Henry, 24, 47
Byrd, William, 25
Byrne, Patrick, 152

Cadell, Thomas, 121, 152, 153, 154, 155, 157, 165, 166, 167, 168, 170, 171, 173, 175, 176, 177, 178
Campbell, Archibald, 162
Caslon, Thomas, 132, 133
Cater, Edward, 42
Cawood, John, 48
Caxton, William, 2, 102
Cecil, William, Lord Burghley, xiii, 11-34, 41, 47
Cecil, Sir Robert, 19
Censorship, in book trade, 41
Chalmers, Alexander, 37
Chalmers, George, 37
Chard, Thomas, 187
Charles I, King, 69, 79
Chesterfield, Earl of, 118, 120, 172, 174
City of London Companies, xiii, xiv,
— see Apothecaries

INDEX

— see Drapers
— see Fishmongers
— see Glovers
— see Goldsmiths
— see Honourable Artillery Company
— see Leathersellers
— see Mercers
— see Merchant Taylors
— see Poulterers
— see Skinners
— see Stationers
Clark, Robert, 173
Clerke, Anthony, 40
Close Rolls, 15
Cockerill, Thomas, 191
Colborne, John, 143
Coles, John, 143
Colledge, Stephen, 8-9
College of Arms, 75
Collins, Arthur, 133
Collins, Benjamin, 173
Colquhoun, Hugh, 152
Confirmation Rolls, 15
Cooke, William, 119, 144
Cooper, Mary, 118
Cooper, Thomas, 118
Copyright Acts, 52, 154, 166, 172, 179
Copyright, disputes over, 50, 51, 155, 156
Corbett, Patrick, 151, 152, 154, 162, 166
Court of Augmentations, 27
Court of Common Council, 45
Court of High Commission, 79, 81, 94, 193
Court of Session, 155, 156, 172, 179
Creech, William, 152, 154, 155, 168, 170, 171, 174, 175, 176, 179
Crooke, Andrew, 6
Crosby, Sir John, 4
Crowley, Robert, 186
Cullen, William, 168, 169
Cummine, John, 162
Cuningham, William, 21
Customs officials, in Scottish book trade see Board of Customs Commissioners
Cymmrodorion Society, 197

Darbishire, James, 119, 144
Darling, William, 173, 174, 175
Davies, Dr John, 196
Davies, Thomas, 133
Davis, Lockyer, 133
Dawbeney, Oliver, 11
Dawson, Gertrude, 67
Dawson, John, 66, 67, 79, 81
Day, John, 16, 17, 20, 21, 22, 23, 46, 47, 49, 185
Day, Richard, 22, 46, 47, 48, 49
Denham, Henry, 46, 47
Denham, Martha, 74
Denham, William, 74
Dennes, Edmund, 117
Desvoeux, Vinchon, 120
Dickson, James, 173, 174, 175, 176
Digby, Sir John, 74

Dight, Walter, 189
Dilly, Charles, 173
Dilly, Edward, 155, 173
Dod, Benjamin, 134
Dodsley, James, 152, 165, 173, 174, 176, 177
Dodsley, Robert, 118
Douglas, George, 173, 174, 175
Douglas, Robert, 175, 176
Dover, Simon, 195
Dow, Daniel, 152, 153, 160, 161, 169, 178, 179
Downing, Anne, 197
Downing, Joseph, 197
Drapers' Company, 20
Dublin, books printed at, 186, 191
Duncan, William, 164
Dunlop, David, 156
Dunlop & Wilson, 152, 153, 174, 176
Dury, Andrew, 133
Dyke, Daniel, 76
Dymott, Richard, 144

Early English Text Society, 38
Edinburgh Booksellers' Society, 166
Edinburgh, book trade at, 155, 166
Edward VI, King, 11, 15, 16, 17, 22
Edwards, John, 192
Edwardes, Evan, 189
Edwyn, Jonathan, 194
Eighteenth Century Short Title Catalogue, 114, 115
Eliot's Court Press, 193
Elizabeth I, Queen, 13, 15, 17, 21, 22, 40, 41, 42, 46, 114
Elliot, Charles, 151, 155, 164, 165, 166, 167, 168, 169, 170, 171, 173, 174, 175, 178, 179
Ellis, Cadwallader, 191
Ellis, Joseph, 190
Eresby, Lawrence, 27, 28
Essex, Earl of, 19, 20
Evans, Matthew, 189
Ewing, Thomas, 151, 165, 167
Eyre, Henry, 116, 119

Fawne, Luke, 66
Fenn, Sir Richard, 66
Ferdinand, C. Y., 188
Flower, Francis, 25
Folingsby, Margaret, 119, 144-5
Forbes, Patrick, 113
Forster, William, 120
Forsyth, Lachlan, 175
Forsythe, Alexander, 169
Foulkes, Edward, 195
Foxe, John, 21, 50
Francis, F. C., 52
Freer, George, 133
Furnivall, F. J., 38

Gadd, Ian, xiv, 45, 51, 93-111
Galbraith, Joseph, 162, 163
Garrett, Magnes, 153, 160, 178
Gataker, Thomas, 120

Gellbrand, Samuel, 195
Geneva Bible, 14, 18, 23
George III, King, 117
Gibbon, Edward, 151, 161
Gilbert, William, 164, 166, 167, 168, 169, 170
Gilman, Anthony, 192
Girvin, John, 153, 154
Glass, D. V., 195
Glovers, 99
Goldsmiths, 2, 75
Gordon, William, 173, 174, 175
Gordon & Millar, 168, 169
Gosling, Robert, 120
Gosson, Henry, 193
Gouge, William, 76
Grafton, Richard, 15
Gray, Thomas, 168
Gray, William, 174, 175
Greg, W. W., 40, 41, 43, 44, 49, 52, 53, 54, 93
Gresham, Sir Thomas, 4
Griffith, Hugh, 187
Gruffydd, Professor Geraint, 186, 193
Gunnery, books on, 77-9
Gwillim, John, 75
Gwillim, Phillip, 191

Hall, William, 192
Hallhead, William, 151, 167, 169
Hamilton, Gavin, 155
Hammersley, Sir Hugh, 66, 69, 73
Hammond, James, 118
Harper, Thomas, 50, 66, 79
Harris, Joseph, 117
Harrison, James, 148
Harrison, William, 98
Hart, John, 48
Harte, Walter, 120
Haviland, John, 73
Hawkins, George, xv, 113-49
Hawkins, Richard, 115
Hay, James, Earl of Carlisle, 77
Hay, James, 161
Hay, John, 167
Hayley, William, 151
Hearne, Thomas, 194
Heath, George, 119, 145
Henry VII, King, 187
Henry VIII, King, 11, 13, 14, 17, 27, 65
Herbert, William, 37, 38
Hills, Henry, 194
Hilker, Anthony, 145
Hitch and Hawes, 134
Hodgson, Sidney, 113
Holmes, William, 47
Holt, R., 195
Honourable Artillery Company, xiv, 46, 65-92
Hooke, Nathaniel, 121, 123
Hooke, Robert, 6
Hooper, Samuel, 134
Howe, Ellic, 113
Hughes, George, 76
Hughes, Henry, 189

Hughes, John, 195
Hughs, John, 148
Hume, David, 155, 161, 166, 176
Hurlock, George, 66, 77

Ilive, Jacob, 122
Ireland, reprinted editions from, xv, 151-83
Islip, Adam, 66, 67, 76, 77

Jackson, C., 152
Jackson, W. A., 44, 45, 49, 53
Jaggard, Thomas, 188
James I, King, 69
James II, King, 51
Jarman, Edward, 6
Johnson, Edward(?), 146
Johnson, John, 35
Johnson, Samuel, 151, 152, 154, 165, 169, 176, 177
Johnston, William, 121, 173
Jones, Huw, 197
Jones, John, 197
Jones, Philip Henry, xv, 185-202
Jones, Richard, 185, 187
Jones, Robert, 194
Jones, Thomas, 192, 196, 197
Jones, W. G., 151
Jones, William, 196
Jugge, Richard, 16, 48

Kay, Thomas, 166
Keyme, John, 27, 28
Keyme, Richard, 27, 28
Killigrew, John, 28
Kincaid, Alexander, 161, 162, 163, 164
King's [Queen's] Typographer, 15, 25
King's [Queen's] Printer, 14, 15, 18, 21, 22, 162, 163, 179
Kingston, John, 189
Kitchen, Thomas, 148
Knapton, John, 134
Knox, James, 161, 174
Kynaston, Edward, 4

Lambert, Richard, 5
Lambert, Sheila, xiv
Langford, Mary, 135
Langford, Thomas, 119, 134-5
Laud, Archbishop, 74, 75, 81
Law books, trade in, 119
Leake, William, 75
Leathersellers, 99
Legge, Cantrell, 50
L'Estrange, Roger, 51
Lewis, William, 135
Leybourne, William, 9
Licensers
 — see Cecil, William
 — see Petre, Sir William
 — see Wotton, Nicholas
Liddell, John, 153, 154, 176
Lintot, Catherine, 120, 148

Lintot, Henry, 120, 148
Lipsius, Justus, 73
Lisle, Laurence, 74
Lloyd, Lodowick, 24
Llwyd, Morgan, 186
London
— book trade in, xv
— Court of Hustings, 4
— 'Inns', 2, 3, 4
— *see also* City of London Companies
Longman, Thomas, 121, 135-6
Losse, Hugh, 27
Lynne, Walter, 15

Mabbe, James, 74, 77
Mabbe, John, 74
Mabbe, Ralph, xiv, 65-92
Mabbe, Stephen, 74
McCaslan, Alexander, 173
McCleish, James, 173, 175
McDonald, Angus, 153, 154
McDougall, Warren, xv, 151-83
Macfarquhar, Colin, 174, 175
MacKenzie, James, 124
McKenzie, Professor D. F., xiv, 35-63, 104, 114, 188, 189
McKerrow, R. B., 53
Macrae, W. D., 43
Magee, James, 164, 167
Magee, John, 165, 167
Manley, Joseph, 79
Mardeley, John, 11
Marks, James, 146
Marshall, Robert, 119, 136
Marshe, Thomas, 23, 24
Martin & Wotherspoon, 175
Mary, Queen, 13, 17, 21, 22, 41
Maslen, K. D., 114
Mathematics, books on, 77-9
Mathewes, Augustine, 192
May, Hugh, 6
'Mechanick', definition of, 97-9
Medical books, trade in, 119, 155
Mercers, 2
Merchant Taylors, 28
Meredith, Luke, 194
Meuros, James, 161, 164
Mierdman, Stephen, 15
Millar, Andrew, 116, 136-7
Millar, William
Miller, John, 146
Miller, Philip, 120
Mills, Peter, 6, 7
Milton, John, 50, 119
Mitchell, Walter, 53
Montagu, Lady Mary Wortley, 161
More, Sir Thomas, 98
Morgan, Paul, 195
Morgan, William, 187, 195
Morison, Robert, and Son, 153, 176, 177, 178
Morris, William, 197
Moxon, Joseph, 103-4

Mundell, Robert, 173
Murray, John, 166
Myddleton, Hugh, 187
Myddleton, Thomas, 187, 193
Myers, Robin, xiv, xv, 35, 36, 38, 53, 113-49
Mylne, Robert, 9

Nelson, James, 97
Newspapers, trade in, 119
News-sheets, printed, 76
Nichols, John, 37, 39, 113, 116
Nicol, George, 170
Noorthouck, John, 37
Northumberland, Duke of, 20, 27
Norton, Bonham, 50
Norton, John, 192
Norton, Thomas, 42
Nourse, John, 120, 137
Nowell, Alexander, 21, 22, 185
Noyes, James, 148

Oakes, John, 66
Oakes, Nicholas, 66, 67
Oakes, William, 66
Oldys, William, 36, 43
Oliver, John, 6
Ordinance on the Regulation of Printing (1643), 94
Orwin, Thomas, 49
Oswald, John, 116
Oswen, John, 15, 196
Oulton, R., 69
Owen, William, 137
Oxford Bible Press, 194

Pace, Richard, 13
Packston, Edward, 79
Pardon Rolls, 15
Parker, Henry, 94
Parker, Matthew, Archbishop, 21, 24
Parry, William, 189
Parsons, Marmaduke, 193
Partridge, Affabel, 74
Partridge, Dionyssus, 74
Patents, related to books, 15, 16, 17, 19, 21, 22, 24, 25, 46, 47
Patent Rolls, 14, 15, 16
Payne, Thomas, 177, 178
Peacock, Miriam, 115
Pearson, Michael, 53, 54
Pembroke, Earl of, 3,
Pembroke Inn, 3, 4
Perez, Antonio, 20
Petre, Sir William, 12, 13, 17, 27
Petyt, William, 116
Philips, R. E., 152, 153, 154, 157
Philips, William, 52
Piracy, of books, 25, 26, 151-83
Pollard, Graham, 35, 40, 41, 43, 44, 49, 51, 52, 54
Ponet, Jon, 20, 21
Pope, Alexander, 119, 120

Potter, Esther, 35
Poulterers, 40, 45
Pount, John, 28
Pratt, Sir Roger, 6
Prichard, Rhys, 186
Prideaux, Sarah, 49
Prince, Daniel, 178
Printers
— see Ackers, Charles
— see Barker, Christopher
— see Barker, Richard
— see Barnes, Joseph
— see Barrie, John
— see Bassingbourne, Ives
— see Beale, John
— see Beale, Thomas
— see Berthelet, Thomas
— see Bettenham, James
— see Birckman, Arnold
— see Bloome, Jacob
— see Bodley, John
— see Bowyer, William
— see Brudenell, Thomas
— see Buck, John
— see Buck, Thomas
— see Butter, Nathaniel
— see Bynneman, Henry
— see Byrne, Patrick
— see Caxton, William
— see Cockerill, Thomas
— see Dawson, Gertrude
— see Dawson, John
— see Day, John
— see Day, Richard
— see Denham, Henry
— see Dight, Walter
— see Dover, Simon
— see Downing, Anne
— see Downing, Joseph
— see Faques, Richard
— see Flower, Francis
— see Grafton, Richard
— see Jugge, Richard
— see Hall, William
— see Harper, Thomas
— see Harrison, James
— see Hart, John
— see Haviland, John
— see Hills, Henry
— see Holmes, William
— see Holt, R.
— see Hughs, John
— see Islip, Adam
— see Jones, John
— see Jones, Richard
— see Jones, Thomas
— see Jones, W. G.
— see Jones, William
— see King's Printer
— see Kingston, John
— see Legge, Cantrell
— see Lintot, Catherine

— see Lintot, Henry
— see Lloyd, Lodowick
— see Lynne, Walter
— see Mabbe, Ralph
— see Manley, Joseph
— see Mardeley, John
— see Marshe, Thomas
— see Mathewes, Augustine
— see Mierdman, Stephen
— see Mundell, Robert
— see Norton, Bonham
— see Norton, John
— see Noyes, James
— see Oakes, Nicholas
— see Oswen, John
— see Oulton, R.
— see Packston, Edward
— see Parry, William
— see Parsons, Marmaduke
— see Purfoote, Thomas
— see Purser, John
— see Pynson, Richard
— see Rastell, Thomas
— see Ratcliffe, Thomas
— see Reid, John
— see Richardson, Samuel
— see Richardson, William
— see Rivington, Charles
— see Rivington, John
— see Roberts, James
— see Roberts, William
— see Robertson, John and James
— see Robinson, Robert
— see Salisbury, John
— see Salisbury, Thomas
— see Say, Charles
— see Seres, William
— see Shelton, Thomas
— see Simmes, Valentine
— see Sowle, Andrew
— see Sowle, Tace
— see Stafford, Simon
— see Strahan, William
— see Thackwell, Roger
— see Thomas, Lewis
— see Torrentinus, Laurence
— see Tottell, Richard
— see Tyler, E.
— see Udall, Nicholas
— see Vautrollier, Thomas
— see Waldegrave, Robert
— see Walkley, Thomas
— see Watkins, Richard
— see Ward, Roger
— see Wayland, John
— see Whitchurch, Edward
— see White, John
— see Wight, Thomas
— see Willison, David
— see Wilson, Alexander, & Sons
— see Wolfe, Reyner
— see Woodfall, Henry

INDEX

— see Yetsweirt, Charles
— see Yetsweirt, Jane
— see Yetsweirt, Nicasius
Printing manuals, 93
Prise, Sir John, 186
Privileges, for printing books, 13, 14, 17, 18, 21, 22, 23, 24, 93
Privy Council, 11, 12, 13, 16, 19, 21, 94
Prynne, William, 193
Puckering, Sir John, 19, 20
Pullein, Octavian, 66
Purfoote, Thomas, 47
Purser, John, 148
Pym, John, 81
Pynson, Richard, 13, 14

Rastell, John, 18, 19, 22
Ratcliffe, Thomas, 189
Rees, Eiluned, 185
Reeve, Elizabeth, 137
Reid, John, 173
Richard, John, 151
Richardson, Samuel, 119, 149
Richardson, William, 149
Rivington, Charles, 37, 38, 39, 49, 51, 52, 149
Rivington, John, 121, 137-8, 149
Robert, Gruffyd, 186
Roberts, James, 16
Roberts, John, 77-9
Roberts, Captain Lewes, 69, 70
Roberts, William, 197, 198
Robertson, John and James, 164, 173, 177, 178
Robertson, William, 155, 156, 157, 176, 177
Robinson, George, 166, 170
Robinson, Robert, 48
Robotham, Robert, 27
Robynson, Ralph, 98
Roger, Owen Ap, 188
Rowe, Owen, 66
Royal Printer see King's Printer
Royston, Richard, 194
Rutte, Robert, 189

St Bartholomew's Hospital, 5
St Pol, Marie de, Countess of Pembroke, 3, 6
Salesbury, William, 186, 195
Salisbury, John, 191, 192
Salisbury, Thomas, 193, 194
Sandby, William, 138
Saunders, Ann, xiv-xv, 1-10
Say, Charles, 149
Sayer, Edward, 138
Sayer, Robert, 139
Schaw, James, 160, 170, 171
Scotland, book trade in, xv, 151-83
Scottish Record Office, 172
Sedden, Thomas, 116
Semple, Robert, 151, 152, 153, 154, 166
Seres, William, 16, 17, 22, 23, 25, 26, 27, 28, 46, 48, 49
Seres, William (junior), 25, 26, 49
Sermons, printed, 75, 76, 120

Seymour, Edward, Duke of Somerset, 11, 12
Shakespeare, in Stationers' Company Records, 37
Shelton, Thomas, 79
Sibbs, Richard, 76
Simmes, Valentine, 48
Simms, John, 52
Simson, Robert, 155
Skelton, Henry, 192
Skinners, 28
Skippon, Major-General Philip, 66
Sleater, James, 167, 168, 169
Smethwick, John, 189
Smith, Adam, 153, 161
Smith, Humphrey, 66
Smith, John, 174
Smith, P., 139
Smith, Sir Thomas, 12, 23, 25, 98
Smollett, Tobias, 174
Somervile, William, 117, 118
Sowle, Andrew, 190
Sowle, Tace, 190, 191
Sparke, Michael, 193
Sparke, William, 28
Society for Promotion of Christian Knowledge (SPCK), 194, 197
Stafford, Simon, 20
Star Chamber, 94
Stationers' Company
— in general, xiii-xvi, 16, 19, 39, 74, 151, 152, 154
— and the Bishop of Oxford, 51
— and William Cecil, 11-34
— and the Honourable Artillery Company, 67
— and the University of Cambridge, 50
— and the University of Oxford, 50, 51
— and Wales, 185-202
— Almanacks, copyright in, 123
— Apprentices, 6, 44, 45, 79, 122, 185, 188-93
— Archives, xiii, xiv, 37, 79, 113, 186
— Charter of Incorporation (1557), 39, 40, 41, 51
— Clerk, 1, 4, 5, 42, 44, 51, 126
— Corporate views, 93-111
— Court, 5, 43, 46, 48, 53, 122, 123
— Court Books, 7, 48
— Court Book A, 43
— Court Book B, 54
— Court Book C, 45, 52, 53, 54
— Court Book D, 5
— Court Minutes, 4, 94
— English Stock, xv, 5, 6, 16, 22, 38, 46, 48, 49, 51, 113, 121, 122
— Freemen, 44, 45
— Hall, xiii, xiv, xv, xvii, 1-10, 29, 79, 103, 113, 122, 155, 173, 175, 177, 178
— 'Humble Remonstrance', 93-111
— Irish Stock, 48
— Latin Stock, 48
— Liber A, xiv, 35-63
— Liber B, 36
— Liber C, 37, 44
— Library, 37, 43
— Livery, 1, 44, 45, 50, 52, 75

— Military service, 46
— Ordinances, 5, 41, 44, 45, 51
— Red Book, 42, 44
— Registers, xv, 117, 121, 126, 155, 171, 173, 178, 185, 187
— Register A, 43, 44
— Register B, 44, 49
— Renter Warden, 5, 191
— Stock Keepers, 48
— Treasurer of the English Stock, 113, 121, 122, 123, 126
— Master, 1, 6, 18, 48, 49, 51, 52
— Under Warden, 43
— Wardens, 1, 5, 6, 9, 18, 40, 42, 44, 47, 48, 49, 51, 52
— White Book, 42
Steevens, George, 37
Sterne, Laurence, 173, 175
Stewart, Thomas, 165, 166, 169
Stevenson, James, 153
Strachey, Henry, 117
Strahan, Andrew, 178
Strahan, William, 121, 149, 152, 153, 154, 155, 157, 165, 171, 175, 176, 177
Strype, John, 9
Subscription lists, 113
Sussex, Giles, 52

Tait, Peter, 174
Tallis, Thomas, 25
Templeman, Mr, 153
Thackwell, Roger, 186
Thom, John, 161
Thomas, Lewis, 194
Thomason, George, 94
Thompson, Thomas, 119
Thomson, Alexander, 160, 161
Thurston, Richard, 139
Tonson, Jacob, 121
Torrentinus, Laurence, 16
Tottell, Richard, 16, 17, 18, 20, 185
Toy, Humphrey, 186
Trade sales, of books, 119
Trussell, Thomas, 67
Tsushima, Jean, xiv, 46, 65-92
Tull, Jethro, 116
Tunstall, Cuthbert, 13
Tyler, E., 195
Tyndale, William, 16

Udall, Nicholas, 15, 16
Upton, John, 117, 118, 119
Urie, Robert, 161, 162

Vaillant, Paul, 120, 139-40
Vautrollier, Thomas, 24, 25

Waldegrave, Robert, 49
Wales, book trade in, xv, 15, 185-202
Walker, Anthony, 149
Walker, James, 152, 171, 172, 174, 175
Walkley, Thomas, 67
Wallace, James, 162, 163
Waller, Captain Henry, 66, 69, 76
Wallis, John, 124
Walsingham, Sir Francis, 17
Wapshott, Robert, 6, 8
Ward, Roger, 46
Ward, Widow, 6
Watkins, Richard, 16, 48
Watkins, Thomas, 192
Watt, John, 153
Wayland, John, 22
Wedgwood, Ralph, 5
Wheeler, Anne, 116
Whiston and White, 140-1
Whitchurch, Edward, 15
White, John, 192
White, Luke, 167, 168, 169, 170, 171
White, Richard, 186
White, Warden (Stationers' Company), 8
Whitestone, 169
Whitgift, Bishop, 49
Wight, Thomas, 16, 19-20
Wilkes, Oliver, 193
Wilkie, John, 126
Williams, James, 167, 169, 173
Williams, Moses, 186, 194, 195, 197
Williams, Rice, 192
Willison, David, 175
Wilson, Alexander, & Sons, 164-5
Wilson, John, 141
Wilson, Thomas, 141
Wilson, William, 151, 167, 168, 169
Wolfe, Reyner, 15, 17, 25
Wolfe, John, 25, 26, 47
Wood, John, 173, 174, 175
Woodcock, Edward, 142
Woodfall, George, 37
Woodfall, Henry, 149
Woodman, Thomas, 116
Woodward, Thomas, 115, 116, 117, 120
Wotton, Nicholas, 12
Wren, Christopher, 6, 8
Wren, John, 142
Wright, Thomas, 124, 125
Wrightson, Keith, 105

Yetsweirt, Charles, 18, 19
Yetsweirt, Jane, 19
Yetsweirt, Nicasius, 17, 18, 19
Young, Edward, 118-19, 120
Young, John, 161